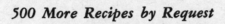

500 More Recipes by Request

500 More Recipes By Request

By

JEANNE M. HALL

BRAMHALL HOUSE • NEW YORK

PROLOGUE

Ten years ago we joyously put together *Five Hundred Recipes By Request From Grandma Anderson's Dutch Kitchens* and happily watched it travel from one end of the United States to the other.

While it wasn't intended that way, the book served as the most lucrative piece of advertising ever put out by the Hotel. It brought new guests by the hundreds.

There is something about the old, quiet air of charm and friendliness at the Anderson Hotel that makes personal friends out of customers. We are so obviously a family hotel in a crossroads country town fortunately located in the Hiawatha Valley which is, and always will be, one of the most beautiful locations in the world! Highway 61 from Minneapolis and St. Paul to La Crosse, Wisconsin is positively unexcelled for breath-taking beauty; literally miles and miles of highway carved out of sheer bluffs and swooping down into picturesque valleys along the Mississippi River and enormous Lake Pepin. This is camera country; when Grandma Anderson came from Pennsylvania, she chose her location well.

The Hotel is well over a hundred years old. It is fortunately located in the residential district of the town and has a big yard, and a gigantic garden. In the back of the Hotel is Grandma Anderson's Preserving Kitchens . . . a small Dutch kitchen where we prepare our jams, jellies, fruit cakes, breads, salad dressings and relishes for resale in our lobby counter.

Our Hotel will never be anything but a family operation. This year my sister, Ann McCaffrey, is running the kitchen and doing most of the cooking. Belle Ebner is a kind of Major General keeping a sharp and piercing eye à la Grandma Anderson on all parts of the management. My mother, Mrs. Verna Anderson McCaffrey, is the smiling Hostess in the Dining Room and here she manages to keep an experienced eye on the little high school and college girls who work for us and still see that everything comes out exactly as Grandma Anderson would want it to be served. Since the last book went to press Margaret has deserted and gone to The Greenbriar at White Sulphur Springs, West Virginia. Other than this the original family group is intact; still running the Hotel with interest, with zest, with friendliness and with love!

When it was time to select the recipes for this new book we found ourselves hemmed in with over two thousand recipes we were sure we couldn't do without! Slowly and painfully they were discarded one by one until only the unusual and super-delectable ones were left to form this book. Again we must thank hundreds and hundreds of our customers who shared their favorite recipes with us. Our only regret is that Grandma Anderson doesn't know that another of her books is going forth to an even larger section of the world than the first one. She would have been enchanted. A woman wasn't a woman in her eyes unless she loved to cook.

My own office has rows and rows of cook books from all over the world. Over six hundred cook books! And yet we keep going back to the rich, old-fashioned and sometimes simple things that Grandma Anderson did so well. Well enough, at any rate, to make her little Hotel Anderson known all over the country.

Here then are more of her recipes. *Bon Appetit!*

PREFACE

Back in 1948 when our first cook book *500 Recipes by Request* was published the book was barely on the newsstand when customers began to shower us with their favorite recipes.

They came in single recipes, groups of recipes, packs of recipes; by mail, in one case by wire, and one batch actually came Air Express.

So we realized that a new book was in the making whether we wanted it or not.

Ten years after, here it is, bigger than the first book, and, like the first book, going out to a greater section of the world.

It isn't meant to be a general cook book in any sense of the word. You won't find simple, elementary recipes because we feel there are already so many excellent books on the market that cover these points. This is a book meant to make a gourmet cook out of any homemaker interested in being one, with the simple, inexpensive products found in any store.

Here and there you'll find a recipe that calls for wine or a vegetable exotic to your part of the country. We include these because we know we have devoted customers in California, Florida, Texas—places where these are in great abundance. We use California wine in our cooking, still feeling that good, old United States of America products are the very best.

We have tried to keep out any recipes that are included in our first book and, after culling and culling, and separating, and cataloging we hope we haven't let one slip in. We sleep, dream and walk around in a world of recipes. Recipes are our job, our hobby, our livelihood and our recreation! Lucky us! We hope the end result is an entirely new experience in good cooking for you.

TABLE OF CONTENTS

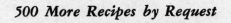

500 More Recipes by Request

APPETIZERS

Grandma Anderson's many handwritten cook books do not show appetizers. But there is a section called "Tid Bits" and these were the things she served in the lobby on cold winter nights when the teams were tied up in the backyard and breath was like white steam on the crisp, below-zero air.

Sometimes there were bits of home-cured sausage on a hot plate, sometimes bowls of pickled cauliflower, pickled pike or summer sausage whipped to a spread with rich spices whipped in, little meat balls in rich gravy, broiled tomato slices with hot buttered crumbs on top, cheese sticks and Sardine Strips with a light cheese sauce.

There was spicy ginger beer to drink and hot mulled cider stirred with a cinnamon stick, and Grandma Anderson made hot cranberry juice long before it was ever thought of commercially. She served it in thick Dutch mugs with crisp cookies or crisp cheese sticks and the weary traveler was sure he was in a gastronomic heaven.

Time has passed and food customs have changed and now we plan heavenly appetizers for our more scrumptious parties. These are the choicest included in this chapter. There are many more, of course, but a book size has a limit, so what is left we'll save for the next book. In the meantime it is good to remember that beautifully executed appetizers can be used as a forerunner for a fairly simple and inexpensive entree—ground round steak broiled to perfection preceded by new and different appetizers can be a culinary triumph for the inexperienced cook! There is eye appeal to be used in cooking as well as taste appeal. We're sure you'll find these simple and elegant!

ANCHOVY CHIP DIP

2 tablespoons anchovy paste
½ cup minced onion
1 tablespoon lemon juice

1 tablespoon tarragon vinegar
½ cup dairy sour cream
1 cup mayonnaise
½ cup finely chopped parsley

Combine all ingredients and mix well. Use as a dip for crackers or potato chips. Yield: 2 cups.

APPETIZER PIE

Cut large round loaves of rye bread in circular slices ¼-inch thick. Spread with butter and soft cream cheese. Place a teaspoon of caviar in center, then surround with a ring of rolled anchovies, a ring of chopped ripe olives, and another ring of cream cheese. Garnish outer edge with small pickled onions, whole stuffed green olives, and halves of shrimps, alternating the foods. Chill until ready to serve, then cut in pie-shaped wedges.

AVOCADO APPETIZERS

Combine in saucepan 1 can (10½ oz.) cream of celery soup, 1 cup sliced fresh mushrooms, ½ cup sliced canned water chestnuts, 1 mashed, peeled ripe avocado, 1 tablespoon lemon juice, 2 tablespoons each chopped pimento, dry white wine, grated Parmesan cheese, pinch each dry mustard, pepper. Fill individual baking shells or dishes. Top each with slices of peeled ripe avocado; sprinkle with fine bread crumbs. Broil 4 inches from heat, 5 to 6 minutes, or until golden brown. Serves 6-8.

BRANDY CHEESE DIP

4 packages (4 ounces each)   8 ounces cream cheese
    Roquefort cheese   ½ cup brandy

Allow cheese to reach room temperature; then mash, add brandy and mix well. Yield: about 3 cups.

CANNIBAL SPREADS

Grind 1 cup raw round steak. Place through the grinder again and add 6 fillets of anchovy, ½ dozen capers, and the riced yolk of two hard-boiled eggs, 1 tablespoon olive oil, and 1 tablespoon finely minced or grated onion. Mix all together, mixing well, and spread quite thickly on rounds of pumpernickel or rye bread.

CAULIFLOWER HORS D'OEUVRES

1 large cauliflower	1 jar large stuffed olives
1 3 oz. jar chipped beef	1 jar sweet gherkins
1 3 oz. package cream cheese	1 jar small dill pickles
1 cup mayonnaise	1 jar pickled mushrooms
Juice of 1 lemon	1 bunch tiny radishes
	1 package quick-frozen shrimp

Loosen cauliflower flowerets, do not break from stem. Wash thoroughly in salty water. Spread chipped beef slices with softened cream cheese; roll up jelly-roll fashion. Cut in 1″ slices. Mix mayonnaise with lemon juice. Dip thawed shrimp in mayonnaise. Place separately on toothpicks: beef rolls, shrimp, olives, gherkins, small dill pickles, pickled mushrooms and radishes. Stick into cauliflower to resemble old-fashioned nosegay. Serve with extra bowl of dipping-mayonnaise. Yields: 16 servings.

CHEESE BUTTER LEAVES

1 cup milk, scalded	3 eggs, well beaten
½ cup butter	5 cups flour, about
1 teaspoon salt	1 cup grated American cheese
¼ cup sugar	2 tablespoons butter
2 ounces yeast	2 tablespoons milk

Pour milk over butter, salt, and sugar; let stand until cooled to lukewarm. Crumble yeast into mixture and let stand for 5 minutes. Add eggs and mix well. Add sifted flour gradually and knead until smooth and elastic. Place in a greased bowl and cover. Let rise until doubled in bulk, knead down, and store in refrigerator if desired, or roll into a rectangle about 14 x 24 inches. Combine remaining ingredients, and heat in double boiler until cheese melts. Spread half of cheese over half of dough. Fold over. Spread half the dough again with remaining cheese mixture and fold again. Cut into 1½-inch squares. Place squares cut side down in greased muffin pans. Let rise until doubled in bulk. Bake in a hot oven, 400 degrees, for 25 minutes. Yield: 3 dozen.

CHEESE DELIGHTS

Cream together 4 tablespoons butter or margraine and 1 cup shredded sharp process cheddar cheese. Add ¾ cup all-purpose flour, dash of salt and ¼ teaspoon celery seed; blend well. Form into small balls. Place on ungreased cooky sheet; flatten with fork to make waffle design; sprinkle with paprika. Chill several hours. Bake in hot oven 450° F. for 8 to 10 minutes. Serve hot. Makes 1 dozen.

CHEESE PUFFS

¼ pound Cheddar cheese
¼ teaspoon oregano

1 tablespoon ketchup
2 teaspoons butter
1 teaspoon minced onion.

Grind cheese and add other ingredients. Spread on crackers or squares of bread, dust with paprika, and toast under broiler until puffed.

GRILLED CRABMEAT BITES

4 finger rolls
1 6½ oz. can crabmeat (flaked)
1 tablespoon chopped onion
1 tablespoon minced parsley
2 tablespoons chopped pimiento
2 tablespoons diced celery

½ teaspoon salt
¼ cup mayonnaise
1 package Velvetta cheese, cut in small pieces
½ cup milk
8 slices bacon

Split rolls in half lengthwise. Mix well the crabmeat, onion, parsley, pimiento, celery, salt and mayonnaise. Spread mixture on rolls. Top each with a slice of bacon. Place on cold broiler grill about 4 inches below flame. Grill at 375° F. about 13 minutes, until bacon is crisp.

About 10 minutes before sandwiches are grilled, put cheese and milk in top of double boiler and stir until cheese is melted and well blended. Serve hot over grilled sandwiches.

LIVER PÂTÉ

Put 1 pound of fresh lean pork and 1 pound of chicken livers (or ½ pound chicken livers and ½ pound calf's liver) several times through the finest blade of the meat grinder. Add 1 chopped shallot, 2 tablespoons chopped parsley, 2 teaspoons freshly ground pepper, ⅔ teaspoon powdered ginger, ¼ teaspoon cinnamon, 2¼ teaspoons salt, 1 tablespoon brandy and 1 tablespoon Madeira wine. Mix all the ingredients together thoroughly.

Line a loaf pan with strips of bacon, pack in the pork-and-liver mixture, and bake the pâté in a 350° oven for about 1½ hours. Cool the pâté under pressure, preferably under another loaf pan containing any handy object heavy enough to pack the meat down to a firm consistency. Chill before serving.

LIVERWURST CANAPÉ

Mix 1 cup of the very best liverwurst available with enough mayonnaise to soften slightly, add 1 heaping teaspoon sweet pickle relish, and 10 or 12 chopped capers. Spread on oblong strips of toast and dredge with very finely chopped chives.

MINIATURE LAMB PIZZAS

4 cups biscuit mix	½ pound Mozzarella cheese,
1 cup milk	sliced
1 8-oz. can tomato sauce	¼ cup grated Parmesan cheese
1 pound ground lamb	2 teaspoons oregano
	1 teaspoon salt

Combine biscuit mix and milk; mix lightly. Turn out on lightly floured surface. Knead gently 10 times. Roll out to ¼-inch thickness. Cut into rounds with floured 3½-inch cutter. Place on baking sheets. Top with tomato sauce, lamp and sliced Mozzarella cheese. Sprinkle with remaining ingredients. Bake in hot oven (425°) 15 to 20 minutes, or until lightly browned. Makes about 24 3½-inch pizzas.

PICKLED MUSHROOMS

1 clove garlic	1 teaspoon salt
¾ cup salad oil	¼ teaspoon pepper
¼ cup olive oil	½ teaspoon dry mustard
½ cup lemon juice	3 bay leaves
1 medium onion, chopped	2 (4-ounce) cans button mushrooms

Rub mixing bowl with cut clove of garlic, pour in oils and lemon juice. Add onion, salt, pepper, mustard, and bay leaves. Drain mushrooms and add to sauce. Put in covered jar to store. Be sure the sauce is sufficient to cover mushrooms. Let stand 24 hours in refrigerator. Before serving, drain mushrooms, lay on paper towel, insert picks. Makes about 80 marinated mushroom buttons.

SARDINE SPREAD CALIFORNIA

2 (3 oz.) packages cream cheese	2 teaspoons wine vinegar
2 (4 oz.) can sardines, drained	2 tablespoons chopped parsley
3 tablespoons sherry	2 tablespoons chopped pimiento
	Onion salt to taste

Place cream cheese in a bowl and mash with a fork; blend in sardines. Gradually blend in sherry and wine vinegar. Add remaining ingredients and store, covered, in refrigerator, several hours to blend flavors. Makes about 1¾ cups spread.

SAUSAGE ROLLS

Slice Cervelat sausage in very thin slices. Fry ½ cup of finely minced or similar cheese, and season with salt, pepper, and a dash of cayenne. Spread thinly on the sliced sausage, and roll. Insert toothpick to fasten and place a small pearl onion or pickled onion on the end of the toothpick.

SARDINE STRIPS

butter
white or rye bread
1 stalk celery
1 slice pimiento
1 can boneless sardines

1 teaspoon prepared horseradish
¼ teaspoon curry powder
1 teaspoon lemon juice
Salt
½ cup whipped cream
2 tablespoons mayonnaise

First, take the butter out of the refrigerator to soften so it will spread smoothly. Then with a sharp knife, trim all signs of crusts off several thin slices of white or rye bread (cutting all slices at once makes them fit together evenly).

Next step: Chop up the celery and pimiento fine with a sharp knife. Mash the drained sardines with a fork and add horseradish, curry powder, lemon juice, salt, whipped cream, mayonnaise and the chopped vegetables. Give this a good stir, then taste to see if it needs a little more of this or that seasoning.

Last step: Spread the filling up to the very edges of half the buttered slices and fit a buttered slice of bread on top. Then bundle several sandwiches together and wrap them in waxed paper to keep in the refrigerator until used. When it's time to serve, cut the slices in narrow strips (a cold sharp knife cuts cold sandwiches fine) and serve them at once.

SHERRIED SHRIMP

24 medium-size fresh shrimp
¼ cup soy sauce
¼ cup sherry wine
½ cup salad oil

1 teaspoon powdered ginger or
1 tablespoon fresh ginger
root, ground
1 clove garlic, finely chopped

Peel and clean shrimp, washing well under cold running water and drying on absorbent toweling.

Combine remaining ingredients. Cover shrimp with soy mixture and allow to stand for an hour or less.

Place the shrimp plus a little of the marinade in a skillet and cook for three or four minutes until shrimp are done. An electric skillet is recommended for this.

SHRIMP CHIP DIP

1 5-ounce can shrimp drained
and chopped
1 cup dairy sour cream
¼ cup chili sauce

2 teaspoons lemon juice
½ teaspoon salt
⅛ teaspoon pepper
1 teaspoon prepared horseradish
Dash tabasco sauce

Cut the shrimp into very small pieces and mix well with the remaining ingredients. Use as a dip or spread for potato chips or crackers. Yield: 1½ cups.

SNAPPY CHEESE ROLLS

½ pound cheese, process American
1 cup chopped celery
⅓ cup dill pickle, minced
2 tablespoons chili sauce

3 tablespoons mayonnaise or
mayonnaise-type salad
dressing
8 frankfurter rolls
1 tablespoon butter, soft

Cut cheese in ¼-inch cubes; add celery and pickle. Stir chili sauce into mayonnaise; mix well. Pour over cheese mixture and toss until all pieces are coated. Slit rolls lengthwise halfway down; remove part of center and fill with cheese mixture. Spread butter on top crusts; place on ungreased shallow baking pan. When ready to serve heat in moderate oven 350° F. for 15 to 20 minutes until rolls are lightly toasted and cheese is melted. Serve hot. Makes 8 servings.

NOTE: These may be made hours ahead, covered with waxed paper and stored in the refrigerator.

STUFFED MUSHROOMS

1 pound large mushrooms
5 tablespoons butter
½ pound chicken livers

1 tablespoon minced onion
1 3-ounce package cream cheese
¼ teaspoon powdered tarragon
Salt and pepper

Remove stems of mushrooms and chop. Sauté caps in three tablespoons butter about five minutes, turning often. Remove from pan.

Add remaining butter to pan and cook chicken livers, mushroom stems and onion till livers are lightly browned. Chop livers. Cool mixture.

Cream the cheese, add liver mixture and season with tarragon and salt and pepper to taste.

Pile into mushroom caps and chill thoroughly.

Yield: 12 servings.

NIBBLER'S DELIGHT

Serve one or more of the following dips in small bowls on a large tray or plate surrounded by several of the following accompaniments; assorted crisp crackers, potato chips and/or pretzels. Garnish with thin wedges of red apples and small clusters of green grapes.

THREE DUNKING SAUCES

1.

1 pint mayonnaise	1 tablespoon Worcestershire sauce
1 cucumber, chopped	1 small onion, minced
	Tabasco

Combine ingredients and mix well.

2.

1 pint sour cream	1 green pepper, minced
1 teaspoon freshly ground pepper	1 tablespoon minced parsley

Combine all ingredients; mix well.

3.

1 cup cooked salad dressing	3 tablespoons grated American
1 3 oz. package cream cheese	Cheddar cheese
	1 chopped pimiento

Blend together cooked dressing, cream cheese and American cheese. Add pimiento.

Ingredients to serve 16.

TINY LAMB KEBABS

1 pound boneless lamb shoulder
1 3½-ounce jar cocktail onions
1 6-ounce can tomato paste

1 tablespoon sugar
½ teaspoon salt
¼ teaspoon pepper

Cut lamb into ½-inch cubes. Drain onions; reserve liquid. Arrange lamb and onions on toothpicks. Broil 3 or 4 inches from source of heat, 4-5 minutes, or until lightly browned. Combine onion liquid and remaining ingredients. Heat to serving temperature, stirring occasionally. Serve tomato mixture as a dip for lamb kebabs. Makes about 3 dozen.

WATERCRESS CANAPÉ

Thoroughly mix the yolks of 2 hard-boiled eggs and add enough highly seasoned mayonnaise to form a good spread. Very finely chop 1 cup watercress from which all stems have been removed, and add this to the egg and mayonnaise combination. Spread on rounds of thinly sliced rye bread and put a border of caviar entirely around the canapé. Squeeze a little lemon or onion juice over the canapé.

SOUPS, BEAUTIFUL SOUPS!

Hotels have a stock pot that is always simmering. Into it goes the bits of vegetables, meat, juices and bones that are cut away as the cooking for the entrees begin.

After hours and hours of simmering, the stock is drained and the good, rich base for the daily soup remains. One reason why many hotel soups are superlative is that they frown on short cuts such as soup bases, artificial flavoring and a variety of other tricks.

I don't think soup base has ever been used in the Anderson Hotel. Our garden is large and abundant and right outside the kitchen door; our cook book shelf includes three cook books dealing exclusively with soups and this doesn't include Grandma Anderson's much thumbed, much used original handwritten cook book!

We love cream soups because so much can be done with them! We love cold fruit soups that are typical of Northern Europe; we love rich broths and old-fashioned barley soups. Most of all we love experimenting and creating our own soup recipes that eventually are considered flawless in our little test kitchen and only then become a part of our permanent recipe file.

It is possible to make a noon luncheon distinguished and memorable by starting with an excellent and elegant soup. A crisp, cold salad, pleasing to the eye, hot little biscuits, a fresh fruit dessert and you've served, with pardonable pride, a charming meal.

Soups are inexpensive for the most part, and once contrived and executed it's almost impossible for them to be ruined. They can be frozen for future sauces, and put in thermos bottles for a filling and vitamin-packed school lunch.

And so to the soups; may you love them as we do.

BEEF GUMBO SOUP

3 to 4 pounds cross-cut beef
    shanks, cut 2 inches thick
2 tablespoons lard or drippings
2 tablespoons salt
2 quarts water
1 onion, quartered
¼ head cabbage, sliced
6 carrots, sliced
1 cup diced potato
½ cup chopped celery

6 green onions, sliced
6 sprigs parsley
1 can (16 ounces) tomatoes
1 10-ounce package frozen lima
    beans
1 10-ounce package frozen cut
    green beans
1 can (16 ounces) whole kernel
    corn
1 can (16 ounces) okra, drained

Brown beef shanks in lard or drippings. Pour off drippings. Add salt, water and onion. Cover tightly and simmer 2½ hours. Add cabbage, carrots, potato, celery, green onions and parsley. Continue cooking 30 minutes. Add tomatoes, lima beans, green beans and corn and simmer until tender, about 20 to 30 minutes. Add okra and heat thoroughly. Yield: 5 quarts.

CARAWAY SOUP

1 carrot
1 small yellow turnip
3 cups chicken stock or canned
    chicken soup

3 tablespoons chicken fat or butter
1 tablespoon flour
2 tablespoons caraway
Salt
Pepper

Wash the vegetables and dice the carrot and turnip. Peel and slice the onion. Cook them in the chicken stock until tender. Strain, and press the vegetables through a sieve. In another saucepan melt the fat, add the flour and the caraway seeds and cook until slightly colored. Stir in the liquid gradually and cook over hot water for one-half an hour. Strain through cheesecloth wrung out in warm water. Reheat if necessary and serve very hot with cheese croutons.

CHEESE SOUP

¼ pound butter	¼ cup finely diced celery
1 cup flour	¼ cup finely diced onions
½ teaspoon salt	¼ cup finely diced peppers
1½ pints milk	¼ cup finely chopped carrots
7 ounces coon or Cheddar cheese	1 pint chicken stock
	Paprika to color

Melt butter and blend in flour, salt and milk. Cook until thickened. Melt cheese in double boiler, parboil vegetables in chicken stock and then combine all ingredients. Bring to a boil, stirring constantly. Serve piping hot. Makes 8 generous helpings.

CREAM OF BROCCOLI SOUP

Wash broccoli carefully and cut into small pieces, add water and cook until tender; use about one pound broccoli, three cups water, one and one-half teaspoon salt; cook for twenty-five minutes, and of the water remaining reserve one cup for the soup.

Make a white sauce as follows: melt one-fourth cup shortening, add one-third cup sifted flour and make a smooth paste; add slowly one quart whole milk (heated previously in the top part of a double boiler); add one-half teaspoon salt; cook and stir until thickened, add the liquid from the broccoli, one tablespoon butter, and a few grains of pepper to season nicely; mix well and, last of all, add the tender, cooked broccoli. Serve hot with crisp cheese wafers.

CREAM OF CAULIFLOWER SOUP

(POTAGE CREME DE CHOUFLEUR)

Wash a cauliflower and break it into pieces. Cook the pieces in boiling salted water until they are soft but still whole, drain off the water and reserve it. Force the cauliflower through a fine sieve and add to it enough liquid (half cauliflower water and half chicken stock) to make a moderately thick soup. Simmer the soup for about 15 minutes, take it off the fire and add gradually 1 cup milk beaten with 2 egg yolks. Add a lump of butter and reheat the soup very slowly, stirring constantly. Do not let it boil or the egg will turn. Serves 4.

GLOUCESTER FISH CHOWDER

3 pounds haddock	4 cups diced potatoes
3 cups hot water	½ cup sliced onion
½ cup salt pork diced	4 cups hot milk

Cut fish into pieces. Add hot water and simmer 20 minutes. Remove skin and bones. Cook pork until crisp; add onion, cook until soft and yellow. Add to fish. Parboil potatoes 5 minutes; add to fish, cook in fish liquid until tender. Add scalded milk and season. Serve hot with crackers.

LOBSTER BISQUE

1 large lobster (2 pounds)	4 tablespoons flour
2 cups cold water	½ teaspoon salt
6 tablespoons butter	¼ teaspoon paprika
	4 cups milk

Boil the lobster for twenty minutes in salted water. Drain and cool sufficiently to handle. Remove the meat from the shell and cut into cubes. Place the body and small claws in a saucepan, cover with the cold water and simmer one-half hour. Strain and reserve the stock. Melt the butter and cook the diced lobster in it about five minutes, then remove the lobster and keep warm. Thicken the remaining butter with the flour, add seasonings and stir in the stock and milk that have been scalded together. Combine with the lobster meat and heat thoroughly. Place an additional teaspoon of butter in each serving dish, pour over it the soup and garnish with a few tiny croutons, a fleck of paprika or one-half a teaspoon of minced parsley. Serves 6.

OYSTER BISQUE LOUISIANA

6 tablespoons butter	4 celery stalks
2 tablespoons flour	2 dozen oysters
2 cups milk	Salt and pepper
Salt	1 pint light cream
4 small carrots	1 teaspoon Worcestershire sauce
2 small turnips	Few sprigs parsley

For cream sauce base melt 2 tablespoons butter, stir in the flour smoothly, add the milk gradually and season the sauce with salt. Cook this slowly until it is smooth and slightly thick, then keep it hot over boiling water.

Next, cut all the vegetables into little pieces, about the size of "the end of your little finger," and cook them slowly in 2 tablespoons of butter in a frying pan until glistening and almost soft. Warning: These little vegetable pieces scorch easily, so be on guard!

Then melt 2 tablespoons of butter in a saucepan, add oysters, oyster liquor and a sprinkling of salt and pepper, and cook only until edges of oysters curl. (Remember, if oysters are overcooked, they get tough.) Finally, heat the cream (making sure its does not boil).

At this point the bisque is ready to be assembled. Vegetables are stirred into the cream sauce and combined with the heated cream; oysters, oyster liquor and Worcestershire sauce are added last of all. This perfectly delicious bisque is then poured into a heated soup tureen (or soup plates), sprinkled with chopped parsley and served piping hot to 8.

OYSTER SOUP, FRENCH STYLE

(Without Milk)

1 tablespoon fat	3 dozen (or 2 cans) medium-
2 tablespoon green onions	size oysters
2 pods garlic	½ cup chopped onions
3 pints cold water	2 tablespoon parsley
	½ teaspoon salt
	⅛ teaspoon black pepper

Melt fat in deep skillet, brown onions and garlic. Add water and bring to boil. Add oysters and other ingredients. Boil 30 minutes. One tablespoon bell pepper may be added. Serves 6.

OYSTER SOUP, YANKEE STYLE

(WITH MILK)

1 cup oyster liquor (or plain water)
2 pods garlic
Tops of 2 green onions

1 pint oysters
1 quart whole milk
2 ounces butter
3 sprigs chopped parsley
Salt and pepper to taste

Put oyster liquor or water, or combination of both, into deep pan. Add garlic and onions chopped fine, and boil 15 minutes on slow fire. Add oysters and boil one minute; then add milk, butter, chopped parsley, salt and pepper, and boil 3 minutes on slow fire. Serve hot with salty crackers.

PHILADELPHIA PEPPER POT

6-7 pounds lean honeycomb tripe
1 knuckle of veal
5 leeks
1 large onion
3-4 sliced carrots
1 large stalk celery, sliced
1 large bunch parsley
Salt
¼ whole fresh or dried red pepper

1 teaspoon whole cloves
1 teaspoon whole black pepper, crushed
1 heaping teaspoon sweet marjoram
1 dessert spoon summer savory
1 dessert spoon sweet basil
1 teaspoon thyme
1½ pints potatoes, diced
3 tablespoons flour
2½ tablespoons butter

Wash and scrub the tripe thoroughly. Cover with about 6 quarts of cold water to which one teaspoon salt has been added. Bring to boil, and then boil moderately for 6-7 hours, until tripe is tender. Keep tripe well covered with water.

Cook knuckle of veal separately in another pot, adding leeks, onion, carrots, celery and parsley. Cover with water and add one-half teaspoon salt and one-quarter whole fresh pepper. Simmer for about 2 hours, or until meat falls from bone. At the end of the first hour add the cloves, pepper, marjoram, savory, thyme and basil, tied in a cheesecloth. Strain, allow to cool, and skim off all grease.

Remove tripe from its pot, saving the liquor. Cut tripe into small pieces (one-quarter inch) and put it into the combined tripe and veal stocks (heated). Dice the potatoes, put them in cold salted water, bring to boil and boil 10 minutes.

Mix flour and butter, dissolving them with a little of the boiling soup, then add to the soup, stirring constantly.

PIQUANT TOMATO SOUP

1 can (No. 2½) tomatoes
2 cups hot water
2 beef bouillon cubes
½ cup chili sauce
1 tablespoon sugar

¼ teaspoon salt
1 bay leaf
1/16 teaspoon celery salt
1/16 teaspoon paprika
　Dash of Tabasco sauce
2 tablespoons lemon juice

Combine all ingredients except Tabasco sauce and lemon juice in a large saucepan. Bring to boiling point and simmer 5 minutes. Mash through a coarse sieve and add remaining ingredients. Serve hot. Yield: 8 servings.

SALMON BISQUE

½ cup onion, minced
¼ cup butter
2 tablespoons flour
1½ teaspoons salt
¼ teaspoon pepper

¾ teaspoon dry mustard
½ cup light cream
4 cups milk
　Liquid and oil of salmon
1 pound can salmon, flaked
　Paprika

Cook onion in butter 5 minutes. Add flour, salt, pepper, and mustard, stir until smooth. Add cream, milk, and liquid of salmon. Cook over hot water until slightly thickened, stirring constantly. Add salmon. Reheat and serve; sprinkle each serving with paprika.

SOUTHERN BISQUE

1½ cups canned corn, creamed
    style
2 cups milk
2 slices onion
3 tablespoons butter
2 tablespoons flour

2 cups tomatoes, pulp and juice
1 teaspoon sugar
1 teaspoon salt
¼ teaspoon pepper
6 cloves
1 teaspoon condiment sauce
1 tablespoon minced parsley

Scald the corn with the milk and onion. Press through a coarse sieve and return to the upper part of the double boiler. Cream together the butter and flour and add to the milk.

Simmer the tomatoes with the sugar, salt, pepper and cloves for ten minutes. Strain and add the condiment sauce. Heat both to the boiling point and pour the tomato mixture into the corn mixture. Serve very hot, garnished with flecks of the parsley.

MEATS AND POULTRY

Grandma Anderson said anybody could cook if they had steaks and roasts to work with every day. But the REAL cook is the one who raised huzzahs from her guests when she served them a frankfurter pie, a turkey casserole, a meat loaf fit for the Gods!

At one time the boarders and roomers at Grandma Anderson's paid $6.00 a week for board and room! They waxed fat and sleek under her loving care and size thirty-eights became size forty-twos in scarcely any time at all!

Last year we won the Lamb Producers National Prize for our Skewered Lamb with Cranberry Burrs. The recipe is included and we hope you'll try it. Served with mounds of wild rice and giant mushroom caps it's indeed a great dish!

Cornish hens are new since Grandma's time but Miss Ann has given them her usual expert care and she wants you to try them with our wonderful Barley Stuffing. The Barley Stuffing is, of course, a Pennsylvania Dutch touch . . . but it goes gloriously with the hens and is much less expensive than wild rice.

You'll find a wide variety of inexpensive recipes in this section, but they all bear the authentic stamp of a gourmet dish if they are prepared exactly as the recipe insists. Don't be a recipe changer! Leave that for the experts! Once you have delved into this chapter you will find that what we say is true . . . it doesn't take a standing Prime Rib Roast or a New York Cut Sirloin to put the stamp of good cooking on a company meal!

FACTS ABOUT FROZEN MEAT

Q. How should meat be prepared for freezing?

A. Roasts and pot-roasts should be cut into convenient sizes for family use and wherever possible bones should be removed. The number of chops, steaks and cutlets packaged together should be determined by the number of persons to be served. Ground meat should be shaped into patties, or packaged in amounts for loaves or other dishes.

Q. How should meat be wrapped for freezing?

A. Meat should be closely wrapped and tightly sealed in a moisture-vapor-proof wrapping to exclude as much air as possible. Steaks, chops, cutlets and patties packaged together should be separated by a layer of the wrapping material.

Q. Should ground meat and sausage be seasoned before freezing?

A. No. Meat should not be seasoned before freezing since the flavor of most seasonings is intensified upon freezer storage. The meat should be seasoned after thawing.

Q. At what temperature should meat be frozen and stored?

A. Meat should be quickly frozen at as low a temperature as possible. Frozen meat should be stored at 0° F. or lower.

Q. What is the recommended maximum storage time for frozen meat?

A. Recommended maximum storage periods for meat held at 0° F. are: sausage and ground meat from 1 to 3 months; fresh pork from 3 to 6 months; lamb and veal from 6 to 9 months; and beef from 6 to 12 months.

Q. How should frozen meat be thawed?

A. The methods of thawing most frequently used are (1) in the refrigerator, (2) at room temperature, (3) during cooking. The method used does not materially affect the flavor, tenderness or juiciness of the cooked meat. Therefore, the method used depends mainly upon its convenience.

Q. How should frozen roasts be cooked?

A. Frozen roasts should be cooked in the same manner as fresh roasts; 300° F., for fresh beef, veal and lamb, and 350° F. for fresh pork. However, frozen roasts require approximately ⅓ to ½ again as long for cooking as thawed roasts.

Q. How should frozen steaks and chops be cooked?

A. Thick frozen steaks and chops must be broiled more slowly than thawed ones in order that the meat is cooked to the desired degree of doneness in the center without becoming too well done on the outside. For this reason partial thawing before cooking is desirable. Frozen steaks and chops to be breaded should be completely thawed before cooking since the coatings will not readily adhere to frozen meat.

Barbecuing for a crowd is no trick at all, if you have a king-sized piece of barbecue equipment (and they do come big enough to serve 25!) and choose the right cuts of meat!

Lamb steaks are different and perfect for a crowd. Ask your meat dealer for a good meaty whole leg of lamb or two. From the sirloin end, have him cut 3 good slices. These are actually lamb sirloin chops, though many call them steaks. Then continue to slice off steaks until the shank end is reached. You should have 4 to 5 good-sized steaks, about 1 inch thick. Have the shank end boned and the meat ground with a bit of kidney fat to use as lamburgers for the younger set. Small fry and teen-agers will love them sandwiched into burger buns with all the "trimmings."

To Prepare Lamb Steaks for Barbecue-Grilling

Cut from the leg, these steaks are tender meat but tangy taste-appeal may be added to the delicate flavor of the lamb by allowing the steaks to stand several hours or overnight, under refrigeration of course, in a marinade of your choice—and you will have a lot of choosing to do when you see the list of these flavor-giving mixtures to be found in cookbooks of all sorts.

These recipes usually start with ¼ cup olive or salad oil to ¾ cup dry red or white wine or lemon juice and wine vinegar or pineapple juice or orange juice, with herbs—fresh or dried—salt, coarse-grind black pepper, garlic, and such items as soy sauce, meat sauce, curry powder, and so on added. You can really start "collecting" these seasoning-sauces, as you would bottles, buttons or snuff boxes. Just as exciting, any day!

The same sauce may be used for basting steaks, chops, or roasts. Brush on with a narrow paint brush or use a long-handled brush designed for basting barbecued meats.

To Grill: Prepare coals and grids as manufacturer of barbecue equipment directs. Rub the grill with cooking fat or a piece of lamb fat pierced with a long fork. Arrange steaks or chops on the grill. Your "barbecue" determines method and time. Some barbecues have a cover which enables cooking with direct heat and shortens the time. With this type, turn only once.

In general, for steaks and chops cut about 1 inch thick, allow about 8 minutes to each side. Use tongs when turning. To determine when the lamb steaks are cooked to your liking, use a small sharp knife and make a slit alongside the bone. The meat should be juicy and a delicate pink inside. Don't overcook by going to the "well-done" stage. The lamb will be dry and tasteless.

When chops are right, season with salt and coarse-grind black pepper. Serve very hot, on hot plates. Top each steak with

LEMON BUTTER

½ cup butter
½ teaspoon salt
 Dash or 2 of Tabasco sauce

2 tablespoons snipped parsley
2 tablespoons lemon juice
 (8 servings)

Let butter stand in bowl until softened. Work with fork or wooden spoon until creamy. Add salt, Tabasco sauce, parsley. Then slowly add the lemon juice, stirring until well blended. Serve a dollop on each lamb steak. Or make in advance; using waxed paper, shape in a roll. Chill. Then roll in minced parsley. Chill again. To serve, slice the chilled roll, allowing a thick slice for each serving.

Partners for Grilled Lamb Steaks: French Fried potatoes and onion slices, a big pot of white beans or baby limas, hot French bread with lots of butter, a mixed green salad, a beverage, and not much else. Save dessert till later in the day!

BEANS AND BURGERS

1½ pound chuck steak, ground
1 small onion, minced
1 tablespoon bottled thick
   meat sauce
1 tablespoon snipped parsley
½ teaspoon dried oregano
½ teaspoon dried rosemary
 Dash paprika
1½ teaspoon salt
¼ teaspoon pepper

¼ cup packaged dried bread
   crumbs
2 tablespoons salad oil
1 8-oz. can tomato sauce
⅓ cup ketchup
½ cup commercial sour cream
¾ teaspoon salt
1 No. 303 can red kidney beans,
   drained, rinsed, then
   drained

1. About 30 minutes before serving: In large bowl, thoroughly mix chuck, onion, meat sauce, parsley, oregano, rosemary, paprika, salt and pepper.

2. Shape meat mixture into 10 or 12 meat balls; roll in bread crumbs; then, in hot oil in large skillet, sauté till browned on all sides.

3. Meanwhile, stir together tomato sauce, ketchup, sour cream, and ¾ teaspoon salt; add, with kidney beans, to browned meat balls in skillet; stir gently. Simmer over low heat, uncovered, 10 min., or until meat is done.

4. Serve, right from skillet, with Toasted French-Bread Wedges (below) and a tossed raw-vegetable salad with cheese dressing. Makes 5 or 6 servings.

TOASTED FRENCH-BREAD WEDGES

About 25 minutes before serving; start heating oven to 425° F. Slice long loaf French bread into wedge-shaped pieces. Spread cut surfaces with soft butter or margarine. Or spread with butter mixed with celery, garlic, or onion salt; grated Parmesan cheese; or celery, poppy, or caraway seeds. Reassemble loaf on cookie sheet. Bake 12 minutes.

BEEF STROGANOFF

3 pounds round steak, cut ½-inch thick	2 cans (4 ounces each) mushrooms
2 tablespoons flour	1 teaspoon paprika
2 teaspoons salt	½ teaspoon pepper
¼ cup lard	2 tablespoons butter
¼ cup water	2 cups dairy sour cream
	1 package (8 ounces) medium noodles, cooked

Cut round steak into strips about ½-inch wide and 3 inches long. Mix flour and salt and dredge meat in seasoned flour. Brown meat in lard in frying pan. Pour off drippings. Add water, cover tightly and simmer for 1½ hours. Remove meat from frying pan, add mushrooms, paprika, pepper and butter. Cover and cook slowly 2 to 3 minutes. Add meat, fold in sour cream. Mix well. Cook until heated through, but do not boil. Serve over cooked noodles. 8 to 10 servings.

BEAN POT STEW

2 pounds beef for stewing,
  cut in 1-inch cubes
¼ cup flour
2½ teaspoons salt
½ teaspoon pepper
3 tablespoons shortening or
  salad oil
1 clove garlic, finely chopped
1 quart boiling water

10 small onions
6 medium carrots, cut in half
5 stalks celery, cut in 2-inch
  pieces
1 tablespoon lemon juice
1 teaspoon Worcestershire sauce
2 bay leaves
1 teaspoon sugar
  Dash cloves
½ teaspoon paprika

Roll meat in flour seasoned with 1 teaspoon of the salt and ¼ teaspoon of the pepper. In large skillet heat shortening or salad oil; add meat, brown on all sides; add garlic. Add rest of ingredients; mix

gently. Turn into greased 2½-quart bean pot or casserole. Cover and bake in moderate oven (350° F.) for 2½ to 3 hours or until meat and vegetables are tender. Add salt and pepper to taste. Serves 6.

BEEF PINWHEELS

1 pound ground beef
1½ teaspoons salt
⅛ teaspoon pepper
1 egg, well beaten
2 tablespoons butter or
  margarine, melted

6 tablespoons bread crumbs, fine,
  dry
2 tablespoons tomato juice
1½ cups mashed potatoes
1½ cups cooked peas

Mix together all ingredients except potatoes and peas, roll with rolling pin between two pieces of waxed paper to form rectangular sheet approximately 6 x 12½ inches thick.

Remove top waxed paper and spread 1½ cups seasoned mashed potatoes (may be left-over) on crosswise half of meat.

Spread other half with mashed peas (canned, quick-frozen or fresh), seasoned with salt, pepper and minced onion.

Roll meat firmly like jelly roll; wrap in waxed paper, chill several hours.

(This preparation may be done as long in advance as 24 hours if roll is kept in refrigerator.)

When ready to cook cut with sharp knife into six 1-inch slices; place on preheated broiler 3 to 4 inches below source of heat; brush with melted butter; broil slowly 12 minutes, turn; brush again with butter and broil 12 minutes on other side. Makes 6 servings.

BEEF SAN MATEO

1½ pounds ground beef
1 clove garlic, minced
1½ teaspoon salt
½ teaspoon Tabasco sauce
1 egg, separated

1 cup cooked rice (add ¼ teaspoon Tabasco per cup water when cooking rice.)
¼ teaspoon ground cloves
¼ cup chopped dried apricots
¼ cup sliced water chestnuts
4 pineapple sticks

Combine beef, garlic, salt, Tabasco, egg white. Form 8 x 11-inch rectangle on foil. Mix egg yolk and other ingredients except pineapple. Spread on meat. Top with pineapple set crosswise. Lifting foil, roll as for jelly roll. Use foil as pan liner. Bake at 350° F. (moderate oven) about 45 minutes. 6 to 8 servings.

SAUCE

Mix ¼ cup each pineapple juice, chopped dried apricots, pineapple, 1 tablespoon brown sugar, dash Tabasco to meat drippings. Bring to boil, pour over meat. Serve flambé if desired.

CREOLE BURGERS

Brown 1 pound ground beef and ½ cup chopped onion in heavy skillet, stirring to separate meat particles. Stir in 1 can Chicken Gumbo Soup, 2 tablespoons each ketchup and prepared mustard, and ¼ teaspoon black pepper. Simmer about 5 minutes. Serve on 8 toasted buttered buns.

BRAISED BEEF CUBES WITH VEGETABLES

3 tablespoons flour
1 teaspoon salt
⅛ teaspoon pepper
2 pounds boneless beef for stew
2 tablespoons lard or drippings
1 cup water
3 large potatoes, quartered

6 medium carrots, cut in half
6 small onions
6 large celery stalks, cut in half
1 package (12 ounces) frozen
green peas
or 1 pound fresh peas
¼ cup enriched flour

Mix flour, salt and pepper. Dredge meat in seasoned flour. Brown meat in lard or drippings. Add water, cover tightly and cook slowly for 1½ hours. Add potatoes, carrots, onions and celery. Cover and cook 30 minutes. Add green peas and cook 30 minutes longer or until meat is tender and vegetables are done. Remove meat and vegetables to serving platter. Add water to cooking liquid to make 2 cups. Thicken liquid with ¼ cup flour for gravy. 6 servings.

CAMPERS' CASSEROLE

1 jar (5 ounces) chipped beef
¾ cup chopped onion
2 tablespoons lard or drippings
⅛ teaspoon pepper
1 package (7 ounces) elbow
spaghetti

3 tablespoons butter or margarine
3 tablespoons flour
2 cups milk
¾ cup grated Cheddar cheese
½ cup chopped ripe olives

Chop chipped beef. Reserve ¼ cup for topping. Brown remaining chipped beef and onions in lard or drippings. Season with pepper. Cook spaghetti (without salt) until tender. Drain.

Melt butter or margarine, add flour and blend together. Add milk gradually. Cook slowly, stirring constantly until sauce thickens. Add cheese and stir until melted.

Combine chipped beef, onions, spaghetti, cheese sauce and olives. Pour into greased 2-quart casserole. Top with ¼ cup chipped beef. Bake in a slow oven (300° F.) for 45 minutes. 6 to 8 servings.

CABBAGE ROLLS WITH CHEESE-TOMATO SAUCE

A food favorite in Near Eastern countries is the "Dolma" or stuffed cabbage leaf. Cabbage leaves are spread with a seasoned rice and meat mixture and then rolled up. They are simmered in a sauce, usually a tomato one, until tender. Mint or allspice are favorite seasonings.

In this recipe a ground beef-rice stuffing is used and the rolls are cooked in tomato sauce. And—cheese is added to the sauce to make it just short of sensational, flavor-wise! Yes, an easy main dish and a favorite.

1 tablespoon cooking fat	¼ teaspoon chili powder
½ cup uncooked white rice	1 large head cabbage
1 pound ground beef	Juice of 1 lemon
½ cup chopped onion	2½ cups boiling water
2 teaspoons salt	2 8-oz. cans tomato sauce
	¼ pound processed cheese spread

Melt fat in a skillet. Add the rice, ground beef and onion. Cook, stirring occasionally, until the beef is browned and the rice begins to turn yellow. Stir in the salt and chili powder.

While the rice and beef cook, remove 12 leaves from cabbage. If necessary to prevent tearing leaves, dip head in boiling water. Cook the leaves in hot water several minutes or until partially tender. Drain. Before stuffing each leaf, cut stiff ridge away from back. Do not split leaf. Place ¼ cup of the rice-meat mixture toward stiff end of each leaf. Begin to roll folding in the sides.

Cut up some of remaining head of cabbage. Place in the bottom of a large soup kettle or Dutch oven. Arrange cabbage rolls in kettle with folds down. Pour lemon juice, boiling water and tomato sauce over the cabbage rolls. Cover and simmer about 1 to 1¼ hours or until the cabbage is tender.

While the rolls cook, cut the cheese into tiny pieces. When the rolls are tender, remove from the sauce and place on a hot platter. Stir some of sauce into cheese. Return to kettle. Heat over a very low heat until the cheese melts. Serve the sauce over the cabbage rolls. This recipe makes 6 to 7 servings.

CHEESE-CRUSTED HAMBURGER PIE

1 small clove garlic	¼ cup flour
3 tablespoons drippings	1 teaspoon salt
1 pound ground beef	1 No. 2 can tomato juice
2 tablespoons chopped green pepper	½ cup chopped celery
	2 tablespoons Worcestershire sauce

CHEESE PASTRY

1½ cups flour	½ cup shortening
½ teaspoon salt	¾ cup shredded American cheese
	3 tablespoons cold water

Sauté garlic in drippings for 5 minutes. Discard garlic. Add beef and green pepper and cook for 10 minutes, stirring frequently. Stir in flour and salt. Add tomato juice and cook until thick, stirring constantly. Add celery and Worcestershire sauce. Pour into a casserole 8 x 8 x 2 inches. Sift flour and salt together. Cut in shortening. Add cheese and sprinkle with water, mixing lightly with fork until all the flour is moistened. Turn out on waxed paper. Gather dough together and press into a ball. Divide dough in half. Roll one piece into an 8-inch square and place on top of meat mixture. Roll remaining piece into an 8-inch square and cut into ½-inch strips. Arrange lattice top on first crust. Bake in a moderately hot oven, 400° F., for 35 minutes. Six servings.

CHUCKWAGON SUPPER

2 flank steaks	1 cup chopped onion
3 tablespoons flour	1 cup chopped celery
¼ teaspoon pepper	1 teaspoon Worcestershire sauce
2 tablespoons lard or drippings	1 can (6 ounces) tomato paste
	1 cup water

Score one side of steaks. Sprinkle scored side with 1 teaspoon salt. Roll and fasten securely with wooden picks. Cut into individual servings 1½ inches thick. Combine flour, 1 teaspoon salt and pepper. Dredge meat in seasoned flour. Brown in lard or drippings. Pour off drippings. Combine onions, celery, Worcestershire sauce, tomato paste and water. Pour over steaks. Cover tightly and simmer 2 hours or until meat is tender. 6 to 8 servings.

CROWN O'GOLD MEAT LOAF

MEAT LOAF

1½ cups fine soft bread crumbs
1½ pounds ground lean
    chuck beef
4 egg yolks
1½ teaspoons salt
2 tablespoons mustard

1½ tablespoons prepared
    horseradish
3 tablespoons finely diced
    green pepper
2 tablespoons minced onion
⅓ cup ketchup

TOPPING

4 egg whites

¼ teaspoon cream of tartar
4 tablespoons mustard

Mix bread crumbs with meat. Combine other ingredients. Blend into meat mix. Pack into 9-inch casserole; bake in moderate oven (325°) 30 minutes. Beat egg whites until foamy; add cream of tartar; beat until very stiff. Fold in mustard gently. Swirl on hot meat; bake 20 to 25 minutes or till tipped with brown. 6 to 8 servings.

DAD'S POT ROAST

3- to 4-pound blade pot roast
3 tablespoons lard
1½ teaspoons salt
¼ teaspoon pepper
½ pound ground beef
½ cup chopped onion
1 4-ounce can sliced mushrooms

1 8-ounce can tomato sauce
½ clove garlic, minced
1½ cups chopped celery
1 tablespoon grated orange rind
¼ teaspoon nutmeg
¼ teaspoon cinnamon
¼ teaspoon cloves
¾ cup water

Brown pot roast in lard. Pour off drippings. Season with salt and pepper. Add remaining ingredients, cover and simmer 3 to 3½ hours, or until tender. 6 to 8 servings.

DUTCH OVEN STEAK

2 pounds round steak, 1-inch
　　thick
1 cup flour
1 tablespoon salt

1 teaspoon black pepper
½ cup shortening
1 large onion, chopped fine
1 can mushroom soup

Pound steak with tenderizer. Pour flour into shallow pan; add salt
and pepper. Press steak into flour mixture and turn several times. Melt
shortening in heated Dutch oven (425° F.). Brown steak well on both
sides, then add chopped onion. Mix mushroom soup with equal parts
of water, stir well, and pour over steak. Turn fire down to 350° and
let simmer for 2 hours. Add more water if necessary. Serves 4 to 6.

HOBO MULLIGAN STEW — IOWA STYLE

2 tablespoons cooking fat
1 to 1½ pounds stew beef, cut
　　in ½-inch cubes
4 cups water
3 teaspoons salt
½ bay leaf
¼ teaspoon chili powder
2 medium carrots, sliced
　　(about 1 cup)

1 medium potato, diced
　　(about 1 cup)
1 large turnip, diced
　　(about 1¼ cups)
2 cups chopped cabbage
1 cup diced celery
½ green pepper, diced
　　(about ½ cup)
1 can tomatoes and juice
　　(1 pound), broken up
½ cup uncooked white rice

Melt fat in a soup kettle or Dutch oven. Add the beef and cook
slowly, until brown. Add additional fat only if necessary to keep from
sticking. Add 1 cup of the water and 1 teaspoon of the salt. Cover and
simmer 1¼ hours. Add the rest of the ingredients and the remaining
3 cups water and 2 teaspoons salt. Cover and cook until the meat and
vegetables are tender, about 45 minutes. Add water if a thinner mixture
is desired. Season to taste with salt and pepper.

Serve piping hot in soup bowls. For an informal party meal, serve
the soup from an iron soup kettle or Dutch oven. Use tin cups or pie

pans for soup bowls and bandana handkerchiefs for napkins. Hot, crusty French or Vienna bread is delicious with the soup. Makes 8 servings.

MUSHROOM MEAT BALLS

1 pound ground beef	1½ teaspoons salt
⅔ cup fine dry bread crumbs	2 cans (2½ cups) condensed
2 tablespoons minced onion	cream of mushroom soup
1 tablespoon minced parsley	¼ cup water
1 egg, slightly beaten	2 tablespoons shortening

Combine ground beef, bread crumbs, onion, parsley, egg and salt. Stir soup until smooth; blend in water. Put ¼ cup of soup mixture into the meat; mix well. Shape into balls about 1 inch in diameter. Brown meat balls in shortening in a skillet; pour in remaining mushroom sauce. Cover and bake in a moderate oven (350° F.) or cook slowly on top of range.

MEAT SAUCE WITH WINE FOR SPAGHETTI

¼ cup olive oil or salad oil	2 cups canned tomatoes or
2 onions, minced	4 fresh tomatoes, cut in pieces
1 clove garlic	1 can tomato paste
1 pound hamburger	Salt, pepper
	2 cups red wine
	1 small can mushrooms

Sauté onion and garlic in oil until lightly browned. Remove garlic. Add hamburger and cook, stirring frequently until well browned. Add tomatoes and tomato paste, salt and pepper to season. Add ¼ cup red wine (Chianti, cabernet, claret, Burgundy, or any other red wine) and continue cooking and adding wine as sauce thickens. Simmer at least 1 hour. Add mushrooms about 10 minutes before the end of the cooking period.

BAKED LIVER AND ONIONS

Peel and slice 6 medium yellow onions. Place in greased 1½-quart casserole. Season with salt and pepper. Wipe with a damp cloth 1 pound beef liver, sliced. Place on top of sliced onions. Season with salt and pepper. Dot with margarine.

Measure 2 tablespoons flour. Add small amount of a 10½ ounce can beef consommé. Mix to a paste. Add remaining consommé. Stir lightly. Pour over liver. Cover. Place in moderate oven (350° F.) and bake for 1 hour and 15 minutes. When ready to serve, remove cover, and sprinkle with 2 tablespoons chopped parsley. Serve from casserole onto rice or broad noodles. Serve with a tossed green salad. Serves 4.

LIVER BACON PATTIES

1½ pounds beef liver, sliced ½-inch thick	1½ teaspoons salt
	¼ teaspoon pepper
2 tablespoons lard	¼ teaspoon thyme
¼ cup minced onion	¼ teaspoon marjoram
1½ cups cooked rice	8 slices bacon
2 eggs, beaten	2 tablespoons lard or drippings

Cook liver in lard until very lightly browned on each side (about 5 minutes). Put through food chopper. Combine liver, onion, rice, eggs and seasonings. Mix well. Shape into 8 patties and wrap a slice of bacon around each. Brown patties on both sides in lard or drippings. Allow 10 to 15 minutes for cooking. 6 to 8 servings.

LIVER LOAF

1½ pounds sliced liver	1 teaspoon salt
2 tablespoons lard or bacon drippings	⅛ teaspoon pepper
	½ teaspoon marjoram
2 slices bacon	1 cup cracker crumbs
1 medium onion	1 cup milk or tomato juice
2 eggs, slightly beaten	½ cup ketchup

Grease a 5 x 9-inch loaf pan. Cook liver in lard or drippings until lightly browned. Grind liver, bacon and onion together. Combine liver mixture, eggs, salt, pepper, marjoram, cracker crumbs and milk or tomato juice. Pour ketchup into loaf pan. Pack liver mixture over ketchup. Bake in a moderate oven (350° F.) for 1 hour. 8 servings.

GOLDEN POTPOURRI

2 pounds veal, cut in 1 to
   1½-inch pieces
3 tablespoons lard or shortening
2½ teaspoons salt
¼ teaspoon pepper
1 can (16 ounces) whole
   kernel corn
½ cup chopped onion
¼ cup chopped green pepper

¼ cup chopped pimiento
4 ounces narrow egg noodles,
   cooked
1 can (10½ ounces)
   mushroom soup
2 tablespoons melted butter
   or margarine
½ cup ½-inch bread cubes,
   toasted

Brown veal in lard. Pour off drippings. Season with salt and pepper. Drain corn and add water to make 1 cup of liquid. Add liquid to veal, cover tightly and simmer 1 hour. Combine veal, corn, onion, green pepper, pimiento, noodles and soup. Place in greased 2-quart casserole. Mix melted butter or margarine and toasted bread cubes and sprinkle over top. Bake in a moderate oven (350° F.) for 45 minutes. 6 to 8 servings.

VEAL ALMOND DIN

2 pounds veal shoulder steaks,
   cut ½-inch thick
2 tablespoons lard or drippings
1 cup sliced celery
1 can (4 ounces) button
   mushrooms, drained
2 cans (4 ounces each) water
   chestnuts, drained and
   sliced thinly
1 large green pepper, cut in
   1-inch pieces

1 cup thawed frozen green beans
⅓ cup pimiento, drained and
   cut into 1-inch squares
2 teaspoons salt
½ teaspoon pepper
½ teaspoon garlic salt
1 bouillon cube
1 cup water
2 tablespoons cornstarch
   Cooked rice
¼ cup toasted, blanched almonds

Cut steaks into strips about 1 inch wide and 2 inches long. Brown meat lightly in lard or drippings. Cover tightly and cook slowly about 30 minutes. Pour off drippings. Cook celery in a small amount of water about 5 minutes. Drain. Add partially cooked celery, mushrooms, water chestnuts, green pepper, green beans, pimiento and seasonings. Stir well. Cover tightly and simmer 10 minutes. Heat ½ cup water to boiling, add bouillon cube and stir until dissolved. Mix cornstarch and remaining ½ cup water. Add bouillon and cornstarch mixture to meat and vegetables and cook, stirring constantly, until thickened. Cover and cook slowly about 5 minutes, stirring occasionally. Serve with cooked rice and top with toasted almonds. 6 to 8 servings.

HERBED LAMB LOAF

2 eggs, unbeaten	¼ cup minced onion
1¼ pounds ground lamb	1½ teaspoons salt
¼ pound ground pork	¼ teaspoon pepper
1 cup rolled oats (quick or old-fashioned, uncooked)	¼ teaspoon sweet basil
¼ cup chicken bouillon (made by dissolving 1 bouillon cube into ¾ cup boiling water)	¼ teaspoon oregano
	Heat oven to 350° F. (moderate)

With fork, beat eggs slightly. Lightly mix in the meat, then rolled oats and remaining ingredients. Combine lightly but well. (Meat will be juicier and more tender if you handle it as little as possible.)

In bowl, shape meat into an oval loaf. Transfer to shallow baking dish or heat-proof platter and smooth into a shapely rectangular-shaped loaf. Place slices of lemon brushed with melted butter on top of the loaf.

Bake for 1 hour in moderate oven. Serve from baking dish or heat-proof platter, spooning off the excess juices to make into a gravy if desired. Or spoon some of the juices over the loaf.

P.S. If you prefer a soft, moist exterior, bake lamb as directed in a 9″ x 5″ x 3″ loaf pan or in a 1½-quart ring mold. Pour juices from pan after baking. Unmold meat loaf onto cake rack. Then place, right side up, on heated platter. If ring mold is used, fill the center with hot buttered or creamed vegetables.

BREAST OF LAMB WITH APRICOT STUFFING

1 breast of lamb with pocket
(about 2 pounds)

Salt and pepper
Lemon juice or garlic

APRICOT STUFFING

6 cups soft bread cubes, small
¾ teaspoon salt
¼ teaspoon pepper
¼ teaspoon powdered thyme
or poultry seasoning

1⅓ cups dried apricots (cut in
small pieces)
½ cup minced onion
1 cup chopped celery
⅓ cup melted butter

Have your meat dealer remove the fell (outside covering) and crack the bones of the breast so that it can easily be carved between the ribs when served. Have a pocket made in the breast by cutting through the flesh close to the ribs. Rub the inside of pocket and outside with salt and pepper; use a little lemon or garlic if you wish additional seasoning.

Prepare bread cubes. Add seasonings. Place apricots in a saucepan and cover with a little water. Cover; when water is boiling, remove from heat and let stand about a minute, or until apricots are slightly tender. Drain off liquid. Cook onions and celery in the melted butter over low heat, until tender but not browned. Add to bread mixture along with the apricots.

Fill lamb pocket with Apricot Stuffing and fasten opening with skewers, or poultry pins and string, as you would a turkey, lacing shoestring fashion. Place breast ribs down in a shallow baking dish. Cook in 325° F. (moderate) oven about 1¾ hours. Serve piping hot with spiced apricots, baked macaroni and cheese, and buttered string beans, with custard and cookies for dessert.

ROTISSERIE-ROAST LAMB

Have your meat dealer prepare for you on order a boned and rolled shoulder or leg of lamb. Additional lamb can be rolled into the boned cut to provide for more servings. You'll need to allow ¼ to ⅓ pound boned roast per serving. Be sure to get the weight of the finished roll. The boned and rolled lamb makes for perfect balancing on the easy handling by the spit, and is sheer joy for the carver.

To Prepare for the Spit

Method 1. Several hours or overnight in advance: Cream together thoroughly ¾ stick butter (6 tablespoons), 2 smallish cloves minced garlic or ½ teaspoon garlic salt, 1½ teaspoons salt, 2 teaspoons monosodium glutamate, ¼ teaspoon coarse-grind pepper, 1 tablespoon lemon juice. Spread this paste over the rolled roast of lamb, completely coating it. Allow to stand in the refrigerator until ready to place on the spit. This serves as a basting sauce while the lamb cooks.

Method 2. Just before barbecuing, insert slivers of garlic in tiny gashes cut at various spots in the roast. Brush with lemon juice, sprinkle liberally with salt and pepper. Or after inserting garlic, mix together ¼ cup granulated sugar, ¼ teaspoon ground cloves, ¼ tablespoon ginger, 1 tablespoon lemon juice. Rub thoroughly into the surface and ends of the roast. Sprinkle with salt and pepper. Run the spit through the exact center of the rolled lamb roast. Place in the roast a short roast meat thermometer, specially designed for rotisserie.

To Roast

Arrange spitted lamb on rotisserie. If you are using a charcoal rotisserie, set at distance above glowing coals as suggested in manufacturer's directions. Start motor for revolving spit.

Time and Temperature

In general, it is well to allow around 25 minutes per pound for meat just taken from the refrigerator, but the best guide is the use of the roast meat thermometer. The accepted internal temperature for roast lamb is 180 to 182° F. which is well-done, but for true enjoyment, do stop the cooking process at 160 to 170° F. The lamb has a delicate pink tinge on the inside, and is tender and juicy in comparison to the somewhat dry texture of "well-done." Some prefer the lamb on the "rare" side—140° internal temperature.

While the lamb is cooking, it may be brushed with a favorite barbecue sauce with a red or white wine and salad oil base or with lemon juice and oil, plus seasonings of your choice, preferably without the usual tomato sauce or catsup addition.

Most motored revolving spits are timed in speed so that they are self-basting, though a drip pan is often provided to catch any errant drippings. Or a pan may be shaped of aluminum foil and placed under the spit. This prevents flare-ups of burning fat. Drippings mixed with a little white wine may be used for basting or for a sauce to serve with the lamb.

To Serve

Always serve lamb piping hot on plates that are not content to be just warm. Gravy should also be served and kept hot. The accompaniments can be many—so many things go with lamb, you know!

Vegetables stuffed with a hearty filling and baked add eye and taste appeal to a humdrum meat-and-potato menu.

INDIAN CURRY

2½ pounds boneless lamb shoulder, cut in 1 to 1½-inch pieces
2 tablespoons lard
1 cup finely chopped onions
1 clove garlic, crushed
2 teaspoons salt
2 bay leaves
⅛ teaspoon thyme
2 teaspoons curry
2 tablespoons tomato sauce
2 cups water
½ cup grated apple
¼ cup chutney, cut in ½-inch pieces
½ cup cream
2 tablespoons cornstarch
¼ cup water
1½ cups rice, cooked

Brown lamb in lard. Add onions and cook until lightly browned. Add garlic, salt, bay leaves, thyme, curry, tomato sauce and water. Cover and simmer for 1½ hours. Remove the bay leaves and add grated apple, chutney and cream. Mix the cornstarch and water, add to the meat mixture and cook for 10 minutes after it has thickened. Serve on hot rice. 8 servings.

Serve with chutney, chopped skinless peanuts, shredded coconut, crisp diced bacon, chopped hard-cooked egg whites, sieved hard-cooked egg yolks and raisins.

CROWN ROAST OF LAMB

To carve: If prepared properly at the market (be sure the backbone is cut off), the crown roast is very easy to carve. The carver steadies the crown by inserting the fork to the left between the ribs. He then makes slices by running knife close to bone of each two ribs, then cutting from tip of roast down to the platter. This double-rib chop and a portion of the stuffing are served to each portion. Always serve lamb piping hot and on hot plates.

To garnish: The crown roast of lamb is so attractive that it needs little more than a few sprigs of parsley to adorn it and the platter. However, using a large platter, an excellent garnish-accompaniment is Chutney-Filled Pears. Fill hollow of pear halves with chutney and dots of butter. Just before serving, place low under the broiler unit to heat through and glaze. Serve very hot.

Accompaniments: Satin-smooth gravy made from the roast drippings, butter-topped broccoli or other green vegetable, a plate of crisp relishes, hot rolls, and rosé wine are good. For dessert, a sherbet with butter cookies or angel, sunshine or chiffon cake.

OLD COUNTRY STUFFING

1 cup minced onions
½ cup (1 stick) butter
8 cups (2 quarts) small bread
    cubes from day-old bread
¾ pound ground lamb
¾ teaspoon salt

2 packages frozen chopped
    spinach, cooked and drained
    (about 2 cups cooked,
    drained, chopped spinach)
1 small clove garlic, minced
½ teaspoon allspice
¼ teaspoon coarse-grind black
    pepper
6 tablespoons grated Parmesan
    or Romano cheese

Cook onions slowly in butter until soft but not browned. Lift from the butter and add to the bread cubes. Cook lamb in butter until a golden brown, stirring frequently. Add salt. Cook spinach, drain well. Add lamb, spinach and remaining ingredients to the bread cubes and onions. Mix lightly with a fork. Place stuffing on heavy aluminum foil.

Use a "drug-store-wrap" to close edges so that stuffing will remain moist during baking. Place in 325° F. oven at the same time as the roast. See roast directions for using stuffing in crown. This stuffing is unusual, with a fine flavor that goes well with lamb. Your favorite stuffing may be used instead.

NOISETTE OF SPRING LAMB

1 saddle lamb, 7 pounds	5 tablespoons butter
1 teaspoon salt	½ bunch tarragon (or 1 teaspoon)
1 pinch ground white pepper	¼ lemon
	1 cup Chablis wine

Select a good saddle of lamb with smooth grained, light-colored meat with some fat, but not too much. Have butcher bone and saddle and cut the kernel into small pieces in style of a filet mignon, removing fat and tendons. Season these tiny noisettes with salt and pepper, sauté in butter until medium-rare. Spring lamb should never be too well cooked. Place the noisettes on a serving platter. Then pour into the pan in which noisettes were prepared about one cup of Chablis. Add chopped fresh tarragon, or dry tarragon if fresh is not available. Reduce by half; add one tablespoon butter. A drop of lemon juice may be added to the sauce at the last moment. Strain through a cheesecloth. Pour over noisettes and serve.

ROAST LAMB, MILANESE

Choose a six-pound leg of yearling lamb, and place on the rack of a roasting pan in a hot oven, 400° F., for fifteen or twenty minutes. Meantime sift a quart can of tomatoes, add one pound of young onions, grated or chopped very fine, also one sweet green pepper, minced, one very small clove of garlic, also minced; heat all together with a cup of good stock or gravy, and pour over the lamb in the roasting pan. After this, reduce the temperature to 325°, and baste the lamb every fifteen minutes with the tomato sauce, for two hours, adding more stock if necessary. Serve on a hot platter with the sauce poured around it, and with it serve one-half pound of Italian spaghetti, cooked in boiling salted water, sprinkled with grated cheese and a dash of paprika.

SAVORY LAMB STUFFING FOR VEGETABLES

1 pound ground lamb
1 cup cooked rice
½ teaspoon powdered or crushed
    dried savory or thyme

1 teaspoon salt
1 can (10½ ounces) condensed
    tomato soup
1 cup shredded American cheese
½ cup chopped onion

Pan-fry the lamb slowly in a skillet until all the pink color disappears. Drain off fat, then combine with other ingredients.

To Stuff Green Peppers

Choose 6 firm well-shaped green peppers. Cut off the stem end. Remove seeds. (The green trimmed-off portion may be chopped and added to the stuffing or used in other dishes.) Boil peppers in salted water for 3 minutes. Drain and stand them up in a muffin tin or other baking pan. Stuff the peppers. Bake in a 350° F. (moderate) oven 35 to 40 minutes. Serve hot with a fruit salad and hot rolls.

Grand Prize-Winner

SKEWERED LAMB WITH CRANBERRY BURRS

½ cup ketchup
¼ cup cranberry juice
2 tablespoons Worcestershire
    sauce
3 tablespoons sugar

2 tablespoons steak sauce
3 tablespoons vinegar
1 teaspoon salt
1½ pounds lamb shoulder in
    1½-inch cubes

Combine all ingredients except the lamb. Heat to the boiling point. String lamb on skewers allowing 3 or 4 cubes to each skewer. Place on the broiler rack. Spoon part of sauce over the cubes. Broil 3 inches from the heat 25 to 35 minutes. Turn and baste every five minutes. Serves 4.

Place skewers of lamb as spokes to a wheel with the center of the wheel filled with Cranberry Burrs. Between the spokes place wild rice and mushrooms.

CRANBERRY BURRS

1 one-pound can jellied
  cranberry sauce
Flour
1 cup all-purpose flour

½ teaspoon salt
⅔ cup milk
2 eggs, well beaten
Cornflakes, crushed
Fat for frying

Chill cranberry sauce thoroughly; remove from the can and cut sauce into balls wtih ball cutter. Roll balls in flour, then in batter made by combining flour, salt, milk, and eggs. Roll in cornflakes and fry in deep fat heated to 390° F. or hot enough to brown a cube of bread in 40 seconds. Drain and serve. Makes 50 small balls and 20 to 25 using larger ball cutter.

This recipe, submitted by the author in the 1957 Lamb and Cranberry Contest, was the Grand Prize-Winner.

SPARERIBS, SAUERKRAUT AND DUMPLINGS

(GERMAN STYLE)

3 pounds salted spareribs
1 pound sauerkraut
½ cup butter
6 large apples, pared and sliced
½ bottle white wine (or water)
  Salt and pepper
  Pinch of sugar

¼ pound ground pork
¼ pound ground veal
1 tablespoon butter
1 teaspoon grated onion
1 egg

Cut the salted spareribs into serving pieces, wash and drain them, then brown on both sides in butter; place them in a Dutch oven or casserole or heavy saucepan. Cover with sauerkraut. Add the butter, apples, white wine, salt and pepper and pinch of sugar. Simmer, covered, for 2 hours. Add little water as original liquid cooks away.

MEAT DUMPLINGS

Mix remaining ingredients together, then work into them enough soaked bread crumbs to make mixture stick together. Form into small

balls, fry in the butter in which spareribs were browned. Place sauerkraut in center of serving platter, arrange the spareribs around it, and
the meat balls on the sauerkraut on top of each other like a tower.
Serves 6.

SURPRISE DRUMSTICKS

1 pound ground pork shoulder	6 to 8 frankfurters
½ cup bread crumbs, fine dry	1 egg, beaten
1 teaspoon salt	1 tablespoon water
Dash pepper	2 tablespoons salad oil or
¼ cup milk	melted fat
¼ cup ketchup	16 gherkin pickles
	16 radishes

Combine pork, crumbs, salt, pepper, milk and ketchup; mix well.
Cut frankfurters into pieces about 1¾ inches long. Divide pork mixture
into 16 equal portions; shape each portion around piece of frankfurter
to form drumstick. Combine egg and water; dip drumstick in egg; then
roll in more fine dry crumbs. Sauté drumsticks in salad oil or fat over
low heat about 15 minutes, turning to brown on all sides. To serve,
insert skewers or wooden sticks through a pickle and a radish, then
through drumstick. Makes 8 servings.

FRANKFURTER BISCUIT PIE

2 tablespoons lard or drippings	¼ cup grated American cheese
6 frankfurters, sliced	¼ cup chili sauce
1 tablespoon finely chopped onion	1 cup canned or cooked green
¼ cup enriched flour	beans
½ teaspoon salt	½ cup canned or cooked whole
2 cups milk	kernel corn

Melt lard or drippings in frying pan, add frankfurters and onions
and brown lightly. Stir in flour, salt and milk; cook until thick, stirring
constantly. Add cheese, chili sauce, green beans and corn. Pour into
8-inch square baking dish. Top with Frankfurter Biscuits. Bake in a
hot oven (425° F.) 30 to 35 minutes. 4 to 6 servings.

FRANKFURTER BISCUITS

1½ cups sifted enriched flour   ¼ cup lard or shortening
2 teaspoon baking powder   ¼ cup grated American cheese
½ teaspoon salt   2 frankfurters sliced
                                       ¾ cup milk

Sift together flour, baking powder and salt. Cut in lard or shortening until mixture has a fine even crumb. Add cheese and frankfurters and mix lightly. Add milk and stir until flour is well moistened. Drop by spoonfuls on above mixture.

HARVEST SAUSAGE PIE

1½ pounds pork sausage links   ⅛ teaspoon pepper
2 tablespoons water   1 cup milk
¼ cup sausage drippings   2 eggs, beaten
3 tablespoons minced green   2 cans (16 ounces each)
     pepper   cream-style corn
2 tablespoons minced onion   1 teaspoon Worcestershire sauce
3 tablespoons flour   1½ cups Homemade Biscuit Mix
1 teaspoon salt   (See recipe page 126)
                                       ¾ cup milk

Place sausage links in frying pan, add 2 tablespoons water. Cover and simmer 15 minutes. Remove sausage links, pour off drippings and save. Cook green pepper and onion in ¼ cup drippings, about 5 minutes. Stir in flour, salt and pepper. Add milk, beaten eggs, corn and Worcestershire sauce. Cook slowly until heated through. Pour into greased 8 x 12-inch baking dish. Arrange sausage links on corn mixture to form 8 squares. Add ¾ cup milk to 1½ cups Homemade Biscuit Mix. Drop a tablespoonful of biscuit mixture in each square. Bake in a hot oven (425° F.) for 30 to 35 minutes. 6 to 8 servings.

HAM ROYALE

½ cup butter or margarine	3 cups diced ham or combination
½ cup flour	of ham and chicken
1 quart milk	½ cup sherry wine
1 pound fresh mushrooms	1½ cups grated sharp cheese
3 tablespoons margarine	2 teaspoons minced onion
	2 teaspoons salt
	½ teaspoon black pepper

Melt margarine in saucepan, add flour to make a smooth paste, add milk gradually; cook and stir constantly until sauce is thickened and smooth. Wash the fresh mushrooms and slice lengthwise. Sauté in the 3 tablespoons margarine about 3 minutes (don't cook too long). Add diced ham or combination of ham and chicken to cream sauce. Stir in sautéed mushrooms, wine, grated cheese. Add minced onion and seasonings and stir thoroughly but gently. Serve in casserole or chafing dish over heat. Sprinkle with slivered almonds if desired. This recipe is fine for a buffet table and will serve 6. Serve on toast points.

HAWAIIAN HAM

2½ to 3 cups diced cooked ham	2 tablespoons cornstarch
1 medium-sized onion	¼ teaspoon salt
1 small green sweet pepper	1 cup syrup from pineapple
1 cup pineapple cubes	⅓ cup vinegar
½ cup dark or golden raisins	1 teaspoon Worcestershire sauce
2 teaspoons dry mustard	1 tablespoon soya sauce
½ cup brown sugar	(optional)
	Cooked rice

Arrange ham in baking dish. Slice both onion and green pepper into rings. Arrange over ham. Add drained pineapple cubes and raisins. Blend mustard, sugar, cornstarch and salt in saucepan. Stir in pineapple syrup and vinegar and cook and stir until mixture boils and is clear. Blend in Worcestershire and soya sauces. Pour over ham mixture. Bake in moderate oven (350° F.) 45 minutes to 1 hour. Serve over rice. Makes 4 to 6 servings.

HAWAIIAN PORK IN BATTER

1 pound boneless pork shoulder, cut in 1-inch cubes	3 green peppers
	½ cup pineapple chunks
1 egg	2½ tablespoons cornstarch
2 tablespoons flour	2½ tablespoons soy sauce
½ teaspoon salt	¼ cup sugar
⅛ teaspoon pepper	¼ cup vinegar
3 tablespoons lard or drippings	½ cup pineapple juice
	Chinese noodles or cooked rice

Beat together egg, flour, salt and pepper. Thoroughly coat cubes of pork in egg-flour batter. Brown on all sides in hot lard or drippings. Cover and cook slowly for about 30 minutes. Pour off drippings. Remove stems and seeds from green peppers. Cut peppers into 1-inch squares. Boil peppers 10 minutes in water to cover. Drain. Add green peppers and pineapple to meat. Cover and simmer 10 minutes. Mix together cornstarch, soy sauce, sugar, vinegar and pineapple juice. Cook, stirring constantly until clear, about 2 minutes. Pour over meat mixture and simmer 5 minutes. Serve over Chinese noodles or cooked rice. Four servings.

PORK CHOP CASSEROLE

4 pork chops, about 1-inch thick	1 can condensed consommé
1 cup uncooked long-grain white rice	½ cup sauterne (or other white table wine)
1 medium onion, chopped	Pinch each of thyme and
½ green pepper, chopped	marjoram)
2 pimientos, chopped	Salt and pepper

Trim excess fat from pork chops. Heat large, heavy skillet, grease with fat from chops; brown slowly on both sides. Mix rice, onion, green pepper and pimientos; spread in bottom of two-quart casserole. Place chops on top. Mix consommé and wine; add water to make 2 cups liquid; add seasonings. Heat to boiling; pour over chops and rice. Cover and bake in moderately hot oven (375° F.) for 30 minutes. Remove chops and stir rice mixture gently with a fork; replace chops. Cover and continue baking about 30 minutes or until chops are tender and rice has absorbed all liquid, turning chops occasionally. Serves 4.

NEW ENGLAND CASSEROLE

6 pork chops (center cut or
   pork steak)
6 medium-sized potatoes, sliced

2 medium-sized onions, sliced
2 tablespoons flour
2 teaspoons poultry seasoning
   Salt and pepper to taste

Grease casserole and casserole lid thoroughly with butter. In bottom of casserole, place 3 chops. Sprinkle with salt and pepper and 1 teaspoon poultry seasoning. On the chops place a layer of sliced onion, then a layer of sliced potatoes, and over these sift 1 tablespoon flour and sprinkle with salt and pepper. Repeat the layers and seasonings, ending with a layer of potatoes with cold water. On top of the potatoes spread the following combination:

6 soda crackers
½ cup boiling water
2 tablespoons butter

1 teaspoon chopped onion
½ teaspoon poultry seasoning
   Salt to taste

Crumble the crackers and soak crumbs in boiling water. Stir in butter while mixture is warm. Add remaining ingredients and mix thoroughly. After topping meat and vegetable mixture with this combination, cover casserole with heavily greased lid and bake 2½ hours at 350° F., removing lid last 30 minutes. Serves 6.

PORK CHOP TREAT

8 rib or loin pork chops, cut
   1-inch thick
1½ tablespoons prepared mustard
2 tablespoons lard or drippings
½ cup hot water
1 No. 303 can cream-style corn

1½ cups soft bread crumbs
2 tablespoons grated onion
1 tablespoon minced green
   pepper
1 teaspoon salt
⅛ teaspoon pepper

Spread pork chops lightly with prepared mustard and brown in melted lard. Arrange browned chops in shallow baking pan. Pour off fat left in frying pan and add ½ cup of hot water, stirring well to loosen bits of meat from the bottom of the pan. Pour over chops.

Combine the corn, bread crumbs, onion, green pepper, salt and pepper and place the mixture in mounds on top of chops. Bake in a moderate oven (350° F.) for 1 hour. 8 servings.

SAVORY HAM PIE

3 tablespoons chopped onion	1 can condensed chicken soup
¼ cup chopped green pepper	1¼ cups milk
6 tablespoons enriched flour	1½ cups cooked ham, cut in pieces
¼ cup shortening	1 tablespoon lemon juice

Cook onion and green pepper in shortening, but do not brown. Rub flour into shortening, add undiluted chicken soup, and the milk. Cook until thickened, stirring constantly. Add ham and lemon juice. Pour into a well-greased casserole and cover with cheese biscuit topping.

CHEESE BISCUIT TOPPING

2 cups sifted enriched flour	½ cup grated cheese
3 teaspoons baking powder	¼ cup shortening
¾ teaspoon salt	¾ cup milk

Sift dry ingredients together, add cheese, then cut in shortening until the consistency of meal. Add milk and stir with a fork until milk is absorbed. Turn onto a lightly floured board and knead lightly for about 20 seconds. Roll to about ½-inch thickness and cut with lightly floured doughnut cutter, making one sharp cut for each biscuit. Arrange on top of ham mixture, filling in corners with extra pieces cut with the small center of the doughnut cutter. Bake in hot oven (450° F.) for 15 minutes, reduce heat to 425° F., and continue to bake 10 to 15 minutes longer. Serves 6.

SLICED BREAST OF TURKEY MORNAY ON TOAST

3 slices turkey	½ teaspoon salt
1 pint milk	2 ounces American cheese
4 ounces butter	1 egg yolk
2 tablespoons flour	Grated cheese

Boil milk and add melted butter, flour, salt, and cheese. Simmer 5 minutes and stir in egg yolk before removing from fire. Cut 3 slices of toast into triangles and place a large slice of turkey on each, then cover with sauce. Sprinkle with grated cheese and brown in oven. Three servings.

CHICKEN AND SPAGHETTI

1 6-pound chicken	2 (or more) cloves garlic
½ cup flour	1 bay leaf
4 tablespoons fat	½ teaspoon thyme
1 #2 can tomatoes	1 tablespoon salt
1 small can tomato paste	¼ teaspoon pepper
1 large onion	1½ pounds spaghetti

Cut chicken into pieces, dredge in flour, brown in fat, and remove from fire. Into the fat put tomatoes and tomato paste, and cook over low flame until thick. Add onion, garlic, bay leaf, thyme, salt, pepper, and 2 quarts hot water. Return chicken to this sauce, cover the pot, and boil slowly for 2 hours. During final period, cook spaghetti in boiling salted water until tender, drain it, and cover it with chicken and sauce. Serve quickly. 12 portions.

CHICKEN CANNELLONI

4 cans chicken broth (7 cups)	5 celery stalks, chopped
¼ cup butter or margarine	2 small onions, chopped
16 packaged tufoli macaroni shells	¾ cup chopped raw spinach
	1 teaspoon salt
3 whole chicken breasts, halved, boned	¼ teaspoon pepper
	3 bay leaves
½ cup sweet butter	¾ teaspoon dried oregano
3 shallots, chopped	½ teaspoon dried thyme
3 cloves garlic, minced	4 egg yolks, unbeaten
	Grated Parmesan cheese

EARLY IN DAY

1. Make Bolognese Sauce; refrigerate. (Recipe below.)
2. In boiling chicken broth and ¼ cup butter in large skillet, cook tufoli (add few extra to allow for breakage), covered, until tender—20 to 30 minutes. Carefully remove; cool.
3. Cut chicken into chunks. Then, in sweet butter in skillet, sauté shallots and garlic 2 minutes. Add chicken, celery, onions, spinach,

salt, pepper, bay leaves, oregano, thyme. Simmer, covered, till tender—about 10 minutes. Quickly stir in egg yolks; remove from heat; discard bay leaves; chop fine; use to stuff tufoli; refrigerate.

ABOUT 45 MINUTES BEFORE SERVING

1. Start heating oven to 375° F. In each of 4 buttered individual shallow casseroles, arrange 4 of the stuffed tufoli; add one-fourth of the Bolognese Sauce; sprinkle generously with Parmesan.

2. Bake until brown on top and heated through, about 25 minutes. If desired, run under broiler to brown top. Serve with crisp crackers. Makes 4 servings.

BOLOGNESE SAUCE

In saucepan, over medium heat, melt 6 tablespoons butter with ¼ cup finely diced cooked ham or prosciutto. Stir in 1 small onion, minced; ¼ cup grated raw carrot. Add ¼ pound chuck, ground, let brown, stirring occasionally. Stir in 1 thin (2 x 1″) piece lemon rind; ⅛ teaspoon nutmeg; 2 tablespoons canned tomato paste; 2 10½-oz. cans condensed beef bouillon, undiluted; 1 teaspoon salt; ¼ teaspoon pepper. Simmer, covered, 1 hour, stirring occasionally. Remove rind; add ¼ cup heavy cream; simmer 2 minutes.

CHICKEN LIVERS AND MUSHROOMS

⅓ cup butter	2 teaspoons A-1 sauce
1 pound fresh or thawed, frozen chicken livers, halved	1 teaspoon Kitchen Bouquet
	¼ cup flour
½ cup minced onion	1 cup water
½ pound fresh mushrooms, sliced (2¾ cups)	1½ teaspoons salt

Melt butter in a skillet, add livers, onion and mushrooms; sprinkle with A-1 sauce and Kitchen Bouquet; cook over low flame until livers are done (about 7 minutes), stirring frequently. Add flour gradually and mix well. Add water gradually and cook until mixture thickens (about 3 minutes), stirring constantly. Add salt and mix well. Yield: 8 servings.

CSIRKEPAPRIKAS

(CHICKEN PAPRIKA)

1 4-pound chicken, or 2½
   pounds lamb or veal
2 tablespoons butter
2 onions, chopped
1 teaspoon paprika

2 tablespoons flour
4 cups water
1 can tomato sauce
4 tablespoons sour cream
1 teaspoon salt
¼ teaspoon pepper

If chicken is used, clean thoroughly and cut into small portions. Lamb or veal should be cut into 1-inch cubes. Heat the butter and brown either chicken or meat; add the chopped onions and, when golden brown, stir in the paprika and flour, and mix well. Slowly add the water and stir until well blended; add the tomato sauce, cream, salt and pepper and cook slowly until chicken or meat is tender.

CHICKEN-VEGETABLE STEW WITH SPECIAL GRAVY

2 medium onions, sliced
¼ cup shortening
2½ pound frying chicken,
   disjointed
1 cup apple juice
1 cup water
1 teaspoon salt

Few grains pepper
1 package quick-frozen
   lima beans
1 package quick-frozen corn
1 package quick-frozen okra
3 tomatoes, quartered
Flour

Brown onions in shortening; remove onions. Brown chicken in same skillet, adding more shortening if necessary. Combine onions, chicken, apple juice, water, salt and pepper. Simmer ¾ hour, or until chicken is almost tender. Add lima beans, corn and okra; cook 20-25 minutes, or until vegetables are tender. Quarter tomatoes; add. Thicken gravy with flour mixed to a smooth paste in cold water. Makes 6 servings.

BARBECUED CHICKEN

4 chicken breasts (about 1
pound each), split
½ cup sifted flour
1½ teaspoons salt
¼ teaspoon pepper
2 teaspoons paprika
¼ cup butter
1 cup ketchup

½ cup sherry wine
⅓ cup water
2 tablespoons lemon juice
½ cup minced onion
1 tablespoon Worcestershire
sauce
2 tablespoons melted butter
1 tablespoon brown sugar

Singe, wash and dry chicken breasts. Mix flour, salt, pepper and paprika in a large paper bag. Shake 2 or 3 pieces at a time in bag to coat thoroughly. Melt ¼ cup butter in large skillet, brown chicken on all sides and transfer to two 1½-quart casseroles. Combine remaining ingredients; add to remaining butter in skillet; bring to boiling point and pour over chicken. Bake, covered, in a preheated oven, basting at the end of 45 minutes. Temperature: 325° F. Time: about 1 hour, 15 minutes. Yield: 8 servings.

CHICKEN À LA FRICASSEE

A can of soup and stuffed olive slices do wonderful things for fried chicken. Serve with hot buttery cornbread sticks.

1 ready-to-cook frying chicken
(3 pounds) cut into serving
pieces
½ cup mlik
1 egg, beaten
½ cup all-purpose flour

1 teaspoon salt
2 teaspoons sesame seeds
⅓ cup shortening (part butter)
1 can condensed undiluted
cream of mushroom soup
1 can (3 oz.) mushrooms
½ cup sliced stuffed olives

Clean chicken. Combine milk, egg, flour, salt, and sesame seeds. Blend thoroughly. Dip chicken pieces into batter. Brown over medium heat in hot shortening, turning pieces carefully. Combine soup and undrained mushrooms and spoon over browned chicken. Sprinkle with sliced olives. Cover and cook over low heat for about 30 minutes. Thin with a little cream, if needed. Remove chicken to warm chop plate and spoon sauce over pieces. Garnish with jumbo stuffed olives. Makes 4 to 6 servings.

CREAMED GIBLETS AND RICE

1¼ pounds chicken giblets	¼ cup celery, sautéed
3 cups cooked rice	1 teaspoon salt
2 cups light cream sauce	¼ teaspoon white pepper
¼ cup onions, sautéed	Crushed potato chips

Clean and wash giblets and cook until tender. Remove from stock and cut into slices or cubes. Mix rice, cream sauce, onions and celery together. Add cut giblets and pour into greased casserole dish. Sprinkle with salt and pepper, top with crushed potato chips and bake in oven at 350° F. for 30 minutes.

FRUIT-DRESSED CHICKEN BREASTS

Who says you can't have fried chicken and dressing, too? Just the thing for hard-to-please company.

6 plump chicken breasts	1½ cups finely crushed corn flakes
1 teaspoon salt	Prune-Apricot Dressing
¼ teaspoon pepper	(recipe below)
¼ teaspoon poultry seasoning	6 cooked pitted prunes
⅔ cup butter	12 cooked dried apricots
	⅓ cup prune juice

Sprinkle chicken breasts with combined seasonings. Melt ⅓ cup of the butter. Coat chicken breasts with butter and roll in crushed corn flakes. Melt remaining ⅓ cup butter in skillet over medium heat. Brown chicken on all sides. Place pieces in greased shallow baking dish. Fill breast cavities with Prune-Apricot Dressing. Spoon any extra stuffing around chicken. Top with cooked prunes and apricots. Bake in slow oven (325°) for about 45 minutes to 1 hour until breasts are tender. Baste occasionally with prune juice. Makes 6 servings.

PRUNE-APRICOT DRESSING

1 quart bread cubes
½ cup diced cooked prunes
½ cup diced apple
½ cup diced celery

1 teaspoon salt
½ teaspoon sage
¼ teaspoon pepper
¾ cup unsweetened prune juice
¼ cup pan drippings

Combine all ingredients, mixing well. Use as directed to stuff chicken breasts.

OVEN-FRIED CHICKEN WITH BLUE CHEESE BISCUITS

Drop wee blue cheese biscuits on easy-in-the-oven chicken . . . the flavor's superb!

1 ready-to-cook frying chicken
(3 pounds) cut into serving
pieces
¼ cup butter (½ stick), melted
Juice of ½ lemon
1 tablespoon instant minced
onion
½ teaspoon monosodium
glutamate

¾ cup seasoned flour
2 teaspoons paprika
⅓ cup soft butter
1 cup coffee cream
2 cups biscuit mix
3 tablespoons blue cheese
⅔ cup milk
Poppy seeds

Combine butter, lemon juice, onion, and monosodium glutamate. Brush mixture on chicken pieces. Refrigerate chicken for several hours or overnight. Combine flour and paprika in paper sack. Add chicken pieces and shake well to coat. Spread butter over bottom of shallow baking dish. Arrange chicken pieces, skin side down, in one layer. Bake in moderate oven (375° F.) for 30 to 40 minutes until nicely browned. Spoon cream over chicken and bake until tender.

Prepare drop biscuits by combining biscuit mix with crumbled cheese and milk. Increase oven temperature to 450° and drop dough over chicken, making 16 to 20 small biscuits. Quickly sprinkle each biscuit with poppy seeds. Bake for 10 to 12 minutes until biscuits are lightly browned. Spoon additional melted butter over biscuits. Serve at once from baking dish. Makes 4 to 6 servings.

TENNESSEE CHICKEN

6 half breasts of chicken	4 tablespoons butter or margarine
6 tablespoons flour	3 tablespoons flour
6 tablespoons shortening	2 cups milk
6 slices country ham	½ cups sherry
6 tablespoons ham fat	6 toast circles
	12 broiled fresh mushrooms

Carefully remove skin and bones from chicken breast; ask meat man to cut breasts, leaving wing bone to first joint. Dredge in flour, shake well to remove loose bits. Brown breasts in shortening in heavy-bottomed frying pan, but do not cook tender. In a separate pan, brown country-ham slices. Remove from pan, trim off fat and add fat back to pan with two tablespoons butter or margarine. Blend in flour, add milk and cook until thickened. Add sherry, stir well, season to taste. Place chicken pieces in sauce, cover the pan tightly and cook in a slow oven (300 to 325° F.) until the chicken is tender. The sauce should have the grace of proper consistency, too thick to run, too thin to clot, just thick enough to cling to the meat. On toast rounds, one to a plate, lay on a slice of country ham, trimmed to fit toast, over the ham the chicken breast, wing tip up. Decorate each breast with two broiled mushroom caps. Pour over gravy. Place in oven until heated thoroughly. Serve immediately. Yield: 6 portions.

CANTONESE DUCK

5 to 6 pounds Long Island-type duckling, dressed weight	¼ cup sherry wine
	¼ cup honey
	1 tablespoon Kitchen Bouquet

With sharp pointed knife cut through duck skin along center of breast from neck to vent. Loosen skin by pulling away from flesh and at the same time running knife underneath. Cut skin where necessary, but keep the flesh intact. Discard skin. Cut skinned duck in serving-size pieces and place in bowl. Combine remaining ingredients and pour over duck meat. Cover and let marinate in cool place for 3 hours, turning occasionally. Place duck and marinade in large covered frying pan and cook over low heat until tender, about 45 minutes to 1 hour. Serve immediately or, if crisp brown crust is desired, place pieces of duck in uncovered baking dish and heat in moderate oven (350° F.) for at least 15 minutes. Serve hot or cold. Makes about 4 servings.

ROAST DUCK

Sprinkle the outside of the prepared duck with salt and pepper and rub the inside with salt. Stuff and truss. Roast in a covered pan in a 300-350° F. oven. The cover of the pan may be removed after the first hour or so, so that the skin becomes crisp. Allow 22 to 30 minutes per pound, the longer period for a small duck and the shorter for a large one.

RICE AND SAUSAGE STUFFING

Mix 1 cup of bread crumbs, which have been moistened in meat broth and then squeezed, with ½ cup milk. Brown 1 medium onion and 1 small clove garlic, both minced, in 1 tablespoon fat and mix with the bread crumbs. Add 4 cups cold boiled rice, 1 tablespoon minced parsley, ½ pound sausage, and salt, pepper, cayenne, sage and poultry seasoning to taste. Toss together and stuff duck.

CORNISH HENS ON COMPANY RICE

2 frozen Rock Cornish hens,
    each about 1¼ pounds
Salt and pepper
Melted butter or margarine
½ cup raw wild rice
1½ cups boiling water
½ teaspoon salt
1 tablespoon butter
2 tablespoons minced onion
1 tablespoon minced green
    pepper
½ 4-oz. can sliced mushrooms,
    drained

½ 10½-oz. can condensed cream
    of mushroom soup,
    undiluted
½ cup heavy cream
⅛ teaspoon dried marjoram
Dash dried basil
Dash dried tarragon
¼ teaspoon curry powder
¼ teaspoon salt
⅛ teaspoon pepper
Few canned sliced mushrooms,
    heated
Fresh dill

Day Before

1. Let Cornish hens thaw overnight in refrigerator; save giblets to serve for lunch.

About 1 Hour Before Serving

1. Start heating oven to 425° F. Sprinkle hens with salt and pepper. Arrange in shallow, open pan without rack; brush liberally with melted butter. Brushing often with melted butter, roast, uncovered, 45 minutes, or until golden and done.

2. Meanwhile, wash rice well in three or four changes of cold water. Then, to boiling water in saucepan, add ½ teaspoon salt; stir in rice. Simmer, covered, 30 minutes, or until rice is done and water absorbed.

3. While rice cooks, in 1 tablespoon hot butter in another saucepan, sauté onion, green pepper, and drained canned mushrooms 5 minutes. Stir in cream of mushroom soup, cream, marjoram, basil, tarragon, curry, ¼ teaspoon salt, and ⅛ teaspoon pepper; heat 10 minutes.

4. Then add cooked wild rice to this mixture, and heat, stirring occasionally.

5. When hens are done, arrange on a bed of the wild rice on serving platter. Top rice with a few heated canned sliced mushrooms; garnish with a ring of fresh dill. Makes 2 servings.

MAIN-DISH ACCOMPANIMENTS

Grandma Anderson was the world's greatest believer in lagniappe, although she probably never knew the word existed, and as a matter of fact I have rarely heard it used outside the plantation south.

Roughly translated it means the thirteenth roll in a dozen, the little extra something, the unlooked for, unpaid for flourish, the exciting unexpected!

Grandma Anderson spent a good bit of her time looking around for lagniappe to surprise her guests. Some days it was a little jar of geranium apple jelly that came to the table with her hot butter crescents. Some days it was a cool green cucumber jelly, some days a slice of poached apple with a delicate pink glaze, or it might be a crème de menthe pear or cinnamon apple sauce with her fresh roast pork. There was always something!

The first fall blast from the Mississippi meant a careful and measured glance towards the garden. Time to bring in the little yellow tomatoes left on the vine, what to do with the rest of the squash, were there still turnips to be dug, and maybe some preserved pumpkin chips from the few pumpkins left? It was the signal for renewed bustle and hustle in the old-fashioned kitchen (now the most modern one in the Valley!) and, of course, it meant more delightful Main Dish Accompaniments. There are some here; we hope they give you the delight they gave Grandma Anderson's guests.

My sister Ann replaces Grandma Anderson at the stoves these days, two generations later. She loves her work, she has an artist's way with food and she could have been a good many other things as successfully as she is a cook. But love of cooking comes naturally to all of us and this is why she chooses to stay as Monarch of the Hotel Anderson Kitchen in a sleepy, but lovely, little country town in the Hiawatha Valley in Minnesota.

SAUCES, DRESSINGS, GARNISHES!

Once upon a time while living in New Orleans I had, ah lucky me, a French Cook! She was a war bride in her late thirties and while she worked for me I had a cuisine unexcelled.

And it was the first time my kitchen budget ever balanced regardless of the amount of entertaining I did, which was a great deal. There is something about New Orleans, an informality, a love of good food that literally makes you say, before you are aware of it, "Why not come home with me to dinner . . ." and usually they do!

There is something about being lucky enough to have a balcony flung out over a beautiful patio that makes it the ideal place to eat, and maybe it does something special for the food!

Geneviev bought what, I suppose, must be called the cheaper cuts of meats. She brought them to the table bubbling with savory sauces, in little copper casseroles, crowned now and then with flaky butter crusts, and my guests generally finished the meal without speaking. She constantly marveled at our selection of California wines and each and every meal was accompanied with the proper wine, something about which I was, at that time, woefully uninformed.

Geneviev's sauces bubbled and simmered for hours at a time with much stirring and tasting, much addition of fresh spices, much testing, and sometimes (I accused her) of much praying over them. Sauces are an important part of French cooking!

She had a hand-written cook book, was a genius at marketing, and had a mild and sweet disposition, as well as a fierce loyalty towards all things French and complete control over my kitchen. I never ate as well or as excitingly. And Geneviev, who had been most unhappy in Minnesota, blossomed in New Orleans, a town where, to her incredulous surprise, they actually spoke a great deal of French!

Many of Geneviev's recipes are in this chapter as best as she could write them out. Every spring when I go to New Orleans Geneviev comes out of retirement and moves into my kitchen, so I find it impossible to stay at some of the hotels where I would love to stay. She finds, somehow, the same apartment for me at 905 Royal. There's a method to my madness for she always has new things to teach me, and we have long talks far into the night on food, cook books, super markets, and Solaris. Famous French Quarter Market. Thank heavens, the talks are now in English!

SAUCES

AU GRATIN SAUCE

In advance cook finely chopped mushrooms in a bit of butter, salt and lemon juice. Then pour ½ cup dry white wine into the top pan of the chafing dish over the direct flame. Add 1 teaspoon minced scallions, and let them simmer until the wine has all but disappeared. Then add the mushrooms and let the mixture boil for 5 minutes. Just before removing from heat, stir in 1 teaspoon minced parsley. (For vegetables.)

BARBECUE GLAZING SAUCE

In the top pan of the chafing dish, over hot water, heat ¼ cup vegetable oil and in it sauté 3 minced garlic cloves. Add 1 teaspoon each of salt and black pepper, ¼ teaspoon oregano, 1 tablespoon chopped fresh thyme, 1½ cups tomato puree, and ¼ cup strained honey. After simmering for 15 minutes, add the juice of 2 limes and ½ cup red wine. After blending the whole mixture well, let it simmer for another 10 minutes.

BASIC A LÀ KING RECIPE

2 cups medium white sauce (made from stock if desired)
1 egg yolk, slightly beaten
1 cup cooked diced meat, poultry or fish

1 cup peas, canned or fresh
½ cup cooked celery, diced
2 tablespoons butter or margarine
¼ cup chopped green pepper and pimiento, mixed
½ pound mushrooms, diced
Salt and pepper

Make sauce in the top of a double boiler and when cooked and smooth, blend in egg yolk. Add meat, cooked peas and celery. Cook pepper, pimiento, and mushrooms in butter over low heat until tender. Add to cream sauce. A few drops of onion juice may be added, if desired. Yield: 6 servings.

BASIC BROWN SAUCE

Melt ¾ tablespoon butter in top pan of the chafing dish over a direct flame, and add 1 slice diced ham, 1 small onion, sliced, and 2 sliced carrots. Sauté ham and vegetable until the onions are tender and brown, then add 1½ tablespoons flour, blend in well, and let it brown. Gradually add 2 cups clean soup stock, ½ bay leaf, and a little thyme, and blend the whole mixture thoroughly. Insert water jacket and let simmer gently for 1 hour.

After that time, peel, seed and chop 1 small tomato and add to the sauce, along with salt and freshly ground black pepper, and ¼ cup sherry wine. Strain after simmering for another half hour. (Use for left-over meat.)

BASIC WHITE SAUCE

In top pan of chafing dish over water jacket, melt 2 tablespoons butter and blend into it an equal amount of flour. After 1 or 2 minutes, add 1 cup milk gradually, stirring all the while as the sauce comes to the boiling point and thickens. Add salt and a dash of white pepper, and enrich by the addition of 3 tablespoons thin cream.

For chicken dishes, substitute 1 cup chicken stock for the milk. Use 1 cup fish stock instead of milk for seafood dishes.

CALIFORNIA SAUCE

Chop 1 onion, 2 shallots, 2 celery stalks, 5 large mushrooms, and 1 small bay leaf, and put them over hot water in the top pan of the chafing dish together with ½ cup each of port and sherry wines. Simmer the mixture until it is reduced to half the original quantity. Chop 2 or 3 chicken or duck livers. Add them to the wine mixture, along with ½ cup chicken broth and the same amount of dry white wine. Then add 2 sprigs watercress, a bay leaf, a pinch of thyme and a dash of curry. Simmer it for about an hour, then thicken with blended flour and butter. Strain through cheesecloth and season. Lastly add ½ teaspoon paprika, 1 tablespoon butter or margarine, 2 teaspoons lemon juice and ¼ cup cognac. (For chicken or meat.)

CHASSEUR

Add ¾ cup mushrooms (caps) sliced to 4 tablespoons butter or margarine in the top pan of the chafing dish over a direct flame. Sprinkle with salt and pepper, and let the mushrooms simmer until quite brown. Add 1 tablespoon minced onion, and ½ cup dry white wine. Cook until the mixture is reduced by half. Then add 1 cup brown sauce, 2 tablespoons tomato sauce, and ½ teaspoon each chopped parsley and thyme. (For vegetables.)

COUNTRY GRAVY

(Milk gravy made after frying chicken, salt pork, or sausage)

2 cups milk	¼ cup drippings
¼ cup flour	Salt, pepper

Make a smooth thin paste with a little of the milk and flour. Add paste to hot drippings, stirring constantly. Add remainder of milk, stir, and cook until gravy is thickened and smooth. Season to taste.

CREAMY MUSTARD SAUCE

¼ cup sugar	¼ cup prepared mustard
½ teaspoon salt	2 tablespoons vinegar
2 egg yolks	½ teaspoon allspice
1 cup milk, scalded	⅛ teaspoon celery salt
	¼ teaspoon paprika

Mix sugar, salt, and egg yolks. Add to scalded milk in top of double boiler. Mix mustard, vinegar, allspice, celery salt, and paprika. Add slowly to milk and egg mixture, stirring until smooth and thickened. Serve hot with ham, lamb, or tongue. Yield: About 2 cups.

CREOLE SAUCE

Good with rice, seafood, roast meats, omelets

¼ cup chopped onion	½ cup water
¼ cup chopped green pepper	1 teaspoon vinegar
2 tablespoons shortening	Dash black pepper
1 can (1¼ cups) condensed	Dash Tabasco sauce
tomato soup	

Cook onion and green pepper until tender in shortening. Add remaining ingredients; cook over low heat about 10 minutes. Makes about 2 cups.

CURRY SAUCE

2 tablespoons butter or margarine	2 tablespoons flour
	½ teaspoon curry powder
1 medium onion, chopped	1 cup beef broth, bouillon or consomme

Melt butter, add onion, and let cook until tender. Stir in flour, let it brown slightly, then add curry and liquid. Cook and stir until sauce is thickened and smooth. A hint of garlic may be added to this sauce by cooking a clove with onion for 1 minute. Good with veal, lamb, or poultry. Yield: 1 cup.

DILL SAUCE

Place 1 minced onion in 1½ tablespoons melted butter or margarine in the top pan of the chafing dish over the water jacket. Stir constantly until the onions are tender, then dust over them 1½ tablespoons flour. Blend well, then add slowly, stirring all the while, 1 cup rich milk. When the mixture thickens and begins to simmer, turn flame low and let it cook for several moments, stirring occasionally. Then add salt and freshly ground pepper to taste, plus a dash each of nutmeg and paprika. A few moments before serving the sauce, add 1 teaspoon chopped dill and let the sauce simmer gently for 2 to 3 minutes. (For fish.)

ENGLISH BREAD SAUCE FOR CHICKEN

1 cup milk	½ tablespoon butter
1 small onion	Salt and pepper
3 slices bread, cubed	1 tablespoon cream

Place milk and onion in saucepan and bring to a boil. Add bread. Simmer, stirring well, until mixture thickens. Remove onion and add cream, butter and salt and pepper to taste. Serve hot.

EXQUISITE EGG SAUCE

Melt 1 tablespoon butter or margarine over a direct flame in the top pan of the chafing dish. Add 6 chopped mushrooms. Let heat for a few moments, then add ¼ cup dry white wine. When this has heated thoroughly, add ¼ cup basic brown sauce, a tablespoon of tomato ketchup, a tablespoon of minced parsley, and a dash of cayenne pepper. Continue cooking until the mixture is well heated and blended, then season to your taste.

HORSERADISH SAUCE

3 tablespoons bread crumbs	3 tablespoons butter
⅓ cup freshly grated horseradish	½ teaspoon lemon juice
1½ cups milk	Salt
	Pepper

Place the bread crumbs, horseradish and scalded milk in a double boiler. Cook for 25 minutes, stirring frequently. Blend in the butter, add the lemon juice and season to taste. Serve with boiled beef.

LYONNAISE SAUCE

Brown 2 chopped onions in 2 tablespoons butter or margarine in the top pan of the chafing dish over a direct flame. Pour in ⅓ cup dry white wine and cook it until it is reduced about ½. After adding 1 cup brown sauce, simmer gently for 15 minutes, then add 1 teaspoon chopped parsley, and salt and fresh black pepper to taste. (A basic sauce.)

MAITRE D'HOTEL BUTTER

Cream 4 tablespoons of butter with a wooden spoon; add ½ teaspoon salt, ⅛ tablespoon finely chopped parsley and slowly ¾ tablespoon lemon juice, continue stirring until well blended. Use for spreading bread for sandwiches when the filling consists chiefly of fish, lobster, shrimps, or crab meat. This butter is also used for spreading over broiled steaks, chops, steaks, fish, etc.

NEVER-FAIL HOLLANDAISE SAUCE

2 egg yolks
½ teaspoon salt

Dash pepper
½ cup melted butter
1 tablespoon lemon juice

Place egg yolks in top of double boiler over warm water and beat until thick and lemon-colored. Add salt and pepper. Then add 3 tablespoons of the butter, a little at a time, beating constantly. Beat in rest of butter alternately with lemon juice.

NEWBURG SAUCE

Melt 2 tablespoons butter or margarine in the top pan of the chafing dish over a direct flame, then blend in 1 tablespoon flour. Slowly add a cup of cream stirring all the while until it is of a thick smooth consistency. Keep the mixture just under the boiling point. Add salt and freshly ground black pepper to your taste. Insert the water jacket and add 2 well-beaten egg yolks. Keep stirring for a few minutes. Then add 2 tablespoons Madeira and remove from heat. (For fish.)

ORANGE SAUCE FOR ROAST DUCK

⅔ cup sugar
¼ teaspoon salt
2 teaspoons cornstarch

1 cup boiling water
1 teaspoon butter
2 oranges, juice and grated rind

Mix sugar, salt, and cornstarch. Pour hot water over mixture, stirring constantly. Cook until thick and clear. Add butter, orange juice, and grated rind just before removing from heat. Stir well and serve with duck. Yield: about 2 cups.

PIXIE SAUCE

Cook 1 chopped onion in ¼ cup vinegar until the mixture is reduced to almost nothing. Then add 1½ cups strained stewed tomatoes, ½ teaspoon salt and a dash of pepper, and cook this mixture for 10 minutes. Then thicken with flour which has been blended with a little cold water. Lastly add 3 tablespoons finely chopped sour pickles and 1 teaspoon chopped barley. (For meat or fowl.)

ROAST BEEF GRAVY

Skim off fat from the roast drippings, leaving about 4 tablespoons in the pan. Add 6 to 8 tablespoons of flour and stir over moderate heat until flour is thoroughly browned. Do not add any water until the flour is very brown, because it won't brown once the liquid has been added. Add 2 cups of water, a little at a time, stirring constantly to keep the gravy smooth. Cook and stir until thickened. Season to taste with salt and pepper. Yield: about 2 cups.

SOUR CREAM MUSHROOM SAUCE

1 cup sour cream	2 tablespoons flour
1 tablespoon grated onion	½ teaspoon salt
½ cup diced canned mushrooms	¼ teaspoon paprika
	2 tablespoons cold water

Heat cream, onion, and mushrooms in top of double boiler. Make a smooth paste of flour, salt, paprika, and cold water. Add to hot mixture gradually, stirring constantly, and cook until thick. Serve with steak, meat balls, or chicken. Yield: Four servings.

TARTARE SAUCE

1 cup mayonnaise	⅓ cup chopped green olives
¼ teaspoon grated onion	1 tablespoon chopped capers
1 tablespoon vinegar	1 teaspoon chopped parsley
⅓ cup sweet-pickle relish	Salt to taste

Blend mayonnaise, onion, and vinegar. Add remaining ingredients and mix. Makes 1½ cups. Serve in tomato flowers. Turn tomato, blossom end down; cut in sections, not clear through; spread to make flower.

TOMATO SAUCE

Melt 1½ tablespoons butter or margarine in the top pan of the chafing dish directly over the flame. Then add 1 tablespoon each chopped carrots and scallions. Let them simmer until the onions are soft. Then blend in 2 tablespoons flour and stir occasionally while it browns. Add 1 cup stewed tomatoes, ¾ cup water, 1 crushed garlic clove, ½ teaspoon sugar, a sprinkling of salt and pepper, a sprig of parsley, 1 celery stalk, ½ bay leaf and a pinch of basil. While this mixture is thickening stir continuously. Then turn heat down and let the sauce simmer for about an hour. During this time stir the sauce through a fine sieve back into the chafing dish. Once again let it come to a boil, this time for 4-5 minutes, stirring all the while. Then pour into a bowl. (For meat and fowl.)

STUFFINGS

GERMAN STUFFING FOR POULTRY

½ cup finely sliced onions	6 cups soft bread crumbs,
½ cup butter, melted	packed tightly
Heart, liver, gizzard, chopped	Salt and pepper
fine	Pinch nutmeg
	3 tablespoons minced parsley
	2 eggs beaten slightly

Sauté the onions in butter until they are light yellow; add chopped giblets, simmer 5 minutes. Pour over the bread crumbs; add other ingredients; stuff mixture into the chicken or turkey, sew or skewer the opening, tie strips of bacon over the opening.

KIDNEY BEAN STUFFING

1 package red kidney beans,	2 cups baked ham sliced in strips
soaked overnight	Bouquet (parsley, bay leaf,
2 cans Italian tomato paste,	thyme, peppercorns)
sharpened with a little	¼ pound butter
vinegar	

Above amounts approximate; proportions can be varied to taste.

Put the soaked (drained and washed) kidney beans in a heavy pot. (Dutch oven good); cover with cold water and bring to a boil. Add the bouquet, cook gently for 1 hour, add a little cold water, salt, cover the pot, and cook till done. This may take 2 to 3 hours, depending on the age of the beans, so allow enough time. When cooked, drain the beans, put them back in the pot with a moistening of the water they have cooked in, and a little butter and olive oil. Simmer gently while you warm the ham in butter. When heated but not cooked, stir in the tomato paste and blend the mixture with the beans. Taste for seasoning.

Let cool enough to handle and stuff the bird. Less than one-quarter pound butter may be used but turkeys are very dry and need added richness.

OYSTER STUFFING FOR TURKEY

¾ cup butter, margarine or turkey fat
2 tablespoons chopped onion
¼ cup chopped parsley

1 cup chopped celery
6 cups bread crumbs
1 pint oysters, coarsely chopped
Oyster liquor
Salt and pepper

Melt the fat and in it cook chopped onion, parsley and celery for a few minutes. Add bread crumbs and oysters and heat thoroughly. Add chopped onion and oyster liquor and seasonings. Mix well. Will stuff a 10-pound turkey.

POULTRY DRESSING

4 tablespoons minced onion
1 cup diced celery
⅔ cup melted butter or margarine
8 cups dry bread cubes

2 teaspoons salt
½ teaspoon pepper
½ teaspoon poultry seasoning
2 teaspoons sage
2 cups broth or stock

Brown onion and celery in butter. Combine with bread and seasonings. Pour broth over bread mixture. Blend thoroughly. Pack dressing lightly into bird just before roasting.

RICE STUFFING

1½ cups rice
½ cup chopped celery leaves
½ cup minced onion
6 fresh mushrooms

2 tablespoons fat
2 teaspoons salt
1 teaspoon poultry seasoning
Water

Wash rice. Brown celery leaves, onion, and chopped mushrooms in fat. Add rice. Brown until rice is a golden color. Add salt and poultry seasoning. Cover with water until water is ½-inch above rice. Cover and steam 10 minutes. Remove from heat. Stuff bird just before roasting. Yield: 6 cups for 6- to 8-pound bird.

SAUERKRAUT STUFFING

1 large onion, grated	½ teaspoon pepper
2 pounds sauerkraut	2 tablespoons salt
1 large potato grated	⅔ cup sherry
6 teaspoons caraway seed	½ cup water
	1 cup tomato sauce

Fry onion in fat, add sauerkraut and grated potato. Then add caraway seed, salt, pepper, sherry, water and tomato sauce. Mix thoroughly and stuff bird.

Note: Sauerkraut stuffing can be used with roast goose, suckling pig, and other fowl which tends to be on the fatty side.

SAUSAGE AND SWEET POTATO STUFFING

1 pound sausage meat	4 cups bread crumbs
4 tablespoons chopped onion	8 cups hot mashed sweet potatoes
2 cups chopped celery	2 teaspoons salt

Cook sausage meat until lightly browned, breaking it into small pieces as it cooks. Remove meat from frying pan and cook onion and celery in the fat for a few minutes. Add bread crumbs, sweet potatoes and salt. Mix well. Will stuff a 12-pound turkey.

SAVORY CORN STUFFING

½ pound sausage meat	2½ quarts bread crumbs
¼ cup sausage fat	1 tablespoon salt
1 cup chopped onions	¾ teaspoon pepper
2 boxes golden sweet corn, thawed	1½ teaspoon poultry seasoning

Fry sausage meat until brown but not hard, crumbling with a fork while cooking.

Drain fat from sausage. Sauté onions in ¼ cup of the fat until golden brown. Add onions and fat to corn. Then add sausage, bread crumbs, salt, pepper and poultry seasoning and mix well. Makes 3½ quarts stuffing, or enough to stuff one 14 to 16 pound turkey. For half turkey, use ½ recipe.

SOUTHERN CORNBREAD DRESSING

3 eggs
2 cups crumbled cornbread
1½ cups dry bread crumbs
3 cups stock

½ cup melted butter or margarine
⅓ cup finely chopped onion
⅛ teaspoon pepper
1 teaspoon salt
1 teaspoon sage

Beat eggs slightly. Combine all ingredients and mix well. Stuff prepared bird.

Note: You may add 1 cup more liquid and bake dressing in a greased baking pan 13″ x 9″. Bake in a moderately slow oven (325° F.) for 1 hour. Yield: 4 cups for 4- to 5-pound bird.

GARNISHES

BAKED BANANAS

6 medium green-topped bananas
2 tablespoons butter, melted

¼ cup lemon juice
¼ cup sugar
1 tablespoon maple syrup

Peel bananas and cut into halves, lengthwise. Place in a buttered baking pan and cover with butter, lemon juice, sugar, and syrup. Bake in a moderate oven (350° F.) for 20 minutes. Baste once during baking time. Yield: Six servings.

COLESLAW IN BEET CUPS

6 cooked beets, medium-sized
½ cup diced celery

½ cup shredded cabbage
½ onion, minced
French dressing

Cut a slice from the bottom of the beets so they will stand securely. Hollow the centers to make cups. Chop the part of the beets removed from the centers and add to the celery, cabbage and onion. Marinate in French dressing. Fill the beet cups with the mixture. Chill and serve.

GREEN CUCUMBER JELLY

Grate enough young cucumbers to make two cups of pulp. Skin and all are grated, but large seeds should be sifted out. Season with two tablespoons of white vinegar or lemon juice, one-half a teaspoon of salt, and a sprinkle of white pepper. Hydrate two tablespoonfuls of gelatine in a little of the liquor from the grated cucumber, dissolve by standing in hot water, and add to the pulp. If the green color is not pronounced, it may be deepened by the addition of spinach green, or a little of one of a green vegetable color. This jelly may be molded in small cones or timbale shapes, or in wee molds to represent four-leaved clovers, or it may be poured to the depth of one-half an inch or more into a shallow pan, and cut in cubes for a salad, to be served on lettuce leaves of delicate green with a pale green mayonnaise.

STUFFED SPICED PRUNES

2 cups prunes	⅓ cup finely chopped onion
1 cup water	¼ cup chopped almonds
2 tablespoons cider vinegar	2 tablespoons chopped preserved
½ teaspoon cinnamon	ginger
¼ teaspoon nutmeg	2 tablespoons chopped chutney
½ cup brown sugar	1 tablespoon catsup

Rinse prunes; combine with water, vinegar, spices, and sugar. Simmer until tender, about 20 minutes. Let stand overnight. Combine remaining ingredients. Stuff pitted prunes. Garnish meat, poultry or fish. Makes 1 pint.

VEGETABLES

Never in her life did Grandma Anderson ever serve a vegetable that was just a vegetable! Green peas were served with little miniature whole onions or fresh chopped mint or dots of pimento. Green beans were served with slivered Brazil nuts or almonds; spinach was carefully blended into a mousse and served with chopped hard-boiled eggs; asparagus spears were served with buttered crumbs or a special light sauce; beets were stuffed, or served with orange sauce; corn was served as corn pudding or corn soufflé or scalloped corn; and potatoes ... ah ... baked and restuffed with pimento and green pepper and a little dash of grated cheese, sliced paper thin and baked in a casserole with lots of country butter; sweet potatoes were french fried, or whipped to an amazing lightness and served in a preserved orange shell; cauliflower was served whole with a can of condensed chicken (cream) soup over the top and shaved nuts over this; eggplant appeared in several guises, stuffed, baked, and cubed in a rich German sauce; carrots were glazed in ginger, or served as carrot coins with fresh chopped mint, or they appeared as the delicate, colorful border on a vegetable plate.

The deadly dull hotel vegetable was wonderfully lacking at Hotel Anderson. Each day was a challenge cheerfully met and never once did a bean appear as a bean, a pea appear as a pea—always the gourmet touch from a woman who loved to cook, who believed that people loved to eat and that there was only one way to prepare food: tastefully, beautifully and with love.

We think you'll love our chapter on vegetables!

Vegetables New and Different

We think the Postillion in Fond du Lac serves the most unusual food in the whole United States of America. We're only sorry they serve so little of it! The Postillion is a French Restaurant in a converted farm house bulging with antique treasures and wonderfully selected things for the home. It is a combination super de luxe café and decorating shop, and it is run with a touch of sheer genius. When we say we're sorry they serve so little of it ... we mean that they are only open every night except Sunday and Monday by reservations only.

And what food! What exciting salads, what wonderful soups, what delightful desserts and what rare and unusual jams and salad dressings, thoughtfully bottled for you to take home if you are so inclined.

Best of all are their vegetables. Liane Kuony, the French proprietess, never serves a vegetable that isn't strictly fresh. The frozen, the canned, the preserved vegetable ... never ever at the Postillion! More than any one Liane Kuony taught me that even the most unexciting vegetable can be a gourmet dish with a little care, a little contrivance, a little patience.

We hope you'll find some unusual vegetable recipes here and we hope that next time you motor past Fond du Lac, Wisconsin, you'll treat yourself to some of the Postillion's fine food! It's worth going a long ways out of your way ... !

ASPARAGUS CHANTILLY

2 egg yolks, slightly beaten
½ cup cream
½ teaspoon salt
⅛ teaspoon nutmeg

2 tablespoons lemon juice
2 tablespoons butter or margarine
1 package frozen asparagus, cooked

Mix all ingredients, except butter and asparagus, in saucepan. Cook 10 minutes. Add butter. Cook 1 minute, stirring constantly. Serve immediately over hot cooked asparagus. Makes 4 servings.

ASPARAGUS PIE

2 cups heavy cream
1 large bay leaf
4 sprigs parsley
4 thin slices onion
Pinch of thyme
Pinch of marjoram
6 peppercorns
1 tablespoon butter

1 can strained junior veal baby food
1 large bunch fresh or 2 pkg. frozen asparagus
9″ baked pie shell
½ teaspoon salt
½ cup Parmesan cheese
¾ cup very fine buttered bread crumbs

Bring cream to scalding point (don't boil) with bay leaf, parsley, onion, thyme, marjoram and peppercorns. Then strain to remove seasonings and return to saucepan.

Meanwhile, heat the butter and stir in the veal baby food. Allow to brown. When brown add the veal to the hot cream, using a bit of cream to facilitate scraping the good crust from bottom of veal pan. Stir the mixture until it begins to boil. Then reduce heat and simmer very, very slowly, stirring occasionally to prevent scorching. Continue cooking, with an occasional stir, for 15 minutes.

Now cook up the fresh asparagus spears in boiling well-salted water. If you use frozen asparagus follow directions on package, again using well-salted water. Line the baked pastry shell with half the cooked asparagus, all points headed away from the center. Pour over them a thin layer of the sauce which you'll notice looks coarse because of the veal. Arrange remaining asparagus, points in this time, on top of sauce.

Take remaining sauce, salt and the Parmesan cheese, and pour over the asparagus. Top the dish with the buttered bread crumbs and brown quickly under the broiler.

A gorgeous dish for Christmas parties and parties the year round.

ORANGE BEETS

1 tablespoon cornstarch	1 cup orange juice
1 tablespoon sugar	1 teaspoon grated orange rind
¾ teaspoon salt	2 tablespoons butter or margarine
	1 (No. 2) can beets, drained

Mix together cornstarch, sugar, and salt in saucepan. Blend in orange juice gradually. Cook over low heat, stirring constantly, until mixture thickens and comes to a boil. Stir in orange rind, butter, and beets; heat thoroughly. Makes 4 servings.

SAUTÉED BROCCOLI

1 bunch broccoli	2-3 tablespoons water
1½-2 tablespoons vegetable oil	½ teaspoon salt
	Grated Parmesan cheese

Wash and drain broccoli. Peel stems of broccoli and cut on the diagonal into one-inch sections.

Slice each floweret into two or three pieces according to size. Heat the oil until very hot in a skillet. Add the broccoli and sauté, covered, for 2 minutes. Add the water and salt. Cook covered for an additional 10 minutes over moderate heat.

Sprinkle with grated Parmesan cheese before serving. Serves 4.

FRESH BROCCOLI SUPREME

1¼ pounds fresh broccoli	⅓ teaspoon salt
2 tablespoons shortening or butter	Pinch of ground black pepper
	Pinch of powdered dry mustard
¼ cup flour	1 hard-cooked egg, chopped
1 pint milk	1 tablespoon parsley, chopped

Wash broccoli carefully. Remove leaves and lower section of stems. Cook in boiling, salted water until just tender. Drain.

Melt shortening or butter. Add flour and cook slowly for 5 minutes. Add hot milk (which has been heated with an onion containing 3 whole cloves) salt, pepper and mustard. Stir until smooth. Cook 15 to 20 minutes on a slow fire. Remove from heat. Strain and add the chopped egg. Ladle sauce over stems of hot broccoli. Dust with chopped parsley.

PENNSYLVANIA DUTCH SOUR CREAM CABBAGE

1 medium head cabbage	2 teaspoons vinegar
2 tablespoons butter	½ teaspoon sugar
2 tablespoons minced onion	¾ teaspoon salt
1 tablespoon flour	Dash pepper
1 cup sour cream	Paprika

Cut cabbage into 6 wedges and cook until just tender in boiling, salted water. Melt butter in a saucepan over low heat. Add onion and cook until tender but not brown. Blend in flour and heat until bubbly. Stir in sour cream, vinegar, and seasonings, except paprika, and cook until thickened, stirring constantly. Pour sauce over cabbage. Sprinkle with paprika. Makes 6 servings.

CABBAGE SAUTÉ

1½ pounds cabbage, shredded
1 ounce bacon
1 small onion, julienne

½ green pepper, diced
1 teaspoon salt
Pinch of ground black pepper

Cook shredded cabbage in boiling salted water for 6 to 8 minutes or until just tender. Drain.

Cook the bacon slowly until crisp. Remove, crumble and reserve bacon.

In the bacon fat lightly brown the onion and green pepper, stirring frequently. Add the cabbage. Season with salt and pepper. Heat well. Serve with crumbled crisp bacon over top.

CARROTS ALAMINTA

12 small carrots
½ teaspoon salt

⅛ teaspoon pepper
½ cup melted butter
1 cup crushed corn flakes

Scrape carrots and cook until just tender. Drain. Add salt and pepper to melted butter. Dip carrots in butter and coat with corn flakes. Arrange in shallow baking pan and bake in moderate oven (350° F.) until lightly browned. Turn once. Serve with hot buttered baby onions. Makes 6 servings.

BLUSHING CAULIFLOWER

1 large cauliflower
Salt
2 tablespoons butter
1 tablespoon minced onion

1 tablespoon curry powder
1 tablespoon cold water
¼ teaspoon salt
1 cup tomato soup (condensed)
Few drops condiment sauce

Select a fine white cauliflower. Remove leaves and stalk. Place the cauliflower upside down in cold water and sprinkle with a tablespoon of salt; allow it to stand one-half an hour. Then place the cauliflower in a kettle of boiling water and cook until just tender; this will vary from ten to twenty minutes. Overcooking will tend to darken the cauliflower. Place the cauliflower on a hot platter and pour over it the Tomato Sauce.

TOMATO SAUCE

Melt the butter and in it cook the onion. Mix the curry powder with the cold water and salt and stir in; add the tomato soup and the condiment sauce. Simmer slowly ten minutes to blend the flavor.

MEXICAN CHEESE DISH

2 tablespoons butter	¾ teaspoon dry mustard
2 tablespoons chopped green pepper	1 cup tomato juice
	1 cup niblet corn
2 tablespoons flour	1½ cups grated sharp cheese
1 teaspoon salt	1 egg, well beaten
Few grains cayenne	Hot toast

Melt butter, add green pepper, and cook until tender. Add flour, salt, cayenne, and mustard and mix well. Add tomato juice slowly, and cook, stirring constantly until thickened. Add corn and cheese and stir until cheese is melted. Remove from heat. Pour over egg slowly, stirring constantly. Serve on toast immediately.

INDIVIDUAL CHEESE SOUFFLÉS

3 tablespoons butter or margarine	¼ cup sherry
4 tablespoons flour	½ teaspoon salt
¾ cup milk	½ teaspoon Worcestershire sauce
1¼ cups grated American or Cheddar cheese	3 eggs, separated

Melt butter and stir in flour; add milk and cook, stirring constantly, until mixture is thickened and smooth. Add cheese and sherry; stir over low heat until cheese is melted; add salt and Worcestershire sauce. Remove from heat and stir in unbeaten egg yolks, pour mixture over the stiffly beaten egg whites and mix gently but thoroughly. Pour into 4 ungreased individual casseroles (1 cup capacity) and bake in a moderate oven (350° F.) for 30 minutes, or until firm. Serve at once.

CHEESE BEAN À LA FALLHALL

2 cans cut yellow wax beans
Butter
Brown sugar

White sauce
½ cup grated cheese
½ cup aged cheese

Drain some juice from beans and cook in a little butter and brown sugar until dry. Combine with a white sauce flavored with ½ cup grated cheese. Place in a buttered casserole dish and cover the top with ½ cup ground aged cheese. Bake 20 minutes in a moderate oven. (To age cheese: dry cheese, grate it until very fine, and pack in glass jars. It keeps indefinitely and has a fine tang.)

SCALLOPED CORN SAUTERNE

3 tablespoons butter or margarine
¼ cup chopped green pepper
2 tablespoons chopped onion
¼ cup flour
1 cup milk
½ cup sauterne or other white
    table wine

1 cup grated Cheddar cheese
1 cup soft bread crumbs
1 (12 oz.) can whole-kernel corn,
    drained (or about 1¾ cups
    cooked corn)
2 eggs, slightly beaten
Salt and pepper to taste
Paprika

Melt butter in saucepan, add green pepper and onion, cook gently for 5 minutes. Blend in flour; add milk and wine; cook, stirring constantly until mixture boils and thickens. Add cheese; stir over low heat until melted. Remove from heat; add bread crumbs, corn, eggs, salt and pepper. Pour into a greased casserole (10 x 6 x 2 inches); sprinkle with paprika. Bake in a moderate oven (350° F.) for about 50 minutes, or until firm in center. Serves 6.

(Note: "Fallhall Glenn" at Black River Falls, Wisconsin is the most beautiful spot in the world! Quaint, rustic cabins flung out over a series of three rushing waterfalls hundreds of feet below. Beds hang by chains that swing and sway like a giant cradle all night long. You are lulled to sleep by the water fall, the whisper of the tall pines and the rustle of all manner of night-prowling animals slipping through the leaves. Mrs. James Hall ... a wonderful, alert, vital 85-year-old Hostess smilingly shows you to your cottage and soon, ah soon you'll be eating marvelous home cooked foods prepared by Lillian Dettinger, Fallhall Glenn's cook of over thirty years. No electric lights, no modern plumbing; time stands still at Fallhall Glenn and the food is of the best!)

SCALLOPED EGGPLANT

1 large eggplant
2 tablespoons butter
1 can mushroom soup

½ cup bread crumbs
1 teaspoon sugar
3 tablespoons grated cheese

Slice eggplant and soak in salt water; drain and drop in boiling water. Cook until tender. Arrange in layers in buttered baking dish, dot with butter and pour can of mushroom soup over it. Sprinkle with bread crumbs, sugar and cheese. Bake in medium oven for 30 minutes.

NOODLES ROMANOFF

⅔ cup noodles
1 cup cottage cheese
1 cup sour cream
¼ cup onion, finely chopped
1 clove garlic, finely cut

2 teaspoons Worcestershire sauce
Dash Tabasco sauce or red
	pepper
½ teaspoon salt
½ cup Wisconsin Natural
	American Cheese, grated

Cook noodles. Add cottage cheese, cream, onion, garlic, Worcestershire sauce, pepper, and salt. Place in buttered baking dish (8-inch). Bake in a moderate oven (350° F.) 30 minutes. Remove from oven, sprinkle with cheese, return to oven for 10 minutes. Serves 6.

FRENCH FRIED ONION RINGS

4 medium-sized mild onions
	Milk
1 cup flour

1 teaspoon salt
⅛ teaspoon pepper
Lard for deep-fat frying

Peel and cut onions into ¼-inch slices. Separate into rings and soak in milk to cover, about 30 minutes. Drain. Mix flour, salt and pepper and dredge onions with seasoned flour. Fry in deep, hot lard (365° F.) until nicely browned. Drain on absorbent paper. Serve immediately. 4 servings.

BAKED GREEN PEPPERS

1 can condensed cream of
    mushroom soup
1¾ cups cooked rice
1 tablespoon chopped pimento

6 whole green peppers, seeded
    and parboiled
6 tablespoons buttered bread
    crumbs

Empty the can of condensed cream of mushroom soup into a saucepan and stir until smooth. Then add cooked rice and chopped pimento. Stuff green peppers, cover with bread crumbs and bake in a moderate oven, 375° F. for 25 to 35 minutes. Serves 6.

BAKED POTATO — STUFFED

1 Idaho potato (80 count)
¼ ounce chopped onions
¼ ounce chopped ham

Pinch of chopped parsley
Grated cheese
Salt and pepper to taste
1 ounce butter

Bake potato in 375° F. oven for ¾ of an hour, then scoop out pulp, add onion, ham, parsley and salt and pepper, and butter, mix well, fill up potato shell compact, flute top with knife, sprinkle with grated cheese and brown in 350° oven until golden brown, serve hot.

IRISH POTATO RING

6 large potatoes
1 package (10 oz.) frozen
    chopped spinach
⅔ cup coffee cream
⅓ cup soft butter

1 egg, beaten
1½ teaspoons salt
¼ teaspoon pepper
½ teaspoon mace
1 tablespoon onion juice

Pare and cook potatoes. Drain and put through ricer. Cook and drain spinach. To hot riced potatoes, add cream, butter, egg, and seasonings. Blend in well-drained spinach. Pile into well-buttered 1½-quart ring mold or casserole. Bake in moderate oven (375° F.) for 15 minutes to 20 minutes. Unmold on serving plate. Fill center with creamed chipped beef and eggs or buttered baby beets. Makes 6 servings.

HASHED BROWN POTATOES

4 potatoes   ½ cup butter or margarine

Scrub potatoes and boil in jackets in salted water to cover. When
potatoes are tender, drain; peel when cool enough to handle. Melt ¼
cup butter or margarine in deep skillet, lay in whole potatoes and mash
down into lumps with wide-tined fork. Fry slowly to a golden crusty
brown. Dot with ¼ cup butter and salt to taste: now place plate over
pan and turn potatoes to plate with the brown side up. Immediately
return potatoes to pan, the unbrowned side down and continue frying
until crusty. Place hot serving plate over pan and turn potatoes to
plate. These should be in cake form about 1½ inches thick. Cut into
wedges. Yield: 4 portions.

RAW POTATO FRITTERS

6 raw potatoes, ground   ½ cup flour
1 small onion, ground   ⅛ teaspoon baking powder
2 eggs, beaten   ½ teaspoon salt
                                Dash of pepper

Combine ingredients and fry in hot fat.

BAKED CREAMED POTATO RING

6 cups diced, cooked potatoes   2 eggs, beaten
1 medium onion, minced   ¾ teaspoon Ac'cent
2 cups thick white sauce   1 cup grated sharp Cheddar
                                   cheese

Combine potatoes and onion. Pour hot white sauce on beaten eggs;
add Ac'cent. Add cheese; stir over low heat until cheese melts. Combine cheese and potato mixtures; mix well. Pack into heavily greased
10-inch ring mold. Set in pan of hot water. Bake in moderate oven
(350° F.) 45 minutes. To unmold, run knife around edges, invert
on large plate, then invert again on serving plate so that browned top
will be uppermost. Fill center with buttered Brussels sprouts or
zucchini. Serves 6 to 8.

MEDITERRANEAN PILAF

¼ cup butter or margarine
1 small onion, chopped
½ cup green pepper, chopped
1 cup rice, uncooked

1 can condensed beef consommé
½ cup water
¼ teaspoon monosodium glutamate
Dash of pepper

Melt butter or margarine in heavy skillet (one with tight-fitting lid); add onion, green pepper and rice. Cook over medium heat until lightly browned, 6 to 8 minutes. Add rest of ingredients; cover and simmer until tender, about 30 minutes. Makes 4 to 6 servings.

NEW ORLEANS RED BEANS AND RICE

Pick over 1½ pounds red kidney beans. Wash in cold water. Place in a large saucepan. Add 3 quarts cold water. Simmer for 1 hour. Add ½ teaspoon baking soda. Simmer for an additional 2½ hours.

Dice 2 (½-pound) slices smoked ham. Heat in a skillet 2 tablespoons oil. Add diced ham, and cook until brown. Remove from skillet and add to beans.

PLACE IN A SKILLET

2-3 medium onions, chopped
4 cloves garlic, peeled and
   chopped

2 tablespoons tomato paste

Cook for 5 minutes, stirring occasionally. Add ½ cup water. Blend well, and cook over low heat for an additional 5 minutes. Add to beans.

ADD

2 tablespoons parsley flakes

2 teaspoons salt
¼ teaspoon pepper

Simmer for 1 hour longer before serving. Serve on rice. Makes 8 to 10 servings.

RED RICE

½ pound bacon
1 pound rice

1 small can tomatoes
Salt and pepper to taste
4 cups chicken broth

Have the bacon sliced and cut in small pieces. Fry it until crisp and remove the bits of bacon. Leave about four tablespoons of the drippings and in this brown the rice, stirring constantly to see that it does not burn. Then add the tomatoes, a teaspoon of salt, and the chicken stock. Cover closely and cook for half an hour or until the rice is tender. Add the bacon bits and serve, seasoning to taste with salt and pepper.

SPINACH SOUFFLÉ

1 package (12 ounces) frozen
　　chopped spinach
3 tablespoons butter
3 tablespoons flour
1 cup milk

1 tablespoon minced onion
2 teaspoon grated lemon peel
1½ teaspoons salt
¼ teaspoon pepper
3 eggs, separated

Cook spinach as directed on package; drain well. Make white sauce of butter, flour, and milk. Stir in onion, lemon peel, and seasonings.

Combine beaten egg yolks, spinach, and white sauce. Fold in stiffly beaten egg whites. Pour into greased 1 to 1¼-quart baking dish about 10 by 6 inches.

Bake soufflé in slow oven (325°) for about 1 hour. 6 servings.

CHICKEN BAKED SQUASH

3 cups cubed yellow squash
2 tablespoons butter
1 can condensed cream of chicken
　　soup, undiluted

½ cup chopped nuts
2 tablespoons chopped pimentos
¼ cup soft bread cubes
2 tablespoons melted butter

Heat oven to 375° F. In 1½-quart casserole, alternate layers of squash, bits of butter, soup, nuts, and pimento. Top with bread cubes and butter, tossed together. Bake 50 minutes. Serves 8.

FRENCH FRIED YAMS

Peel raw yams; trim and slice in ½- to ¾-inch strips. Dip in ice water to prevent discoloring. Drain well and dry. Fry in deep hot shortening (365° F.) for 3 to 5 minutes until browned. Drain on paper toweling; sprinkle with sugar.

For extra flavor and texture preheat yams 15 minutes in very hot water (170° to 180°) before peeling. Do not dip in ice water.

SAVORY STUFFED TOMATOES

8 large tomatoes	1¼ cups canned applesauce
⅔ cup finely chopped onion	½ teaspoon sage
2½ tablespoons butter	¾ teaspoon salt
⅔ cup dry bread crumbs	Few grains pepper
	⅓ cup grated Parmesan cheese

Wash tomatoes thoroughly. Cut a slice from top of each tomato; carefully scoop out centers. Use centers for stewed tomatoes, do not use in filling. Sauté onion in butter until lightly browned. Add bread crumbs, applesauce, sage, salt and pepper. Place filling into tomatoes. Sprinkle with grated Parmesan cheese and bake in moderate oven, 350° F., 25-30 minutes. Serve with chicken. Yield: 8 servings.

SALADS

A limp salad means, generally speaking, a limp hostess!

The basic requirement for salads is that they must be served Cold. COLD, COLD, COLD. The colder the better. The crisper, the better. And for a real treat try using clear glass salad plates, put them in the refrigerator with the salads on them, bring them to the table after the guests are seated, and what a delight to find a frosted salad plate! It shows that you CARE about the proper way to serve your food!

Serving lettuce? Strangle the impulse to use the wilted outside leaves. Wash them, put them in the refrigerator and bring them out later as Baked Lettuce Mornay. (Shredded, cooked in a rich cheese sauce and served as a Vegetable Timbale.) For an artist's touch serve bowls of mixed Bib lettuce, leaf lettuce, fresh spinach, watercress and romaine. Ahh—cries of delight will greet the appearance of this dish. Go all the way and serve a choice of three or four wonderful salad dressings. Using a Basic French Dressing, there are a hundred tricks to give you a hundred different dressings! Have the dressing COLD!

Learn to marinate your fruits, learn to combine them with artistry and skill. Learn to use up odds and ends in jellied salads that look gay and colorful. Buy a French wicker basket to wash your greens in. And in cleaning lettuce NEVER cut out the bottom with a knife. It will cause the rest of the lettuce to rust! Use your hands, tear out the bottom and tear up the rest of the lettuce as needed.

The new jellied bases for salads are more creative than they were ten years ago. Did they have apple, peach and watermelon gelatin then? The molds are inexpensive and elegant ... how wonderful to find a jellied Tuna Mold in its original fish shape! With a ripe olive for an eye and resting on a bed of endive!

Salads can be served as an entire meal, as companion to a meal or even as a sandwich. However it is served it must be cold, it must be fresh, it must be crisp. And it must mirror the abilities of the gal who prepares it!

APRICOT SALAD DRESSING

1 tablespoon sugar
Few grains salt
2 tablespoons and 1 teaspoon
  cornstarch

1½ cups apricot nectar
2 teaspoons butter
1 teaspoon lemon juice

Sift together sugar, salt, cornstarch, and add gradually the apricot nectar (apricot juice and pulp mixed and sweetened); stir with a wooden spoon and cook carefully until clear and completely thickened; remove from the fire and add butter and lemon juice. Let cool and serve with fruit salad, or a pear and lettuce salad.

BACON DRESSING FOR RAW SPINACH SALAD

3 tablespoons bacon fat
2 tablespoons flour
1 tablespoon grated onion
¾ teaspoon dry mustard
1½ teaspoons salt

⅛ teaspoon black pepper
¼ teaspoon sugar
2 teaspoons salad mustard
2 tablespoons vinegar
1 cup water

Melt bacon fat; stir in flour. Add onion; cook slowly 1 minute. Add seasonings, sugar, mustard and vinegar; blend. Add water, continuing to stir. Cook, stirring constantly until thickened. Yield: approximately 1 cup.

CALIFORNIA FRENCH DRESSING

½ cup ketchup
3 tablespoons powdered sugar
1 cup salad oil
½ cup vinegar
¼ teaspoon garlic seasoning

¼ teaspoon onion seasoning
¼ teaspoon celery salt
¼ teaspoon salt
¼ teaspoon black pepper
1 teaspoon dry mustard
4 teaspoons Worcestershire sauce

Measure all ingredients into mixing bowl. Beat with rotary egg beater. Pour into covered pint jar. Shake well before serving. Yield: about 1¾ cups.

COOKED LIME DRESSING

2 teaspoons salt
1½ teaspoons dry mustard
4 teaspoons sugar
  Cayenne pepper

1 cup sour cream
2 tablespoons flour
2 eggs
1 cup scalded milk
½ cup lime juice

Mix dry ingredients and add eggs. Add milk and lime and cook over hot water. Stir constantly. Cool and add sour cream.

CUCUMBER SALAD DRESSING

1 cup mayonnaise
  Juice of 1 lemon
1 clove garlic mashed
2 small cans anchovies mashed

1 cucumber (cut lengthwise,
    then slice across fine)
1 cup chopped parsley
2 heads lettuce cut in bite sizes

Mix mayonnaise, lemon juice, garlic and anchovies. Fold in cucumber and parsley. Pour over chilled lettuce and toss. Serve immediately. Serves 8.

FRUIT SALAD DRESSING

1 cup sugar
2 tablespoons flour
½ teaspoon mustard
¼ teaspoon salt

2 eggs (beaten)
½ cup pineapple juice
¼ cup orange juice
¼ cup lemon juice
1 cup heavy cream whipped

Combine sugar, flour, mustard, salt and eggs in a saucepan. Slowly add fruit juices and mix well. Cook slowly until thickened (about 10 minutes) stirring constantly. Remove from heat, pour into pint jar and cool. When ready to serve, fold in whipped cream.

$1,000.00 MAINE SARDINE SALAD DRESSING

(Note: This recipe, an original family recipe, won the $1,000.00 first prize recipe contest sponsored by the Maine Sardine Industry in 1953.)

1 cup of mayonnaise
1 cup Maine sardines, well
　　drained
½ cup parsley

1 tablespoon tarragon vinegar
¼ cup of celery
½ bar of Philadelphia cream
　　cheese (4 oz.)
½ cup of milk

Put all ingredients into a blender. Blend thoroughly at high speed until all ingredients are liquefied. Refrigerate until used. If it thickens in storage, thin with milk. Serve on chilled greens with hard-boiled egg slices, tomato wedges and sliced celery.

PIMIENTO SALAD DRESSING

1 (3¼ oz.) package pimiento
　　cheese
⅓ cup salad oil
2 tablespoons lemon juice

¼ cup sherry
2 tablespoons chopped parsley
½ teaspoon Worcestershire sauce
¼ teaspoon onion salt
¼ teaspoon garlic salt

With a fork, mash cheese and gradually blend in salad oil, lemon juice and sherry, beating until mixture is smooth. Add rest of ingredients, mix well. Delicious over hearts of letuce or with any fruit or vegetable salad that takes kindly to a cheese flavor.

PIQUANT VINEGAR

Chop into rough slices one head of garlic and place in a large, wide-mouthed bottle. Add one tablespoonful of cayenne, and one-fourth cup of tomato ketchup. Pour over all one pint of vinegar, add paprika to color—one or two tablespoonfuls—and let all stand for a month to infuse. Strain off the liquid, let settle until clear, and decant into small two-ounce bottles. Cork and seal. Use to season soups and sauces, or to sprinkle over baked or broiled fish. It is delicious in salad dressings.

ROQUEFORT CHEESE DRESSING

6 egg yolks
¼ cup olive oil
¼ cup vegetable oil
¼ cup lemon juice
Dash of Tabasco

½ teaspoon Worcestershire sauce
1 teaspoon salt
¼ teaspoon paprika
1 cup crumbled Roquefort
¼ cup light cream

Whip egg yolks until thick. Slowly add blended oils and continue the beating until the mass starts to thicken. Keep thinning with lemon juice, adding a dribble at a time. When thoroughly smooth, add dash of Tabasco, Worcestershire sauce, salt and paprika. Now crumble in Roquefort, add cream and whip until smooth. The dressing should be thick but not too thick to pour. Serve over greens or a Chef's Salad; delicious sauce for shrimp cocktail; a love match with the avocado. Yield: 3 cups.

SOUR CREAM SALAD DRESSING

3 tablespoons sugar
3 tablespoons flour
1 teaspoon salt
⅛ teaspoon white pepper
¼ teaspoon paprika

1 teaspoon dry mustard
2 eggs, slightly beaten
½ cup vinegar
2 tablespoons butter
1½ cups dairy sour cream

Mix dry ingredients. Add eggs to vinegar; add to dry ingredients. Cook over low heat, stirring constantly until smooth and thick. Add butter; blend. Remove from heat; stir in sour cream. Chill. Yield: 2¼ cups.

TOMATO FRENCH DRESSING

2 tablespoons sugar
2 teaspoons dry mustard
1 teaspoon salt
½ teaspoon black pepper
1 can (1¼ cups) condensed tomato soup

½ soup can vinegar (½ cup plus 2 tablespoons)
½ soup can salad oil (½ cup plus 2 tablespoons)
2 tablespoons minced onion

Combine dry ingredients in a 1-quart jar; add remaining ingredients and shake well. Store in refrigerator until needed; shake well before using. Makes about 2⅔ cups dressing.

FRENCH DRESSING VARIATIONS

To 1 cup of Basic Tomato French Dressing, add any one of the following:

Bacon Dressing: 2 slices bacon, cooked and crumbled ... for sliced egg, mixed greens, potatoes.

Blue Cheese Dressing: 1 tablespoon crumbled blue cheese ... for fresh fruit, sliced tomatoes, lettuce wedges.

Garlic Dressing: Allow 1 medium clove of garlic to stand in dressing over night, and then remove ... for sliced cucumbers, mixed greens, cooked vegetables.

Herb Dressing: ½ teaspoon ground herb (rosemary, sage, savory, marjoram or thyme) ... for sliced tomatoes, lettuce wedges, chicken.

Sweet Pickle Relish Dressing: 1 tablespoon sweet pickle relish—for sliced egg, avocado, lettuce wedges, cottage cheese.

Chiffonade: 1 hard-cooked egg chopped fine, 1 tablespoon each minced green pepper and pimiento ... lettuce wedges.

CURRIED LOBSTER SALAD

1 lobster	1 teaspoon curry paste
1 cucumber	1 teaspoon celery salt
3 tablespoons salad oil	Salt and pepper
½ lemon	Cayenne
1 teaspoon shallot, minced	Lettuce
1 teaspoon mango chutney	Endive

Cook the lobster, cool, remove the meat and cut it in pieces. Pare the cucumber and slice thin. Make a dressing by combining the oil and the juice of the lemon; add the shallot, chutney, curry paste and celery salt. Season well with salt, pepper and a few grains of cayenne. Marinate the lobster with the dressing. When ready to serve, place on nests of lettuce, surround the lobster with the slices of cucumber and garnish with endive. Yield: Serves 4.

GREENS WITH SOUR-CREAM DRESSING

1 head lettuce	⅛ teaspoon pepper
½ pound young spinach or	2 teaspoons vinegar
dandelions	2 hard-cooked eggs, chopped
1 teaspoon salt	1 cup sour cream

Wash greens thoroughly. Drain and shake dry in clean cloth. Break greens into small pieces with fingers. Add seasonings and eggs to sour cream. Fold greens into dressing just before serving. Yield: 4 portions.

HARRY'S SALAD

(From "Harry's"—Minneapolis, Minn.)

Put into a salad bowl:

½ head each of romaine, chicory,	½ cup cut-up shrimp
and head lettuce, broken	8 anchovies rolled with capers
into chunks	1 hard-cooked egg, coarsely
1 cucumber, sliced thin	chopped
2 tomatoes, quartered	6 ripe olives and 6 green olives,
½ cup lobster meat	sliced

Just before serving toss salad with dressing of 2 parts olive oil to one part vinegar to which are added mustard, salt, pepper and paprika to taste. Yield: 4 to 6 servings.

HEARTY BEEF SALAD

2 cups diced cooked beef	½ cup coarsely grated carrots
½ cup French dressing	¼ cup chopped sweet pickle
½ cup diced cooked potatoes	2 hard-cooked eggs, diced
½ cup cooked green beans	½ cup mayonnaise
	4 to 6 lettuce cups

Pour French dressing over beef cubes and chill for 1 hour or longer. Chill remaining ingredients. Combine beef, French dressing, carrots, potatoes, green beans, pickles and hard-cooked eggs. Add mayonnaise and mix lightly. Serve salad in lettuce cups. 4 to 6 servings.

JULY SALAD BOWL

3 cups shredded cabbage
½ medium cucumber, diced
½ green pepper, minced
¼ cup chopped celery
1 beet, minced

1 tablespoon minced onion
½ cup mild vinegar
1 teaspoon salt
⅛ teaspoon pepper
½ cup light cream

Wash and prepare the vegetables as indicated. Pour over the vinegar and season with salt and pepper. Chill and allow to stand an hour. Add the light cream and serve in a large salad bowl. Yield: 6 servings.

MEXICAN SALAD

1 head of lettuce
1 cooked cauliflower
2 medium-sized alligator pears

2 ripe tomatoes
1 onion
3 tablespoons lemon juice
6 tablespoons olive oil

Arrange the washed and crisped lettuce in a salad bowl. On it place the head of cauliflower and pour over it a dressing made from the lemon juice and the olive oil. Peel the onion and mince very fine. Pare the alligator pear and mash the pulp. Dice the tomatoes. Combine these three, season with a little salt and blend to the consistency of a paste. Arrange in little mounds around the cauliflower. Chill thoroughly and serve. Yield: 4 to 6 servings.

NETHERLAND SALAD AND DRESSING

¾ head lettuce, cut julienne
½ cup julienne of chicken

½ cup julienne of baked ham
⅓ cup julienne tomatoes
1 tablespoon chopped pickle

DRESSING

1 teaspoon finely chopped chives
1 hard-boiled egg, chopped
3 tablespoons mayonnaise

2 tablespoons vinegar
3 tablespoons olive oil
1 teaspoon Worcestershire sauce

Mix well and serve well chilled on dinner plate. Do not use leaves of lettuce to serve on, but put directly on plate. Yield: Serves 4.

SUNDAY FRANKFURT SALAD

10 frankfurters
3 cups cooked potatoes
¼ cup chopped onion
⅓ cup chopped green pepper

¾ cup diced cucumber
1 cup mayonnaise
⅓ cup chili sauce
1 teaspoon prepared mustard

Slice 7 frankfurters for the salad and add to vegetables. Make dressing by mixing mayonnaise, chili sauce and prepared mustard. Add dressing to frankfurters and vegetables and toss lightly. When ready to serve, split the 3 remaining frankfurters almost through to the center and then cut in half. Arrange the frankfurter halves on salad. Chill and serve. 6 servings.

GELATIN SALADS

FROZEN FRUIT SALAD

1 teaspoon plain gelatin
1 cup table cream
2 tablespoons lemon juice
2 tablespoons sugar
⅛ teaspoon salt
½ teaspoon mild prepared mustard

¼ teaspoon Worcestershire sauce
1 cup apricot whole fruit nectar
½ cup finely diced fresh or
    cooked fruit
Salad greens
French dressing

Soften gelatin in ¼ cup cream. Heat remaining cream to just below boiling and dissolve gelatin in it. Chill thoroughly. Beat well. Combine lemon juice, sugar, salt, mustard, and Worcestershire sauce, and whip into cream a small portion at a time. Pour into refrigerator tray, place in freezing compartment with control set at lowest temperature and freeze to a mush consistency. Remove to chilled bowl and beat nectar and fruit into cream, blending thoroughly. Return to compartment and freeze until firm. Reset temperature control to normal. Serve on shredded salad greens dressed with French dressing. Serves 4 to 5.

GOLDEN SUMMER SALAD

1 (12-ounce) can apricot whole
    fruit nectar
¼ cup water
¼ package lemon-flavored gelatin
    Few grains salt
2 teaspoons mild prepared
    horseradish

Juice of 1 lemon
1 cup grated carrot
½ cup chopped blanched almonds
    Shredded lettuce
    French dressing

Heat nectar and water to just below boiling. Dissolve gelatin in hot liquid. Add salt, horseradish and lemon juice. Chill until thick but not firm. Blend in carrot and almonds. Turn into individual molds or large mold and chill until firm. Unmold on shredded lettuce, dressed with French dressing. Top with mayonnaise, if desired. Serves 6.

HOLIDAY FRUIT MOLD

1½ cups apricot whole fruit nectar
¼ cup grapefruit juice
1 package lemon-flavored gelatin
⅛ teaspoon salt

1 cup grapefruit segments
¼ cup finely chopped blanched
    almonds
    Salad greens for garnish
    Sour cream dressing

Heat nectar and grapefruit juice to boiling and dissolve gelatin and salt in it. Chill until thick but not firm. Whip until light and frothy. Fold in grapefruit and almonds. Pour into a mold or pan and chill until firm. Unmold and serve on garnished salad plates. Top with Sour Cream Dressing. Serves 6 or more.

NECTAR MELON SALAD

1½ cups apricot whole fruit nectar
1 envelope plain gelatin
¼ cup cold water
1½ tablespoons lemon juice

¼ teaspoon salt
1 cup diced cantaloupe
⅓ cup ripe olives
    Lettuce
    Mayonnaise

Heat nectar to just below boiling. Soften gelatin in cold water and dissolve in hot nectar. Blend in lemon juice and salt. Chill until slightly thickened; whip until light. Stir in cantaloupe and olives cut into medium-sized pieces. Turn into individual molds and chill until firm. Unmold and serve in crisp lettuce cups. Top with mayonnaise. Serves 6.

RASPBERRY TANG SALAD

1 package prepared raspberry
    gelatin
½ cup boiling water
1 cream cheese
¼ cup salad dressing

1 small can crushed pineapple
1 banana, diced
¼ cup shredded coconut
½ cup pecan meats, chopped
1 cup cream, whipped

Dissolve the gelatin in boiling water and set aside to cool. Soften the cream cheese with the salad dressing. Add gradually, so that the mixture will be smooth, the pineapple, banana, coconut and pecans. When the gelatin mixture begins to congeal, add the cheese mixture to it. Place in individual molds and chill until firm. Unmold on nests of cress or lettuce and serve with brown bread sandwiches for a bridge, tea or supper.

SUPREME SALAD

1 package lemon-flavored gelatin
1 cup hot water
½ cup sugar
½ cup diced orange sections
1½ cups diced celery
2 cups chopped pitted plumped
    prunes (pour hot water
    over them and let stand
    until plump)

¼ cup slivered toasted almonds
Crisp chicory
1 8 oz. package cream cheese
Slivered toasted almonds
Pitted whole plumped prunes
Mayonnaise or French Dressing

Dissolve gelatin in hot water; add sugar. Stir until dissolved. Cool. Combine diced orange sections, celery, chopped prunes and slivered almonds; add cooled gelatin. Pour into mold; chill until firm. Unmold on chicory. Cut cream cheese into squares, stud with slivered almonds; place on chicory around mold, interspersed with pitted prunes. Serve with mayonnaise or French dressing. Makes 8 servings.

WALDORF CIDER SALADS

½ cup seedless raisins	Dash salt
1 envelope (1 tablespoon) plain gelatin	1 large red apple ¾ cup diced celery
2 tablespoons lemon juice	Salad greens
1¾ cups apple cider	Salad dressing

Rinse raisins, cover with water and boil 5 minutes. Drain and cool. Soften gelatin in lemon juice. Heat cider to boiling, and dissolve gelatin in it. Blend in salt. Cool until slightly thickened. Core and dice apple. Fold raisins, apples and celery into gelatin. Spoon into individual molds and chill until firm. Unmold on crisp salad greens. Serve with dressing made by blending equal parts of mayonnaise and commercial sour cream. Makes 6 (6-ounce) molds.

ROQUEFORT SALAD

4 tablespoons gelatin	⅓ cup salad dressing
1 cup cold water	⅛ teaspoon salt
2½ cups boiling water	½ cup American cheese
1 cup cream	½ cup Roquefort cheese
6 4-ounce packages cream cheese	Pimiento

Allow two tablespoons of plain gelatin to soften in one-half cup of cold water; add one cup of boiling water, stir until dissolved. Let cool until thickened, whip until fluffy and fold in cream beaten stiff. Fold in the cream cheese, softened in a warm room, and the salad dressing. The gelatin must have the proper consistency in order that one may fold in these ingredients without losing lightness. The mixture may be chilled in a pan of cracked ice.

Meanwhile, soften two additional tablespoons of plain gelatin in one-half cup of cold water, add one and one-half cups of hot water;

stir until dissolved; let cool until thickened. Season with salt, whip very light and fold in the previous mixture.

Divide into three parts; leave one plain, add diced American cheese to one portion, and crumbled Roquefort cheese to the third portion. Pour into separate molds, or fill each mold with two kinds of mousse as desired. Let chill, unmold, decorate with pieces of pimiento. Provide shredded lettuce and French dressing. Yield: 8 to 10 servings.

SHRIMP-TOMATO SALAD

1 envelope unflavored gelatin
¼ cup water
1 can tomato soup, undiluted
1 tablespoon lemon juice
¼ teaspoon Worcestershire sauce
¼ teaspoon onion salt
1 cup finely diced celery
½ cup sliced, stuffed olives
½ cup salad dressing
2 cans (4½-ounce size) cleaned shrimp, drained

Soften gelatin in water. Heat with soup until dissolved. Remove from heat; let cool. Stir in remaining ingredients, except garnish. Pour into 1-quart mold or individual serving-size molds; chill until firm. Cover; freeze. Use within 2 weeks.

Thaw in refrigerator overnight. Unmold on lettuce; garnish as desired. 6 servings.

BREAD

We're in love with our chapter on Bread. We very frankly specialize in Breads at the Hotel Anderson because we are sick to death of traveling ten thousand miles each year, in and out of all the places recommended and not recommended, and practically never finding a roll that looks as though it might be homemade. We can spot a baker's roll ten miles away and we can spot the ones that are being gussied up in the warming oven for the second and third day in a row!

It's why we have a Bread Tray at the Hotel Anderson that is passed and re-passed, meal after meal, literally bulging with a glorious variety of sweet rolls, hard rolls, fruit and nut breads, native breads, bread sticks, coffee cakes and muffins.

We love seeing the incredulous wonder in a first-visit customer's eye. It's worth the getting up at 5:00 A.M. to put the dough a-rising! It's worth stationing one girl at the ovens, meal after meal, so that breads can be brought out popping hot and oven fresh!

We couldn't close our preface on breads without a bouquet to the Pillsbury People who publish their own book of one hundred prize-winning recipes after each Pillsbury Bake-Off in the fall of the year. They have been most cordial in letting us reprint many of the recipes that we use at Hotel Anderson day after day. We hope they NEVER stop printing these delightful and original books, they are among the finest books available. We buy twenty-five copies every year and at the end of the year they are in shambles—used so much, each one better than the last. To Pillsbury's, then, all the orchids in the world for doing so much to further the cause of good creative cooking and good baking.

We ask that you take this book to bed with you some night and spend one whole hour on our Bread section . . . we think it's that good. And once inspired you'll find that baking is easy, and baking bread is fun, when there is such a wide variety of recipes to choose from.

113

We think you'll never buy another loaf of baker's bread once you bake your own, if for no other reason than the indescribable aroma of freshly baked bread that is bound to float through your house. It's new fashioned to be old-fashioned where baking your own bread is concerned!

ANADAMA BREAD

3 cups water
1 teaspoon salt
⅓ cup corn meal, yellow
⅓ cup molasses
1½ tablespoons shortening

¼ cup warm (not hot) water
1 package or cake yeast, active
   dry or compressed
4 cups (about) all-purpose flour
1 tablespoon butter, melted

In pan combine water and salt, bring to boil; slowly stir in corn meal, bring to boil again, stirring constantly. Remove from heat, pour into large bowl; add molasses and shortening; stir until melted; cool to lukewarm. Measure warm water into small bowl; sprinkle or crumble in yeast; stir until dissolved; blend into corn-meal mixture. Add 2 cups flour; beat until smooth. Gradually add remaining flour to make soft dough. Turn out on floured board; knead until smooth and springy. Place in large greased bowl, turning over to grease entire surface. Cover with towel, let rise in warm place (85° F.) until double in bulk, about 1½ hours. Punch down, turn out on lightly floured board; shape into loaf. Place in greased loaf pan, 9 by 5 by 3″. Cover with towel; let rise in warm place until double in bulk, about 1 hour. Brush with butter or margarine and sprinkle with about 1 teaspoon of uncooked corn meal. Bake in moderate oven (375°) for 40 to 45 minutes. Turn out of pan and cool thoroughly on rack. Makes 1 loaf.

APPLE CORN BREAD

2 tart apples
1 cup corn meal
1 cup flour
3 teaspoons baking powder

¾ teaspoon salt
¼ cup sugar
1 egg
1 cup milk
2 tablespoons melted fat

Quarter the apples, remove the cores and pare. Cut in thin slices. Sift together the corn meal, flour, baking powder, salt and sugar. Beat the egg and add it to the milk. Stir the liquid ingredients into the dry ingredients, add melted fat and pour into a well-greased pan. Place the apples on top of the corn bread so that the slices overlap slightly and the rows of apples are parallel. Bake at 375° F. for 25 minutes.

APPLE MUFFINS

2 cups flour	1 cup apples, chopped
½ cup sugar	1 egg, beaten
3 teaspoons baking powder	1 cup milk
¼ teaspoon salt	3 tablespoons butter, melted

Sift dry ingredients together, add apples, mix. Add combined liquid ingredients, mixing just enough to moisten. Pour into buttered muffin pans, filling two-thirds full. Sprinkle with the following crunch: ⅓ cup brown sugar, ⅓ cup nut meats, chopped, ½ teaspoon cinnamon. Bake in a hot oven (400° F.) 15 minutes. 12 to 16 muffins.

APRICOT BREAD

½ cup dried apricots	1 cup sugar
1 large orange	2 tablespoons butter
½ cup raisins	1 teaspoon vanilla
Boiling water (amount given later in method)	1 egg, beaten
	2 cups sifted all-purpose flour
¼ teaspoon salt	2 teaspoons baking powder
1 teaspoon soda	½ cup chopped nuts

Soak apricots in small amount of water for one-half hour. Squeeze out as much water as you can before putting through food grinder. Squeeze juice of orange into a cup and fill with boiling water. Put orange rind, apricots and raisins through food chopper. Add orange juice and water. Add soda, sugar, melted butter, vanilla and beaten egg. Add dry ingredients and nut meats. Bake in oiled bread pan 1 hour at 350° F.

BANANA TEA BREAD

1¾ cups sifted flour	⅓ cup shortening
2 teaspoons baking powder	⅔ cup sugar
¼ teaspoon baking soda	2 eggs, well beaten
½ teaspoon salt	1 cup mashed ripe bananas*
	(2 to 3 bananas)

(Use either fully ripe or all-yellow bananas.)

Sift together flour, baking powder, soda and salt. Beat shortening until creamy in mixing bowl. Add sugar gradually and conitnue beating until light and fluffy. Add eggs and beat well. Add flour mixture alternately with bananas, a small amount at a time, beating after each addition until smooth. Turn into a well-greased bread pan (8½ x 4½ x 3 inches) and bake in a moderate oven (350° F.) about 1 hour 10 minutes or until bread is done. Makes 1 loaf.

BARBECUED FRENCH BREAD

¾ cup finely chopped onion	2 teaspoons brown sugar
2 tablespoons butter	½ teaspoon celery salt
⅔ cup chili sauce	¾ teaspoon dry mustard
2 tablespoons vinegar	1 loaf French or Vienna bread
1 tablespoon Worcestershire sauce	½ cup shredded process American cheese

Cook onion in butter until tender. Add other ingredients except bread and cheese; simmer until thickened. Without cutting through bottom crust, slice bread, making each slice about ¾-inch thick; spread a tablespoon of sauce on each. Sprinkle slices and top with shredded cheese. Wrap in heavy foil; freeze. To serve, heat wrapped loaf in hot oven (400°) for 20 to 25 minutes. 6 servings.

BATTER BREAD OR SPOON BREAD

4 eggs, beaten separately (fewer
    eggs may be used at high
    altitudes)
1 cup cooked hominy grits
4 tablespoons cornmeal (white)

1 pint milk
1 teaspoon sugar
1 teaspoon salt
1 teaspoon baking powder
1 tablespoon melted butter

Mix all ingredients, then fold in whites of eggs last. Bake in greased pan till thoroughly done, about thirty to forty-five minutes. Serve hot with plenty of butter. Maple syrup may be used if desired. This should be soft enough to be cut from the pan with a spoon.

BELGARDIN BROD

1¼ cups strained honey
¾ cup butter or margarine
¼ cup orange juice
    Grated rind of 1 lemon
    Grated rind of 1 orange
2 cups chopped almonds

10 cups sifted cake flour
2 cups sugar
1 teaspoon cloves
1 teaspoon cinnamon
2 teaspoons nutmeg
1 teaspoon salt
4 teaspoons baking powder

Melt honey and butter or margarine over hot water. Remove from heat and add orange juice, lemon and orange rind and almonds.

Now sift all the dry ingredients together and mix thoroughly with the warm honey-butter mixture. Chill in refrigerator several hours (tastes even better after mellowing several days). To bake, roll on a lightly floured board ⅛″ thick, cut in strips and place on a greased baking sheet. Bake 10 minutes in a 325° F. or slow oven.

While cookies are still warm, brush with a thin glaze of ½ cup confectioners' sugar mixed with 1 tablespoon cream. Makes 200.

BISHOP'S BREAD

4 eggs, separated
1 cup sugar
1 teaspoon vanilla
1 cup flour
2 teaspoons baking powder

1 cup raisins
1 cup almonds, blanched and
    chopped
Pinch salt
Powdered sugar

Beat yolks of eggs until light and lemon-colored; then add sugar, and cream well. Add the vanilla. Sift the dry ingredients together and stir into the egg mixture. Add the nuts and raisins. Fold in the stiffly beaten egg whites. Pour into an oblong buttered pan and bake in a moderate oven (350° F.) for 20 minutes. While cake is still hot, cut into squares and cover with powdered sugar.

BLUEBERRY-ORANGE BREAD

3 cups sifted all-purpose flour
4½ teaspoons baking powder
¼ teaspoon baking soda
1½ teaspoons salt
½ cup sugar
1 cup blueberries, fresh,
    canned or frozen

1 egg slightly beaten
1 cup milk
⅓ cup orange juice
1 tablespoon orange rind, grated
½ cup salad oil or melted
    shortening

Sift flour, baking powder, soda, salt and sugar; sift again into large bowl. Add blueberries and toss lightly until berries are thoroughly coated and evenly distributed through flour mixture. Combine egg, milk, orange juice, rind and salad oil or shortening (slightly cooled); pour into flour mixture and stir just enough to moisten all the flour. Turn into oiled loaf pan, 9 x 5 x 3 inches, and bake at 350° F. about 1 hour. Cool 5 minutes; remove from pan and set on cake rack to cool thoroughly.

BRAN BUTTERMILK BISCUITS

½ cup bran
¾ cup buttermilk
1½ cups flour

1 teaspoon baking powder
1 teaspoon salt
½ teaspoon soda
⅓ cup shortening

Soak the bran in buttermilk. Sift the flour, baking powder, salt and soda together. Cut in the shortening until the mixture is like coarse corn meal. Add the soaked bran; stir until well blended. Turn onto a floured board, knead lightly a few seconds; roll or pat to one-half-inch thickness and cut with floured cutter.

BUCKWHEAT CAKES

2 cups milk
2 cups boiling water
1 yeast cake
4 cups buckwheat flour

½ teaspoon soda, dissolved in
1 cup hot water
1 teaspoon salt
1 tablespoon molasses

Scald the milk and add the boiling water. Cool to body temperature and dissolve the yeast cake in mixture. Sift in enough flour (using more than 4 cups, if necessary) to make a batter thin enough to pour. Let rise overnight in an earthen crock. In the morning, add the dissolved soda, molasses and salt. Fry on a hot greased griddle. Keep about ½ cup of this batter as a sponge for the following day. Keep in a cool place until night and then add enough flour to make a stiff batter. In the morning, proceed as usual adding the molasses, salt and dissolved soda.

CHEESE BISCUITS

2 cups flour
4 teaspoons baking powder
½ teaspoon salt

3 tablespoons butter
¾ cup Wisconsin Natural
American Cheese, grated
⅔ cup milk

Sift dry ingredients together, work or cut in butter and cheese. Add milk, beat until well mixed. Roll ½-inch thick and cut into biscuits. Bake in a hot oven (400° F.) 15 minutes.

CORN-MEAL POTATO MUFFINS

Cream a tablespoon of brown sugar with two tablespoons butter or chicken fat, and add one beaten egg. Sift a cup of fine, yellow corn meal with four teaspoons baking powder and one-half teaspoon salt, mix with a cup mashed potatoes and a cup rich milk, and combine with the mixture of butter, sugar and egg. Beat well for a minute or two, and baked in greased muffin tins. Bake at 375° F. The quantities given should make a dozen muffins, and the flavor is uncommon and very good.

CRUNCHY BROWN SUGAR COFFEE RING

½ cup light or dark raisins
2½ cups biscuit mix
⅓ cup sugar
¾ cup light cream or half and
   half

⅓ cup brown sugar (packed)
½ teaspoon cinnamon
3 tablespoons butter or
   margarine

Rinse and drain raisins. Combine with biscuit mix and sugar. Stir in cream to make moderately stiff dough. Heat brown sugar, cinnamon and butter together until butter melts. Drop dough by small spoonfuls into well-greased 8½-inch ring mold. Drizzle brown sugar mixture over top. Bake in moderately hot oven (375° F.) about 25 minutes. Turn out and serve hot. Makes about 6 servings.

DANISH GINGER ROLLS

This is an old family recipe brought from Denmark. Subtle ginger flavor lends a special appeal.

Dissolve 1 cake compressed yeast (or 1 package dry granular yeast) in ¼ cup lukewarm water.

Beat 2 eggs in large bowl until light and fluffy. Blend in ½ cup milk, 2 tablespoons melted butter or shortening, 3 tablespoons sugar, 1½ teaspoons ginger, 1½ teaspoons salt and dissolved yeast. Mix well. Add 3 cups sifted enriched flour. Mix to a soft dough. Place in greased bowl. Cover. Let rise in warm place (85° to 90° F.) until double in bulk, about 1 hour. Punch dough down. Let rise in warm place until double in bulk, about 30 minutes.

Roll out on lightly floured board to about ¼-inch thickness. Cut into rounds with 3-inch cutter. Brush with melted butter. Mark a crease with dull edge of knife to one side of center of each round. Fold small part over large; press edge to seal. Place on greased baking sheet. Let rise in warm place about 30 minutes.

Bake in moderately hot oven (400° F.) 15 to 20 minutes. Makes about 18 rolls.

DARK ORANGE RAISIN BREAD

Heat ¼ cup sugar in heavy skillet over low heat, stirring constantly, until sugar melts and turns dark golden brown. Add very slowly ⅓ cup hot water, a few drops at a time at first, stirring constantly until sugar is completely dissolved. Cool.

Soften 2 cakes compressed yeast in ½ cup lukewarm water in large bowl. (Or substitute 2 packages dry yeast softened in ½ cup very warm, not hot, water.) Let stand 5 minutes. Add ⅓ cup firmly packed brown sugar, 2 cups sifted rye flour, 1 tablespoon salt, 1½ cups warm water, ¼ cup melted shortening, 1 cup raisins, 2 tablespoons grated orange rind and the burnt sugar. Beat well. Add gradually 4 to 4½ cups sifted enriched flour to form a stiff dough. Knead on floured board until smooth and satiny, 5 to 8 minutes. (To knead, fold the dough over on itself and push it lightly with the palms of the hands. Repeat this process rhythmically, turning the dough one quarter way around on the board each time.) Place in a greased bowl and cover. Let rise in warm place (85° to 90° F.) until light and doubled in size, about 2 hours. Punch down; let rise again for ½ hour.

Divide into three parts. Shape into round or long loaves and place on greased baking sheets or in small loaf pans. Cover. Let rise in warm place until light and doubled in size, 30 to 60 minutes. Bake in moderate oven (350° F.) 40 to 45 minutes. Makes 3 loaves.

DUTCH BREAKFAST CAKE

1 cup milk	½ cup sugar
½ yeast cake	⅓ cup melted butter
3 cups flour	2 tablespoons butter, softened
½ teaspoon salt	⅓ cup chopped walnut meats
1 egg, well beaten	2 tablespoons brown sugar
	1 teaspoon cinnamon

Scald the milk and cool to lukewarm; crumble the yeast cake into it and allow to soften. Stir in half the flour, the salt, egg, sugar, and melted butter. Add the remaining flour and toss the dough onto a lightly floured board. Knead and allow to rise until double in bulk.

Knead again and place in a shallow buttered pan. Brush the top with the softened butter, sprinkle with nuts and sugar mixed with the cinnamon. Bake. Cut in squares and serve hot. Temperature: 350° F. Time: 35 minutes.

FASTNACHTS

2 cups milk	3 eggs
1 yeast cake	½ teaspoon nutmeg
1 cup warm water	¼ cup melted butter
6½ cups flour, approx.	¼ teaspoon salt
1 cup sugar	Deep fat

Scald milk and set aside to cool. Dissolve yeast in water and add ½ cup flour and mix to a batter. Add the scalded milk and, when mixture is lukewarm, stir in 1 teaspoon sugar and about 3 cups flour. Set in a warm place to rise overnight. In morning add eggs, well beaten, nutmeg, butter, remaining sugar, salt. Mix thoroughly. Stir in flour until batter can't be stirred with a spoon. Set aside to rise until light. Roll on a well-floured board and cut with a doughnut cutter. Let rise again and then fry in hot fat until golden brown.

FLANNEL CAKES

Preparation time: about ½ hour.

1 cup sifted all-purpose flour	2 egg yolks
¼ teaspoon salt	½ teaspoon baking soda
1¼ cups buttermilk	2 egg whites
1 tablespoon melted butter or margarine	Shortening for griddle
	Butter and syrup for serving

Sift flour and salt into a 2-quart bowl. Pour buttermilk in gradually, beating hard, and add melted butter.

Beat the egg yolks and add to the batter along with the soda. Mix thoroughly. Beat the egg whites stiff and fold into the batter.

Heat a heavy griddle over medium heat. When the griddle is hot, add enough shortening to make the surface glossy. Pour enough batter on griddle to make 4-inch pancakes. When brown on the underside, turn.

As soon as the second side is brown, lift pancakes out onto a hot plate or pan. Stack and keep warm in a slow oven (300° F.) until all are made.

Serve 4 pancakes per person on a hot plate, with butter and syrup. Makes 16 pancakes.

FRENCH DOUGHNUTS

1 cup hot water	1 cup sifted enriched flour
3 tablespoons lard	3 eggs
¼ teaspoon salt	Lard for deep-fat frying
	Confectioners' frosting

To hot water add lard and salt and bring to a boil. Add flour all at once and stir vigorously until mixture forms a ball. Cool. Add eggs, one at a time, beating thoroughly after each addition. Chill dough 1 hour or longer. Press dough through a pastry tube onto 3-inch rounds of brown paper which have been greased. Have lard heated to 365° F. and lower doughnuts into lard with the paper side up. Fry until brown on one side. Remove paper, turn and brown on second side. Cool on cake rack and sprinkle with confectioners' sugar or glaze with a thin confectioners' sugar frosting. Yield: 10 to 12 doughnuts.

CONFECTIONERS' FROSTING

1 cup sifted confectioners' sugar	Dash of salt
	2 tablespoons water
	½ teaspoon vanilla

Combine ingredients and mix until smooth. Spread on doughnuts.

GOLDEN WAFFLES

Sift together:

2 cups sifted all-purpose flour	3 teaspoons cream of tartar baking powder
	¾ teaspoon salt

Combine and add

   2 egg yolks, slightly beaten   1¾ cups milk
                                         ¼ cup margarine, melted

Stir just enough to mix well.

Fold in
   2 egg whites, stiffly beaten

Drop by spoonfuls on hot waffle iron. Bake until brown, about 4 minutes.

SOUR MILK WAFFLES

Add ¼ teaspoon soda and 3 tablespoons sugar to dry ingredients. Substitute 1¾ cups sour milk or buttermilk for 1¾ cups milk. Proceed as for Golden Waffles.

CHEESE WAFFLES

Fold in 1½ cups grated cheese into Golden Waffle batter. Proceed as for Golden Waffles.

BACON WAFFLES

Drop Golden Waffle batter by spoonfuls on hot waffle iron. Sprinkle 2 tablespoons minced, uncooked bacon on top of each waffle. Proceed as for Golden Waffles.

GRAHAM NUT BREAD

1 cup flour
½ teaspoon soda
½ teaspoon baking powder
½ teaspoon salt
1 cup brown sugar

1 cup graham flour
½ cup nut meats, chopped
½ cup raisins
1 egg, beaten
1 cup sour milk
2 tablespoons butter, melted

Sift first 4 ingredients together, add brown sugar, graham flour, nut meats, and raisins; mix well. Add combined egg, milk, and butter. Bake in buttered pan (4x10x2 inches) or two 1-pound loaf pans in a moderate oven (350° F.) 45 to 55 minutes. 2 loaves.

GRAPE NUT BREAD

1 cup flour	½ cup graham flour
1 teaspoon baking powder	½ cup grape nuts
1 teaspoon soda	1 cup nut meats
½ cup sugar	1 egg, beaten
½ teaspoon salt	1 cup sour milk
	2 tablespoons butter, melted

Sift first 5 ingredients together, add graham flour, grape nuts, and nut meats. Add combined liquid ingredients, mixing just enough to moisten. Bake in buttered loaf pan in a moderate oven (350° F.) 45 to 55 minutes, or muffin tins in a hot oven (400° F.) 25 to 30 minutes. Yield: 1 loaf.

HARD DINNER ROLLS

½ cake compressed	4 teaspoons sugar
or	1¼ teaspoons salt
½ package dry granular yeast	1 egg
¼ cup lukewarm water	3½ cups sifted flour, about
1 cup milk, scalded	3 tablespoons melted shortening

Soften yeast in lukewarm water. Combine milk, sugar and salt and stir until sugar and salt are dissolved; cool to lukewarm; add softened yeast and beaten egg. Add about ½ of the flour and beat until smooth. Add melted shortening and beat well. Add remaining flour gradually and knead until smooth and satiny. Place dough in a lightly greased bowl, grease surface lightly, cover and allow to rise in a warm place until doubled in bulk (about 1¾ hours). Turn out on lightly floured board, punch down and divide into 24 parts; press each part flat, cover with a cloth and allow to rest about 10 minutes. Shape each part into an oval, 3 inches in length, tapering the ends. Place rolls at least 2 inches apart on greased baking sheet, cover and allow to rise in a warm place until doubled in bulk (about 1½ hours). Bake in a preheated oven, then turn off heat and dry in oven about 20 minutes. Temperature: 400 degrees F. Time: about 15 minutes. Yield: about 2 dozen.

HICKORY NUT SWIRLS

(Full of Sugar and Spice and All Things Nice)

1 cup milk	3⅔ cups (about) fine whole-
¼ cup shortening	wheat flour of high grade
1⅓ teaspoons salt	Cinnamon and sugar
¼ cup sugar	mixture
1 cake compressed yeast	Raisins
1 egg	Molasses
	Hickory nut meats

Heat the milk, remove from the fire; add the shortening, salt and sugar, stir until dissolved. Let cool to lukewarm temperature; add about one-half cup of the mixture to the crumbled yeast; stir until smooth and return to the bowl; mix well and add the egg well beaten. Sift the flour, be sure to add any bran which is too coarse to go through the sifter. Add one-half of the flour and beat thoroughly; then add more flour to make a stiff dough. Turn out onto remaining flour and knead gently and lightly, but thoroughly. Put the dough in an oiled bowl; turn it over to oil the top. Cover, and let rise until doubled in bulk. Knead well, roll out flat, sprinkle with cinnamon, sugar and raisins; roll up and slice off the end to form swirls. Grease a baking dish, pour a thin layer of sorghum molasses over the bottom, sprinkle with hickory nutmeats and lay the swirls on them. Let rise until doubled in bulk. Bake about fifteen minutes in a fully preheated oven at 375° F. Turn from the baking dish while warm.

HOMEMADE BISCUIT MIX

8 cups sifted enriched flour	1 cup lard for soft wheat or
¼ cup baking powder	1½ cups lard for hard
4 teaspoons salt	wheat flour

Sift together flour, baking powder and salt. Cut in lard until the mixture has a fine even crumb. Cover closely and store in the refrigerator until ready to use. This mixture will keep at least a month in the refrigerator. Yield: 5 batches biscuits with 2 cups of the mixture to the batch.

To make biscuits, add ½ cup milk to 2 cups Homemade Biscuit Mix. Turn onto a lightly floured surface and knead gently for ½ minute. Pat or roll ½-inch thick and cut with a medium-sized biscuit cutter, dipped in flour. Bake in a hot oven (450° F.) 12 to 15 minutes. Yield: 10 to 12 biscuits.

HONEY-FILLED BISCUITS

(It's the spread that gives them style.)

2 cups flour	¾ teaspoon salt
3 teaspoons baking powder	4 tablespoons shortening
	⅔ cup milk or less

Sift together flour, baking powder and salt. Cut in shortening with two knives or a pastry blender. Stir in milk lightly to make a soft dough. Turn dough onto a lightly-floured board and knead it just enough to make the surface smooth. Roll into a rectangle about one-half inch in thickness. Spread surface with Honey Spread and roll like a jelly roll. With a sharp knife cut slices one-inch thick from the end of roll; place in well-greased muffin tins or, if preferred, on a greased baking sheet. Bake in a quick oven at 400° F. for fifteen to twenty minutes.

HONEY SPREAD

¼ cup butter	¼ cup chopped dates
¼ cup honey or more	¼ cup chopped walnut meats

Cream together butter and honey; add dates and walnut meats and blend thoroughly. Add additional honey if necessary to make the mixture of right consistency to spread.

HUCKLEBERRY PANCAKES

2½ cups flour	1 egg, well beaten
1 teaspoon soda	2 cups sour milk
½ teaspoon salt	1½ tablespoons butter, melted
1½ tablespoons sugar	2 cups huckleberries

Sift the dry ingredients together. Combine the egg and milk and add slowly to the dry ingredients, beating the mixture until smooth. Stir in the butter and then the berries. Pour by tablespoons on a hot greased griddle. Fry on both sides until brown. Serve with powdered sugar.

ITALIAN CHRISTMAS BREAD

1 package active dry or compressed yeast	½ teaspoon anise flavoring or 1 teaspoon nutmeg
¼ cup lukewarm water	About 4 cups sifted all-purpose flour
1¾ cups milk	
1 tablespoon sugar	½ cup seedless raisins
2 cups sifted all-purpose flour	½ cup finely sliced citron
⅓ cup shortening	1 cup coarsely chopped walnuts
1 cup sugar	
2 eggs	1 egg
1½ teaspoons salt	1 tablespoon water

Dissolve yeast in lukewarm water. Meanwhile, heat milk until a film forms on top (do not boil), remove from heat, add 1 tablespoon sugar and cool. When lukewarm, stir in yeast and 2 cups flour.

Now work or cream shortening and gradually work in the cup of sugar. Add well-beaten eggs, yeast mixture, salt, flavoring and 4 cups flour. Mix thoroughly, cover with tea towel and let rise in a warm spot until bread has doubled in size. Then stir in raisins, citron, nuts and knead lightly on a floured board for a few minutes.

Put back in the bowl, brush a little shortening over the top, cover and let rise the second time until double in size. Shape dough into 2 or 3 round loaves (depending on the size loaves you prefer), place on greased baking sheet or pie pans and brush tops with egg that has been beaten with water. Let rise until double, then bake in a 400° F. or moderately hot oven for 15 minutes, then reduce temperature to 350° or moderate and bake until done—15 to 20 minutes for small loaf; 20 to 25 minutes for larger one.

JOHNNY CAKES

Preparation time: about 20 minutes

1 cup white corn meal
1 teaspoon salt
2 tablespoons syrup
1 cup boiling water
½ cup sifted all-purpose flour
1 teaspoon baking powder
1 egg
½ cup milk

2 tablespoons melted butter or margarine shortening, for griddle
2 (12-oz) pkgs. frozen sliced peaches, thawed, or 1 (1 lb. 14 oz.) can sliced peaches
Butter, for serving

Mix the corn meal, salt and syrup in a 2-quart bowl. Stir in boiling water and let stand 10 minutes.

Meanwhile, sift flour and baking powder together. Beat egg and add milk and melted butter. Pour liquid into corn meal mixture. Add flour and baking powder and mix thoroughly.

Heat a heavy griddle over medium heat. When the griddle is hot, add enough shortening to it to make the surface glossy, tilting the griddle to and fro. Pour enough batter on griddle to make 4-inch pancakes. When brown on the underside, turn.

As soon as the second side is brown, lift pancakes out onto a preheated plate or pan. Stack and keep warm in slow oven (300° F.) until all are made.

Serve 4 pancakes per person on a hot plate with peaches and butter. Number of servings: 4 (16 pancakes in all).

KIEVA'S KIFFLES

1 package active dry or compressed yeast
2 tablespoons lukewarm water

½ pound butter or margarine
2 egg yolks
2 cups sifted all-purpose flour
½ cup light cream

Dissolve yeast in lukewarm water. Then cream or work butter or margarine until soft, stir in unbeaten egg yolks, yeast, flour and cream. Divide into 4 parts and cool in refrigerator at least 4 hours. Better yet, overnight. Now make up this filling:

½ pound shelled walnuts	1 tablespoon cream
1 egg white	1 teaspoon rum or vanilla
1 tablespoon sugar	extract

Grind walnuts fine through food chopper. Beat egg white until it stands in peaks. Now mix nuts, egg white and other ingredients together.

Roll first part of dough out paper thin on a board sprinkled with half confectioners' sugar and half flour. Cut this into 2½" squares with a sharp knife. Put 1 teaspoon of nut filling on each square, and roll up neatly. Use up remaining dough in the same fashion. Bake on greased baking sheet in 325° F. or moderately slow oven for 8 to 10 minutes. Sprinkle with confectioners' sugar while still warm. Makes 80 little rolls.

KAFFEEKLATSCH CINNAMON-PECAN MINUTE MUFFINS

⅔ cup uncooked white rice	⅓ cup beet or cane sugar
1⅓ cups water	½ teaspoon cinnamon
1 teaspoon salt	½ cup chopped pecans
2 tablespoons margarine or butter	½ cup sifted all-purpose flour
	2 eggs, separated
	½ cup milk

Put the rice, water and salt in a 2-quart saucepan. Bring to a boil. Turn heat down. Cover. Simmer 14 minutes. Remove from heat and let stand, covered, 10 minutes.

Cut up the margarine or butter and add to the rice. Stir in the sugar, cinnamon and nuts. Cool. Stir in the flour. Cover and store in the refrigerator until meal time. Store overnight if desired.

Turn on oven and set at 375° F. Beat the egg yolks. Stir in the milk. Stir into the rice-flour mixture. Beat the egg whites until stiff but not dry. Fold into the rice-flour mixture. Spoon into well-greased muffin tins. Fill ¾ full. Bake about 25 to 35 minutes or until brown on top and around edges. Serve immediately. This recipe makes 16 to 18 muffins about 2¼ inches in diameter.

LOUISIANA GRIDDLE CAKES

1½ cups sifted all-purpose flour
3½ teaspoons baking powder
1 teaspoon salt
½ teaspoon nutmeg

1¼ cups mashed cooked
   Louisiana yams—fresh
   or canned
2 eggs, well beaten
1½ cups milk
¼ cup melted butter or
   margarine

Sift flour, baking powder, salt and nutmeg together. Combine remaining ingredients and mix well; add to dry ingredients and mix only until ingredients are blended. Drop by spoonfuls on hot griddle. Bake on both sides until browned. Serve with butter and jelly or syrup, as desired. Makes 4 servings.

LOUISIANA YAM NUT MUFFINS

1¾ cups sifted all-purpose flour
1 teaspoon salt
2 tablespoons brown sugar
3 teaspoons baking powder
½ cup coarsely chopped
   walnuts
2 eggs, well beaten

¾ cup milk
1¼ cups mashed cooked
   Louisiana yams—fresh
   or canned
¼ cup melted butter or
   margarine
Cinnamon
Sugar

Sift flour, salt, brown sugar and baking powder together. Add walnuts and mix well. Combine eggs, milk, yams and butter or margarine; mix well. Add yam mixture to dry ingredients all at once and mix only until ingredients are combined. Fill greased 2-inch muffin pans two-thirds full. Sprinkle lightly with cinnamon and sugar. Bake in hot oven (425° F.) 35 to 40 minutes, or until done.

Yield: 12 2-inch muffins.

MAINE RYE PANCAKES

1 cup flour	6 tablespoons molasses
1 cup rye flour	1 cup sour milk
1 egg	1 teaspoon soda

Sift the rye and white flour together, beat the egg and mix with the molasses and sour milk in which the soda has been dissolved. Mix with the dry ingredients to form a stiff batter. Drop teaspoonfuls of the batter into deep hot fat and fry until brown. Serve with maple syrup.

OATMEAL MUFFINS

1 cup milk, scalded	½ teaspoon salt
2 tablespoons butter	½ teaspoon salt
¾ cup oatmeal, uncooked	1 egg, well beaten
3 tablespoons sugar	1½ cups flour
	4 teaspoons baking powder

Melt butter in hot milk, pour over oatmeal, let stand 3 minutes. Add sugar, salt, and egg. Add sifted dry ingredients, mixing just enough to moisten. Bake in buttered muffin pans in a hot oven (400° F.) 20 to 25 minutes. 12 to 16 muffins.

OLD PLANTATION ROLLS

You don't have to knead these rich, tender cloverleaf rolls. And you can store the dough in your refrigerator if you like, then bake fresh rolls as needed.

Combine 1 cup scalded milk, ¼ cup suger, ½ cup shortening. Cool to lukewarm by adding 1 cup water. (The water used to dissolve dry yeast should be subtracted from water in recipe.) Add 1 egg, unbeaten; 1 cake compressed yeast, crumbled (or 1 package dry granular yeast dissolved as directed on package); mix well. Blend in 3 cups sifted enriched flour; let stand 20 minutes. If you use Pillsbury's Enriched Self-Rising Flour, omit baking powder, soda and salt.

Sift together 2½ cups sifted enriched flour, 1 teaspoon double-acting baking powder, ½ teaspoon soda, 1½ teaspoons salt. Add to soft dough.

Place in lightly greased bowl; cover. Let rise in warm place (85° to 90° F.) about 1 hour.

Shape dough into 24 cloverleaf rolls. Place in greased muffin cups. Let rise in warm place until light, about 1 hour. Bake in moderately hot oven (400° F.) 15 to 20 minutes. Makes 24 large rolls.

ONION SQUARES

2 cups sliced onions	4 teaspoons baking powder
2 tablespoons margarine	1 teaspoon salt
½ teaspoon salt	5 tablespoons shortening
¼ teaspoon pepper	¾ cup milk
2 cups flour	1 egg, well beaten
	¾ cup dairy sour cream

Cook onions in margarine until delicately browned. Season with ½ teaspoon salt and ¼ teaspoon pepper. Sift flour, baking powder, and salt together. Cut in shortening until mixture resembles coarse crumbs. Add milk and mix to a soft dough. Spread in a greased pan about 11 x 7 inches. Top dough with onions. Mix eggs with sour cream and pour over onions. Bake in a hot oven (450° F.) for 20 minutes. Serve in squares with roasts. Yield: 12 servings.

ORANGE BISCUITS

Make a biscuit dough by your favorite recipe. Roll one-half inch thick; cut in strips six inches wide; then spread with orange paste; roll like a jelly roll and with a sharp knife cut in one-inch slices; place these in greased muffin tins or on a baking sheet; bake in a hot oven.

ORANGE PASTE FILLING:

6 tablespoons butter	⅓ cup orange juice
2 tablespoons flour	1 orange rind, grated
	½ cup sugar

In a double boiler cook all the ingredients except the sugar. When thickened, add sugar and remove from fire. Allow to cool before spreading. This may be made in advance and kept in the refrigerator.

ORANGE GRIDDLE CAKES

1 cup flour	1 egg, well beaten
2½ teaspoons baking powder	1¼ cups milk
¾ teaspoon salt	3 tablespoons butter, melted
1 tablespoon sugar	1⅓ cups corn flakes
	Grated rind of 1 orange

Sauce:

½ cup honey   ½ cup orange juice

Sift dry ingredients together. Combine egg and milk and add gradually to dry ingredients, mixing only until smooth. Add butter, corn flakes and rind. Bake on hot griddle. Serve immediately with sauce made by combining honey and orange juice.

PEANUT BUTTER BISCUITS

2 cups flour	3 teaspoons baking powder
½ teaspoon salt	4 tablespoons shortening
2 tablespoons sugar	⅔ cup milk, approximately
	Peanut butter

Sift together the flour, salt, sugar and baking powder. Cut in the fat. Stir in the milk quickly, blending with a fork. Add more milk quickly, blending with a fork. Add more milk if necessary to form a light, soft dough. Toss the dough onto a board that has been lightly floured, knead the dough until the surface is smooth, roll to one-fourth inch thickness, and cut with an oval-shaped cutter. Spread the tops of the biscuits with peanut butter, and fold over, place close together on a greased baking sheet and bake at 425° F. ten to twelve minutes depending on the size.

PENNSYLVANIA DUTCH APPLE BUTTER BRAN BREAD

1 cup ready-to-eat bran	1 egg
1½ cups apple butter	1¾ cups sifted flour
1 teaspoon lemon juice	2 teaspoons baking powder
¼ cup shortening	½ teaspoon soda
½ cup sugar	½ teaspoon salt
	½ cup seedless raisins

Combine bran with apple butter and lemon juice; let soak about 5 minutes. Blend shortening and sugar thoroughly; add eggs and beat well. Stir in bran mixture. Sift flour with baking powder, soda and salt. Stir in raisins. Add to other ingredients, stirring only until combined. Pour into greased loaf pan and bake in preheated slow oven (325° F.) for 1 hour and 10 minutes. Cool before slicing. Makes 1 loaf (5¼ x 9⅓ inch pan). Glaze with fruit glaze.

PINEAPPLE COFFEE CAKE

1½ cups sifted flour	1 egg, beaten
2 teaspoons baking powder	1 cup dairy sour cream
½ teaspoon soda	½ cup drained crushed
½ teaspoon salt	pineapple
½ teaspoon cinnamon	½ cup brown sugar, firmly
¼ teaspoon nutmeg	packed

TOPPING:

¼ cup light corn syrup	½ cup chopped walnuts
	⅓ cup shredded coconut

Sift dry ingredients together. Combine egg, sour cream, pineapple, and brown sugar; add to dry ingredients stirring only until flour is moistened. Brush bottom of a buttered 8-inch square pan with corn syrup; sprinkle nuts and coconut over syrup. Spread batter over topping. Bake at 375° for 25-30 minutes. Cut into squares and serve warm. 8" square pan. Yield: 9 servings.

PLUM BISCUITS

3 heaping tablespoons butter
4 tablespoons sugar
Pinch of salt
Grated rind of one lemon

1 beaten egg yolk in ½
cup cream
2 cups sifted flour mixed with
4 tablespoons baking
powder

Mix and roll out about 1 inch thick. If dough is inclined to be a little bit soft to hold its shape, a little additional flour can be sprinkled on and worked in to give it the necessary firmness. Cut with large size (3-inch) biscuit cutter. Make a depression in the center of each biscuit and place a half of either a blue or red plum with the inside up in this depression. Sprinkle top of biscuit liberally with sugar and fill the inside of each half plum with about 1 heaping teaspoon of sugar. If plums are extra ripe, sugar can be cut down and a very little lemon juice sprinkled to bring out the plum flavor. Dot with several dots of butter and bake in a moderate oven at 350° F. for 30 to 45 minutes, or until plums are done.

POPPY SEED YEAST COFFEE CAKE

1 cake compressed or 1 package
dry granular yeast
¼ cup lukewarm water
¼ cup milk, scalded
½ cup butter
¼ cup sugar

2 eggs
¼ teaspoon salt
2 tablespoons orange juice
1 tablespoon grated orange rind
3 cups sifted flour
Poppy Seed Filling
Confectioners' Sugar Frosting

Soften yeast in lukewarm water. Cool milk to lukewarm. Cream butter well, add sugar gradually and continue creaming until light and fluffy; add well-beaten eggs, salt, orange juice and rind and mix well. Add about ½ of the flour and beat until smooth. Add softened yeast and milk and mix well. Add remaining flour gradually and knead until smooth and satiny. Roll into a rectangle, 16 x 20 inches. Spread with Poppy Seed Filling (recipe follows) and roll as for a jelly roll (16 inches long); join ends to form a ring. Place sealed edge down in a greased 9-inch ring mold; cover and allow to rise in a warm place until doubled in bulk (about 3 hours). Bake in a preheated oven. Cool slightly on wire cooling rack. Frost with Confectioners' Sugar Frosting, page 123. Yield: 1 coffee cake. Temperature 375° F. Time. about 40 minutes.

Poppy Seed Filling

1 cup poppy seed, crushed (¼ pound)	2 tablespoons sugar
	2 tablespoons milk
⅔ cup pared and grated apple	¼ teaspoon salt

Combine ingredients and mix well. Yield: 1 coffee cake. Temperature: 375 degrees F. Time: about 40 minutes.

PRUNE BREAD

2⅓ cups sifted all-purpose flour	¼ cup butter, softened
1 teaspoon baking powder	1 cup sugar
½ teaspoon baking soda	1 teaspoon vanilla
1 teaspoon allspice	3 eggs
½ teaspoon cloves	½ cup cultured sour cream
1 teaspoon cinnamon	1 cup chopped, cooked prunes (or 1 cup mixed fruit)

Sift together dry ingredients. Cream butter, sugar and vanilla together; add eggs, one at a time, mixing well after each addition. Carefully add sour cream and mix until smooth and well blended. Add dry ingredients; mix well. Add prunes and mix. Pour into oiled 9 x 5 x 3 inch loaf pan and bake at 350° F. for 50 minutes to 1 hour. Remove from pan when done and cool on cake rack.

PRUNE PINWHEELS

1¼ cups chopped pitted
plumped prunes
¼ cup sugar
½ cup chopped pecans
⅛ teaspoon salt
½ teaspoon cinnamon
¼ teaspoon allspice

2 teaspoons grated orange rind
2 tablespoons orange juice
3 cups biscuit mix
⅓ cup butter or margarine
3 tablespoons sugar
1 egg, beaten
½ to ⅔ cup milk

Combine prunes, ¼ cup sugar, pecans, salt, cinnamon, allspice, orange rind and juice. Mix well. Combine biscuit mix, butter or margarine, 3 tablespoons sugar, egg and enough milk to make a rather stiff dough. Knead 30 seconds. Roll out dough on lightly floured board 18″ x 3″. Spread with prune mixture. Roll up jelly-roll fashion beginning with long side. Cut into 15 to 18 slices. Place, cut sides down, on greased baking sheet about 2″ apart. Bake in moderately hot oven, 375° F., 18-20 minutes. Serve hot.

QUICK COFFEE CAKE

¼ cup butter
½ cup sugar
2 eggs, beaten well
1½ cups flour
½ teaspoon salt
2 teaspoons baking pwoder

1 cup milk
½ cup brown sugar
½ cup nut meats, chopped
1 teaspoon cinnamon
1 tablespoon butter
1 tablespoon flour

Cream butter and sugar, add eggs. Add sifted dry ingredients alternately with milk. Put half of dough in buttered pan. Combine remaining ingredients, put half of this nut mixture on dough, cover with remaining dough and sprinkle with remaining nut mixture. Bake in buttered pan (8 x 8″) in a moderate oven (350° to 375° F.) 30 to 45 minutes.

RAISIN BRAN MUFFINS

1 cup bran cereal
1 cup milk
1 egg, lightly beaten
2 tablespoons melted shortening

1 cup seedless raisins
1 cup sifted all-purpose flour
4 teaspoons baking powder
½ teaspoon salt

Soak bran in milk 5 minutes. Add lightly beaten egg, shortening and raisins. Sift together flour, baking powder, salt; add all at once to first mixture, stirring only to moisten. Fill greased muffin pans ⅔ full. Bake in hot oven (400°) 20 to 25 minutes. Makes 12 to 15 medium-sized muffins.

RAISIN TWISTS

½ cup light or dark raisins	1 egg
2 cups biscuit mix	½ cup light cream
2 tablespoons soft butter	Milk
3 tablespoons brown sugar	1 cup chopped nuts
1 teaspoon grated orange rind	Sugar
½ teaspoon cinnamon	Candied cherries

Rinse and dry raisins. Combine biscuit mix, butter, sugar, rind, spice, egg, cream and raisins. Mix well. Turn out on floured board; pat into 12 x 6″ oblong. Cut into 12 strips and roll to 6 to 8-inch lengths. Brush with milk, roll in nuts. Shape each into a figure 8 on greased baking sheet. Sprinkle with sugar and place a cherry in center of each twist. Bake in hot oven (400° F.) 10 to 15 minutes. Serve hot. Makes about 1 dozen.

SNOW RING

There are almonds, citron and currants between the braids of this coffee cake. The bread itself is wonderfully rich and good, made with eggs and butter. It may be decorated for seasonal holidays as desired, but is delicious by itself for any occasion.

Dissolve 1 cake comressed yeast (or 1 package dry granular yeast) in 2 tablespoons lukewarm water. Add 1 cup scalded milk, cooled to lukewarm, 2 teaspoons sugar, 1½ cups sifted enriched flour. Beat until smooth. Let rise in warm place (85 to 90° F.) until light, about 30 minutes.

Cream ½ cup butter (half shortening may be used) with 1 cup confectioners' sugar. Beat in 1 egg, 1 egg yolk and 1½ teaspoons salt. Add to risen yeast mixture. Blend in 2½ cups sifted enriched flour. Beat for 2 minutes. Let rise in warm place until light, about 1 hour. Punch down dough with fist. Let rise in warm place about 30 minutes.

Divide dough into three parts. Roll each part between floured hands to make strips about 18 inches long. Lay dough on floured board and flatten slightly. Place ¼ cup blanched almonds down center of one strip, ¼ cup diced citron down center of next strip, ¼ cup currants down center of last strip. Seal fillings into dough by pinching edges together. Braid the three strips of dough and form in a circle on greased baking sheet; insert ¼ cup almonds in dough between strips. Let rise in warm place until light, about 20 to 25 minutes.

Combine 1 egg white, 1 tablespoon water and brush over dough.

Bake in moderate oven (350° F.) 25 to 30 minutes. Sprinkle with confectioners' sugar while warm. Makes one large coffee cake.

SOUR MILK GINGER BREAD

¼ cup butter	1 teaspoon baking soda
½ cup sugar	1 teaspoon ginger
1 egg, beaten	½ teaspoon salt
½ cup molasses	½ cup sour milk
1⅔ cups flour	2 tablespoons sugar
½ teaspoon soda	1 teaspoon cinnamon

Cream butter and sugar thoroughly, add egg and molasses, blend. Add sifted dry ingredients alternately with milk, beat until smooth. Pour into buttered pan and sprinkle top with sugar and cinnamon. Bake in a moderate oven (350° F.) 45 minutes. Serves 12.

SOUR CREAM NUT BREAD

2 cups sifted flour	¼ teaspoon nutmeg
1 teaspoon baking powder	1 egg beaten
1 teaspoon baking soda	1 cup brown sugar, firmly
1 teaspoon salt	packed
¼ teaspoon cinnamon	1 cup dairy sour cream
¼ teaspoon cloves	1 cup broken nut meats

Sift flour, baking powder, soda and spices together. Beat egg. Add sugar and mix well. Stir in sour cream carefully. Add dry ingredients, stirring only enough to moisten them. Add the nut meats. Pour into a well buttered loaf pan and bake in 350° F. preheated oven for 1 hour. Good served warm or cold. 2½ x 3½ x 7¾ inch pan. Yield: 1 loaf.

SOUR MILK WHEAT CAKES

2 cups sour milk
2 eggs, well beaten
2 cups flour

2 teaspoons baking powder
1 teaspoon soda
¼ teaspoon salt
2 tablespoons melted butter

Mix the milk and well beaten eggs; sift flour, soda and baking powder. Gradually add to the eggs and milk and beat until smooth. Drop by spoonfuls on buttered hot griddle. When nicely browned turn and cook on the other side. Turn only once.

SUGAR PLUM RING

1 package active dry yeast or
   1 cake compressed yeast
¼ cup water
1 cup milk, scalded
⅓ cup sugar
¼ cup shortening
1½ teaspoons salt
4 to 4½ cups sifted
   all-purpose flour
2 eggs
½ teaspoon vanilla

¼ teaspoon nutmeg
1 3-ounce can (½ cup)
   candied chopped mixed
   fruits and peels
½ cup chopped candied
   cherries
1 cup seedless raisins
⅓ cup sugar
½ teaspoon cinnamon
¼ cup broken walnuts
3 tablespoons butter, melted

Soften active yeast in warm water or compressed yeast in lukewarm water. Combine milk, sugar, shortening, and salt. Cool to lukewarm. Stir in about 1½ cups flour. Beat vigorously. Add eggs and beat well. Stir in softened yeast, vanilla, and nutmeg. Add fruits, then remaining flour, to make soft dough. Cover and let rest 10 minutes. Knead on well-floured surface till smooth and elastic (6 to 8 minutes). Place in lightly greased bowl, turning once to grease surface. Cover; let rise in warm place till double (about 2 hours). Punch down. Let rest 10 minutes. For Sugar Plum Ring, pinch off balls of dough about 1¼ inches in diameter. Combine sugar, cinnamon, and nuts. Dip tops of balls in melted butter, then in sugar mixture. Place balls in layers in 2 oiled 8-inch ring molds. Allow room between balls for rising. Cover; let rise till almost double. Bake at 350° about 20 to 25 minutes. Cool slightly before removing from pan. Serve warm. Glaze if desired.

SWEDISH PANCAKES WITH LINGONBERRY PRESERVES

⅔ cup sifted flour	2 tablespoons melted butter
1 teaspoon salt	1 teaspoon grated orange rind
2 tablespoons sugar	4 eggs
1 teaspoon nutmeg	¼ cup melted butter
1¾ cups milk	Lingonberry preserves

Sift together dry ingredients. Blend in milk and beat well. Add butter and orange rind. Beat eggs until thick, add to mixture, blend well. Set aside for 2 hours. Grease and heat a 7-inch skillet. Pour ¼ cup of batter into skillet, tipping pan so that batter spreads evenly over pan. Fry pancakes until golden brown. Remove from pan, brush with melted butter. Spread with lingonberry preserves, roll up. Sprinkle with confectioners' sugar. Serves 4 to 6.

SWEDISH RYE BREAD

(Wonderful for a Smorgasbord or every day meal)

2 cups milk	½ cup molasses
2 tablespoons sugar	2 tablespoons shortening
1 cake yeast or 1 pkg. granular	(melted)
yeast (use according to	1 tablespoon salt
package directions)	3 cups sifted enriched flour
	3 cups medium rye flour

Scald milk, add sugar and let cool to lukewarm (80° F.). Add yeast and let stand about 5 minutes to dissolve. Add molasses, shortening and salt. Blend well. Add three cups of white flour and beat well to make a smooth dough. Add the rye flour. Knead on lightly floured board. Put in greased bowl, cover and let rise until double in bulk (about 1½ to 2 hours). Punch and let rise again until light (about

¾ hour). Divide into 2 loaves, let rise until doubled. Bake in moderately hot oven (375° F.) for 10 minutes, then reduce heat to 350° F. and bake 35 to 40 minutes longer.

Note: the dough may be shaped into a braid or twist. A glaze may be added by brushing bread with beaten egg. Sesame seeds may be sprinkled over the glaze.

UPSIDE-DOWN CINNAMON ROLLS

½ cup milk	⅔ cup brown sugar, firmly packed
2 cups biscuit mix	½ teaspoon cinnamon
4 tablespoons butter or margarine	1 tablespoon water
	⅔ cup seedless raisins

Stir milk into biscuit mix. Roll on lightly floured board to rectangle about 7 x 12 inches. Blend together butter, sugar and cinnamon. Spread half the mixture over biscuit dough, half in bottom of 8-inch round pan. Sprinkle water over mixture in pan. Spread raisins over mixture on biscuit dough. Roll as for jelly roll, from short side, to make 12-inch roll. Cut into 1-inch slices and place cut side down in sugar-coated pan. Bake in moderately hot oven (375° F.) about 35 minutes. Invert pan over serving dish and allow syrup to drain over rolls. Serve warm. Makes 12 small rolls.

DESSERTS AND ICES

Mention our name in Constantinople and they'll know about our desserts and ices! We're that famous for them! Grandma Anderson used to turn her nose up at a menu that listed only ice cream and sherbets for dessert. In her eyes a meal was not a meal unless as much care and thought went into the ending as went into the beginning.

And what desserts! Shortcakes, tortes, baked puddings, frozen desserts, cream puffs, frozen cakes—there wasn't a limit to the endless list of things that appeared on Grandma Anderson's menus.

When she turned the Hotel over to my Mother, many years ago, she made several reconnaisance missions a week to see if her traditions were being kept as had been promised. There HAD to be Apple Pie in some form or another; there had to be a Pennsylvania Dutch cobbler or a hot pudding! Baked Apples had to be done with éclat and flair ... not just a Baked Apple. They had to be stuffed with Maple Syrup and Raisins and Nuts. And how did she keep them bright, shiny and red? She colored the syrup!

You should hear the moans and groans and sighs when the visitor makes his first appearance at Hotel Anderson and sees our dessert menu! Diets go by the boards—a truce is declared and the taste testing is on. Ann will prepare a dessert tray on request with smaller portions of each dessert—for a family it's wonderful! And we are not modest about our desserts and our pastries. We are thrilled when they are praised and each compliment is another spur to greater heights in the dessert line.

You'll find this a fat chapter because it contains so many of our special concoctions. Good eating!

SWISS DIVINITY

3 whole eggs
4 egg yolks
¾ cup milk
⅓ cup sugar
1 tablespoon cornstarch
¼ teaspoon salt

1 envelope unflavored gelatin
¼ cup cold water
4 egg whites
¼ cup confectioners' sugar
2 to 3 tablespoons brandy
Whipped cream for topping

In top of double boiler combine whole eggs, yolks and milk. Blend sugar, cornstarch and salt; add to egg-milk mixture.

Beat with rotary beater or electric hand mixer until well mixed; then set over very hot (not boiling) water and continue beating until custard mixture is thick and doubled in volume, about 10 to 15 minutes.

Soften gelatin in cold water, and stir it into hot custard mixture. Chill quickly by putting saucepan into bowl containing cracked ice and water. Continue slow beating with beater or mixer until custard is well chilled and about to set.

Beat egg whites until frothy; gradually add sugar, 1 tablespoon at a time, beating well after each addition and continue beating until whites form soft peaks. Gently fold in custard mixture. Add brandy, ¼ teaspoon at a time, until desired flavor is acquired. Chill thoroughly.

When ready to serve, beat slowly until smooth; spoon into dessert dishes, snow-cap with whipped cream, and top with Raspberry Sauce. Makes 4 servings.

RASPBERRY SAUCE

1 (10 oz.) pkg. frozen
    raspberries, thawed

2 tablespoons water
2 teaspoons sugar
1 teaspoon cornstarch

Put thawed raspberries through fine sieve. Add water. Blend sugar and cornstarch; stir into raspberry juice. Cook over low heat, stirring constantly, until sauce is clear and slightly thickened. Chill.

APPLE AND PRUNE BETTY

⅓ cup butter or margarine
3 cups toasted bread cubes
2 cups pitted diced prunes
1 cup sliced canned apples
½ cup firmly-packed brown sugar

½ teaspoon cinnamon
½ cup prune cooking water
Few grains salt
1 tablespoon lemon juice
1 teaspoon grated lemon rind
¼ cup slivered toasted almonds

Melt butter or margarine; toss with bread cubes. Combine prunes, apple slices, brown sugar, cinnamon, prune water, salt, lemon juice and rind. Arrange in casserole in alternate layers, bread cubes and fruit mixture, ending with bread and nut meats. Bake in moderately hot oven, 375° F., 45 minutes. Serve hot with lemon sauce or whipped cream. Makes 6 servings.

APPLE BROWN BETTY

3 tablespoons butter
2 cups dry bread crumbs
½ to ¾ cup sugar
¼ teaspoon cinnamon

½ teaspoon nutmeg
½ lemon (juice and grated rind)
3 to 4 cups apples chopped or
    sliced thin
½ cup water

Melt the butter in a saucepan, stir in the crumbs, sugar and spices, and mix well but do not brown. Place a layer of apples in a buttered baking dish, add a layer of the bread crumb mixture, then another layer of apples and another layer of crumbs. Add the lemon juice and water. Bake in a covered dish in a moderate oven (375° F.) for twenty minutes. Remove cover and continue baking until the apples are tender and the crumbs are brown. Serve hot with hard sauce or cream.

APPLE TREASURES

2½ cups Homemade Pastry Mix
    (see page 269)
4 to 6 tablespoons water
6 medium cooking apples

½ cup sugar
1½ teaspoons cinnamon
2 tablespoons butter or
    margarine

SAUCE

1 cup sugar	3 tablespoons butter or margarine
¼ teaspoon cinnamon	2 tablespoons lemon juice
	1 cup water

Add water to Homemade Pastry Mix a small amount at a time, mixing quickly and evenly with a fork until pastry just holds in a ball. Roll pastry in a rectangle 12 x 18 inches. Cut in six 6-inch squares.

Peel and core apples. Combine ½ cup sugar and 1½ teaspoons cinnamon. Roll apples in sugar and cinnamon mixture. Place an apple on center of each square of pastry. Fill centers of apples with remaining sugar and cinnamon mixture and dot with butter or margarine. Fold corners of pastry to center up over each apple, moisten corners, and pinch together so whole apple is covered. Place in 8 x 12 inch baking dish.

Combine sugar, cinnamon, butter or margarine, lemon juice and water. Bring to a boil. Pour hot syrup around dumplings. Bake in a hot oven (400° F.) 40 to 45 minutes or until pastry is browned. 6 servings.

APRICOT TORTE

TORTE CRUST

1¼ cups sifted enriched flour	⅓ cup lard
¼ teaspoon salt	2 egg yolks
½ teaspoon baking powder	2 tablespoons cold water
1 tablespoon sugar	½ cup currant jelly
	Apricot Filling (recipe below)

Sift together flour, salt, baking powder and sugar. Cut in lard with a fork or pastry blender until mixture has a fine even crumb. Mix egg yolks with the 2 tablespoons water and stir into mixture until dough just holds in a ball. Roll between 2 sheets of waxed paper and line a 9-inch pie pan. Bake in a hot oven (400° F.) for 10 minutes. Spread bottom of crust with currant jelly and fill with Apricot Filling. Cover with meringue and return torte to oven for about 4 minutes or until meringue is browned.

APRICOT FILLING

1 pound dried apricots
2 cups water

¾ to 1 cup sugar
1½ tablespoons cornstarch

Wash and drain apricots. Cook with 2 cups water until tender, about 30 to 40 minutes. Combine sugar and cornstarch and add to cooked, undrained apricots and cook until mixture is thickened. Cool.

To make meringue, beat 2 egg whites and ⅛ teaspoon cream of tartar until stiff. Gradually add ¼ cup sugar and beat until the mixture stands in peaks.

BAKED APPLES WITH CRANBERRIES

6 apples

2½ cups cranberry sauce
6 tablespoons sugar

Wash and core the apples and place in a baking dish. Fill centers with the prepared cranberry sauce, pouring the remaining sauce around the sides of the apples. Sprinkle the sugar over the top of the apples, and bake in a moderate oven (350° F.) about 40 minutes or until apples are soft. Baste the apples frequently with the cranberry sauce.

BANANA CRUMBLES

4 bananas
¼ cup lemon juice

1 cup brown sugar
1 cup flour
½ cup butter

Peel the bananas and cut in slices crosswise; arrange in a well-buttered baking dish. Sprinkle with the lemon juice and one-half a cup of the sugar. Blend the remaining sugar with the flour and cut in the butter. Pat the mixture over the top of the bananas and bake. Serve with Spiced Hard Sauce, page 00. Temperature: 350° F. Time: 45 minutes.

BAVARIAN CREAM DESSERT

1 envelope unflavored gelatin	2 eggs, separated
½ cup sugar, divided	1¼ cups milk
⅛ teaspoon salt	½ teaspoon vanilla
	1 cup heavy cream, whipped

Mix together gelatin, ¼ cup of the sugar and salt in top of double boiler. Beat together egg yolks and milk; add to gelatin mixture. Place over boiling water and cook, stirring constantly, until gelatin dissolves and mixture thickens slightly, about 5 minutes. Remove from heat; add vanilla. Chill until mixture is slightly thicker than the consistency of unbeaten egg white. Beat egg whites until stiff, but not dry. Gradually add remaining ¼ cup sugar and beat until very stiff. Fold into gelatin mixture; fold in whipped cream. Turn into a dessert dish. Chill until firm. Garnish with whipped cream, shaved chocolate, chopped nuts and pieces of maraschino cherry. Yield: 6 to 8 servings. Note: Dessert may be turned into 5-cup mold or individual molds.

BERRY BAVARIAN CROWN

1 package strawberry-flavored gelatine	2 packages (10 oz. size) frozen or 2½ cups sliced, sweetened fresh strawberries
1 cup hot water	2 cups whipping cream, whipped
½ cup ice water	1 angel food cake (10-inch size) Ruby Glaze

Dissolve gelatin in hot water. Add ice water and chill until slightly congealed. Beat until light and fluffy. Drain berries and reserve juice for glaze. Fold in strawberries and whipped cream. With fork, tear angel food cake into pieces, being careful not to use the browned edge of the cake. Alternate cake pieces and gelatin mixture in a 10-inch angel food cake pan. Chill until firm. Unmold on serving plate; drizzle with Ruby Glaze. Chill. Makes 12 servings.

RUBY GLAZE

1 cup strawberry juice
1 tablespoon cornstrach

2 to 3 drops red food coloring
1 teaspoon soft butter

Blend cornstarch with a little juice. Gradually add to juice in saucepan. Cook until clear, 3 to 5 minutes. Remove from heat and add food coloring and butter. Cool. Drizzle over Bavarian mold. Chill.

BLANC MANGE

1 quart milk
8 tablespoons cornstarch

½ cup of sugar
¼ teaspoon salt

Put the milk on to boil. Moisten the cornstarch with a little cold milk, then add to the boiling milk, and stir until it thickens; add the sugar and salt, take away from fire, pour it into custard cups, and put in refrigerator to harden. Serve with cream sauce. This will serve five persons.

BLUEBERRY TARTLETS

4 tablespoons shortening
1 cup flour
½ teaspoon salt
Cold water

1 pint fresh blueberries
½ cup sugar
½ package cream cheese

Cut half the shortening into the flour and salt. Using a fork, stir in just enough water to make the particles stick together. Form into a ball, toss on to a lightly floured board and roll to one-fourth inch thickness, shaping as nearly square a sheet as possible. Spread with bits of the remaining shortening, fold and roll; repeat a second and a third time. Chill and roll one-eighth an inch thick. Cut rounds to fit six fluted molds, place over the inverted pans, arrange on a baking sheet and bake as indicated.

Pick over and wash blueberries; place in a saucepan with the sugar. Simmer gently for ten minutes. Cool. When ready to serve, fill the shells and pipe with the cream cheese moistened with cream to the right consistency. Temperature: 450° F.

BLUEBERRY TORTE

1⅓ cups graham cracker or
    zwieback crumbs
¼ cup sugar
½ cup soft butter
1 pkg. (8 ounces) cream cheese
2 eggs

½ cup sugar
½ teaspoon vanilla extract
Cinnamon
Blueberry Filling
1 cup heavy cream, chilled
    (optional)

Combine crumbs, ¼ cup sugar and butter; press mixture on bottom and up one inch on sides of a greased pan (7 by 11 inches). Allow cheese to reach room temperature. Work cheese with a spoon; add well-beaten eggs gradually and mix well. Add sugar and extract and mix. Pour over crumb mixture in pan. Sprinkle with cinnamon. Bake in a preheated oven at 375° F. for about 30 minutes. Chill. Cover with cooled Blueberry Filling. Chill thoroughly in refrigerator. Serve garnished with whipped cream, if desired.

BLUEBERRY FILLING

½ cup sugar
2 tablespoons cornstarch
¼ teaspoon salt

2 tablespoons and 2 teaspoons
    lemon juice
1 can (14½ ounces) blueberries,
    packed in heavy syrup

Mix sugar, cornstarch and salt in saucepan; add lemon juice and blueberries and mix well. Boil until thick (about 5 minutes), stirring constantly. Cool. Yield: 8 servings.

BRANDIED FRUIT

2 grapefruit, large
4 oranges, large
2 cups grapes, cut in half and
    seeded

¼ cup almonds, blanched
2 tablespoons sugar
3 tablespoons brandy

Pare the grapefruit and oranges with a sharp knife, removing all white inner skin. Then cut the fruit into sections, saving all the juice in a separate dish. Next a mound of grapes goes in center of shallow serving dish. A circle of grapefruit and orange sections goes around the grapes and a sprinkling of almonds. Add sugar and brandy to the juice and stir until sugar is dissolved. This is poured over the fruit and the dessert is chilled for several hours. Enough for 6 to 8 servings.

CHERRY CHEESE CAKE

CRUST

Combine 1¼ cups zwieback crumbs, ¼ cup sugar and 2 teaspoons cinnamon. Blend in ⅓ cup melted butter. Press to bottom and sides of a 9-inch spring form pan; chill thoroughly.

FILLING

2 envelopes gelatin	24 ounces cream cheese
½ cup cold water	1 tablespoon lemon juice
3 eggs, slightly beaten	1 teaspoon lemon rind, grated
1 cup sugar	2 teaspoons vanilla
1½ cups undiluted evaporated milk	½ teaspoon salt
	½ cup heavy cream

Sprinkle gelatin on cold water to soften. In saucepan combine eggs, sugar and 1 cup of evaporated milk. Add gelatin; cook over low heat, stirring constantly, until mixture coats spoon. Soften cream cheese with remaining ½ cup of milk. Then gradually add custard mixture, stirring until thoroughly blended. Stir in lemon juice and rind, vanilla and salt; chill until mixture starts to thicken. Whip cream; fold into gelatin mixture and pour into chilled crust; chill several hours or overnight.

To serve: Remove sides of spring form pan and spoon about ½ cup cherry preserves around edge of cake allowing syrup to run down sides.

CHOCOLATE CREAM ROLL WITH FUDGE SAUCE

Beat one cup of cream and one-half teaspoon vanilla until firm. Have ready one carton of "famous" chocolate wafers, or very thin chocolate cookies made from your own recipe, and measuring two and three-fourths inches in diameter. Spread a tablespoon of the whipped cream evenly over the surface of a cookie, then place another cookie above it; repeat the process until all of the cream is used. (It will take about thirty cookies.) Place this roll lengthwise on a serving dish.

Beat one cup of cream until firm and use it to mask completely the roll of cookies-and-cream. Place in the ice box overnight. When serving, cut slices diagonally, about one inch thick and serve with

FUDGE SAUCE

In the top of a double boiler, set over rapidly boiling water, melt one and one-half squares of Premium chocolate and one teaspoon butter; add one and one-half cups confectioners' sugar which has been blended with two teaspoons cornstarch; stir until smooth; add one cup boiling water and stir again, mixing all ingredients. Cover and let cook twelve minutes, stirring occasionally. Before serving, add one-half teaspoon vanilla extract. Yield: 10 to 12 portions.

CHOCOLATE ICEBOX CAKE

1 cup sugar	¼ cup boiling water
2 eggs, separated	1½ teaspoons double-acting
1 teaspoon vanilla	baking powder
1½ cups sifted all-purpose flour	½ teaspoon salt

FILLING

4 squares bitter chocolate	4 eggs, separated
1½ cups confectioners' sugar	¼ cup boiling water

Beat sugar and egg yolks together until creamy. Add vanilla and two tablespoons flour, stirring in well. Add boiling water. Sift together and add baking powder, salt and remaining flour. Beat egg whites until stiff but not dry; fold into batter and turn into a 11 x 7-inch greased cake pan which is wax-paper covered, and then the paper well greased and dusted with flour.

Bake in a slow oven (325° F.) for about 25 minutes. Watch it now, don't get it too brown for the cake must be soft. Place clean dish towel over rack, turn out cake and cool while making the sauce. Remove wax paper. For filling: Melt chocolate in top of double boiler over hot water. Beat into melted chocolate ¾ cup sugar, sifted to remove lumps. Add water. Beat egg yolks until smooth in bowl with remaining sugar. Add chocolate mixture, stirring well. Beat egg whites until stiff but not quite dry and fold into batter. Take cake, cut into thirds, then each piece into three layers, making nine layers in all. Line two pans, 8½ x 4½ x 2¾ inches, with heavy waxed paper, lay in a layer of cake, a layer of chocolate filling and keep repeating with layers until filled. There should be four layers at least and be sure to end with the chocolate. Place in refrigerator for 8 hours or longer. The finished cake will keep for two weeks. Serve sliced with whipped cream or ice cream. If it's ice cream, you may top with butterscotch sauce.

COCONUT BALLS WITH STRAWBERRIES

1 quart fresh bread, cut in ¼-inch cubes

1 15-ounce can sweetened condensed milk

1 4-ounce package shredded coconut

1 12-ounce package quick-frozen sliced strawberries

Combine bread cubes and condensed milk; mix well. Shape into 24 balls; roll each in coconut, pressing with hand. Place on greased cooky sheet. Bake in moderate oven 300° F., for 20 to 25 minutes until lightly toasted. Remove from sheet and cool. Place 3 in individual serving dish and pour on strawberries that are just thawed.

COFFEE CORONET

2 tablespoons unflavored gelatin
½ cup strong, cold coffee
1½ cups strong, hot coffee
1 cup sugar
2 dozen ladyfingers (about)

½ pkg. (3 oz.) semi-sweet chocolate pieces, melted
2 cups heavy cream
1 cup broken pecans
1 tablespoon vanilla or rum flavoring

Sprinkle gelatin on cold coffee. Add hot coffee and sugar; stir until sugar and gelatin dissolve. Chill until consistency of unbeaten egg white. Meanwhile split 9 or 10 ladyfingers and dip one end of each segment in melted chocolate. Whip chilled gelatin mixture until light and fluffy. Whip cream and fold in with pecans and flavoring. Spoon into spring form pan to a depth of about half an inch. Stand chocolate-tipped ladyfingers upright around edge of pan, chocolate tips upmost. Add about ⅓ gelatin mixture and layer with plain split ladyfingers. Add another third of gelatin mixture, another layer of split ladyfingers and a top layer of gelatin. Chill until firm. Remove from pan. Just before serving, sprinkle with a mixture of 3 teaspoons sugar and 1 teaspoon very finely ground coffee. Garnish with additional whipped cream and sugar-coffee mixture. Makes 12 servings.

COFFEE CREAM PUFFS

⅓ cup butter or margarine
1 cup hot coffee

4 eggs
1 cup sifted flour
¼ teaspoon salt

Melt butter or margarine in hot coffee. Add flour and salt all at one time and stir vigorously over low heat until mixture is smooth and leaves the sides of the pan. Remove from heat. Stir in unbeaten eggs one at a time. Continue beating until mixture is very thick. Drop by tablespoons on greased baking sheet, 1½ inches apart, piling dough high. Bake in hot oven, 450° F., 20 minutes. Reduce heat to moderate, 350° F., and bake 20 minutes more. Remove from baking sheet and cool. Make a cut on each side and fill with Coffee Whipped Cream Filling. Makes 12 medium-sized puffs or 8 large ones.

COFFEE WHIPPED CREAM FILLING

1 teaspoon unflavored gelatin
2 tablespoons double-strength,
   cold coffee

1 cup heavy cream
½ teaspoon vanilla
6 tablespoons very fine sugar

Soften gelatin in cold coffee. Set over boiling water and stir until dissolved. Add to cream with vanilla and sugar and beat until stiff. Chill. Spoon into cream puffs, made from above recipe. This filling is sufficient for 12 medium-sized puffs.

COFFEE JELLY PARFAIT

1 tablespoon unflavored gelatin
2¼ cups strong, cold coffee
⅓ cup sugar

1 tablespoon brandy flavoring
1 cup heavy cream
½ cup chopped salted almonds

Soften gelatin in ¼ cup of the cold coffee. Heat remaining coffee to boiling point. Add softened gelatin and sugar and stir until gelatin dissolves. Add flavoring. Pour into jelly roll pan or any shallow pan, to a depth of about half an inch. Chill until firm. Cut into ½-inch cubes. Whip cream and sweeten to taste. Arrange alternating layers of coffee jelly cubes, whipped cream and almonds in tall dessert glasses. Makes 6 servings.

COFFEE SOUFFLÉ

⅓ cup all-purpose flour
3 tablespoons cocoa
¼ teaspoon salt

1 cup coffee
4 egg yolks
½ cup sugar
4 egg whites

Mix flour, cocoa and salt. Stir in coffee slowly and when well blended, cook over low heat, stirring vigorously until mixture is very thick. Beat in one egg yolk at a time, and stir in sugar. Grease a quart casserole with softened, not melted, butter or margarine and coat with granulated sugar. Fold well-beaten egg whites into mixture, pour into casserole and bake about 25 minutes in moderately hot oven, 425° F. Serve at once. Makes 6 servings.

THE COLONEL'S FRUIT DELIGHT

¾ cup milk
1 egg yolk, slightly beaten
¼ cup sugar
1 tablespoon flour
Dash salt
½ teaspoon vanilla
1½ teaspoons lemon juice

2 tablespoons rum
¼ cup seeded raisins, chopped
¼ cup candied cherries, chopped
¼ cup almonds, blanched,
    chopped
¼ cup crushed pineapple,
    well drained
2 cups whipping cream

Scald the milk, stir it gradually into egg yolk. Sugar, flour and salt are combined and added to egg mixture. Cook this over boiling water, stir it constantly until the mixture thickens. Then take it from heat, stir in vanilla, lemon juice and rum and chill thoroughly, about 45 minutes. At this time set the cold control of refrigerator at its coldest position and put a deep 2-quart bowl and a rotary beater on shelf to chill. Mix raisins, cherries, almonds and pineapple, chill until needed. Then, using the chilled bowl and beater, whip cream until stiff, stir in the well-chilled custard and divide equally into 2 freezing trays. Freeze this to a mush, stir half the chopped fruit into each tray and continue freezing to serving consistency. This takes about 2 hours, and at that time turn the control to normal setting to keep pudding frozen until serving time. Makes about 1 quart.

"DEEP SOUTH" BANANA PUDDING

¾ cup sugar
1 tablespoon flour
¼ teaspoon salt
2 cups milk

3 eggs, separated
1 teaspoon vanilla
Vanilla Wafers
6 bananas

Combine ½ cup sugar, flour and salt in top of double boiler; stir in milk. Cook over hot water, stirring constantly, until thickened. Cook, uncovered, 15 minutes more, stirring occasionally. Beat egg yolks; gradually stir in a little of the hot mixture. Return to rest of mixture in double boiler, cook 5 minutes, stirring constantly. Remove from heat; add vanilla. Line bottom of casserole with vanilla wafers; top with a layer of sliced bananas. Pour a portion of custard over the bananas. Continue to layer wafers, bananas and custard, ending with custard on top. Beat egg whites stiff, but not dry; gradually add remaining ¼ cup sugar and beat until mixture forms stiff peaks. Pile on top of pudding in casserole. Bake in hot oven (425° F.) 5 minutes, or until delicately browned. Served warm or chilled. Serves 6 to 8. Note: For a delicious variation try substituting canned crushed pineapple for the bananas. Use #2 can; drain well.

DELMONICO PUDDING

1 pint milk	1 envelope plain gelatin
3 eggs, separated	½ cup cold water
1 cup sugar	1 teaspoon vanilla
	1 dozen almond macaroons

Scald milk in double boiler. Mix together yolks of eggs and sugar and gradually add scalded milk. Cook in top of double boiler, stirring constantly until mixture coats spoon. Soften gelatin in cold water five minutes and dissolve in hot custard. Remove from heat, fold in stiffly beaten egg whites and vanilla. Line pudding mold with macaroons and pour hot mixture over. Chill overnight. Unmold, top with whipped cream, add a sprinkle of nutmeg. The pudding shows a top of macaroons, a caramel-like gelatin center, a Bavarian base. Yield: 8 portions.

FRESH BLUEBERRY REFRIGERATOR CAKE

1⅓ cups (1 can) sweetened condensed milk	2½ cups fresh blueberries
¼ cup lemon juice	2 egg whites, beaten stiff
¼ teaspoon lemon extract	24 ladyfingers, or narrow strips of sponge cake

Blend together sweetened condensed milk, lemon juice and lemon extract. Stir until mixture thickens. Add blueberries. Beat egg whites until stiff and fold into mixture. Line narrow, oblong pan with waxed paper; cover with filling. Add layer of lady fingers, alternating in this way until filling is used; finishing with layer of ladyfingers. Chill in refrigerator twelve hours or longer. To serve, turn out on small platter and carefully remove waxed paper. Cut in slices, serve with whipped cream garnished with a few fresh blueberries reserved for the purpose.

FROSTED MELON SUPREME

1 medium-size cantaloupe
2 teaspoons unflavored gelatin
2 tablespoons cold water
1 tablespoon orange or lemon juice

Approximately ½ cup fruit purée
⅛ teaspoon salt
Sugar to taste
2 (3-ounce) packages cream cheese
Shredded coconut

Peel melon. Cut about a 2-inch slice from top. Scoop out seeds. Dice top slice. Soften gelatin in cold water, then dissolve over boiling water. Stir in fruit purée and lemon juice, salt and sugar. Let chill until slightly thickened. Fold in diced melon. Pour gelatin into cavity. Wrap in aluminum foil and chill several hours. Lay melon on its side, cutting small slice from side it rests on. Soften 2 packages cream cheese with a little milk. Cover melon with creamed mixture. Sprinkle with coconut.

FROZEN PRUNE DELIGHT

Remove pits from cooked prunes, cut the flesh into very small pieces, and measure two cups. Soften two teaspoons granulated gelatin in two tablespoons cold water. Beat four eggs until very thick and light. Heat one-half cup table syrup, add the gelatin, stir until dissolved, then pour gradually over the beaten eggs, beating constantly. Add one-eighth teaspoon salt, one teaspoon vanilla, and the prunes; mix well. Pour into molds and freeze in the refrigerator pan. Unmold and serve with iced tea or coffee.

CANTONESE GINGER ALE SHERBET

⅓ cup sugar
½ cup warm water
2 tablespoons orange juice
3 tablespoons lemon juice

2 tablespoons unsweetened
    pineapple juice
1 egg white
1 tablespoon sugar
1 pint ginger ale

Allow sugar to dissolve in warm water, let cool, add orange juice, unsweetened pineapple juice and lemon juice, mix and let chill.

Prepare eight or ten pounds of chipped ice and mix with two pounds of coarse ice-cream salt. Assemble the freezer ready for use, and pack with salt, ice, and any brine which may be have accumulated. Let stand five minutes to chill the container, turn the crank several times to settle the ice, then add more of the ice and salt.

Pour fruit juice mixture into the container and let chill thoroughly for two or three minutes, turning the crank a few times to prevent the mixture from caking on sides of container. Then start turning the crank slowly and freeze to a mush, remove dasher, fold in egg white, beaten stiff and sweetened with one tablespoon of sugar, then open a pint of chilled ginger ale, and add it to the mixture. Finish freezing the mixture to the consistency of sherbet, remove dasher, push the mixture down lightly in the container; cover and let stand until time to serve.

GLAMOROUS MACAROON PUDDING

1 8-ounce jar Maraschino
    cherries
1 envelope unflavored gelatin
3 tablespoons water

2½ cups milk
8 almond macaroons, small
1 cup sugar
4 eggs
¼ teaspoon vanilla

First the drained cherries are cut in half and arranged, cut-side up, in bottom of 6-cup star mold (or in a bread pan). Then soften the gelatin in water. Milk is then scalded in top of double boiler. Half a cup of the milk goes in a small bowl; macaroons are whisked in and out of the milk and put on a plate ready to use later. The softened gelatin and sugar are added to remaining 2 cups of milk, stirred until dissolved. Next separate egg whites from yolks, beat until stiff and put them aside. Beat the yolks, stir in a small amount of the hot milk mixture, put this back with remaining milk mixture and cook over hot, not boiling, water, stirring constantly until it's slightly thickened and coats a metal spoon. Pour this gradually over beaten egg whites, cutting and folding with a gentle hand until completely mixed. Vanilla goes in now. About half of custard mixture goes over cherries in mold —carefully! Macaroons are arranged in layer on the custard and remaining custard is poured over them. Chill for 5 or 6 hours. Unmold before serving. Serve with great dollops of whipped cream garnished with slivers of well-drained maraschino cherries. Makes 8-10 servings.

GLAZED CHERRY-WINE TARTS

1½ tablespoons cornstarch	½ cup Port wine
3 tablespoons sugar	1 (3 oz.) pkg. cream cheese
Dash of cinnamon	1 tablespoon milk
Dash of salt	8 baked tart shells
½ cup syrup from canned red sour pitted cherries	3 cups drained canned red sour pitted cherries

Mix cornstarch, sugar, cinnamon and salt in a sauce pan; gradually add cherry syrup and Port, stirring until mixture is smooth. Stir over medium heat until sauce is thick and clear. Remove from heat; mash cream cheese with a fork; blend in milk; spread mixture evenly over bottom of tart shells. Place cherries in shells; pour sauce over cherries. Chill thoroughly before serving. Top with whipped cream.

GOLD COAST BAKED APPLES

6 baking apples	½ cup sugar
¼ cup seedless raisins	½ cup water
¼ cup canned slivered blanched almonds	1 teaspoon grated orange peel
	¼ cup orange juice
1 tablespoon orange marmalade	1 tablespoon butter

Core apples, being careful not to cut all the way through. Peel about ⅓ of the way down from stem end. Combine raisins, almonds and marmalade; fill apple centers with this mixture. Combine remaining ingredients in saucepan; stir over low heat until sugar dissolves; simmer 5 minutes. Place apples in baking pan, pour syrup over them. Cover; bake in moderate oven, 350° F., 45 minutes to 1 hour, basting frequently with syrup in pan. When tender, baste once more and run under broiler to glaze. Serve with whipped cream.

GRAPES IN SOUR CREAM

Use a deep silver platter. On this put a layer 1½ inches deep of green seedless grapes. On top of these place a layer (same thickness) of sour cream and sprinkle heavily with brown sugar. Place in icebox for two hours, before serving, to allow the cream and sugar to seep through the grapes. Pass extra brown sugar with the dish.

HEAVENLY APRICOT ROLL

1 package angel food cake mix or recipe for 10-inch angel food cake	¼ teaspoon almond extract Apricot-Almond Filling Apricot slices for garnish

Prepare cake batter acording to directions. Fold in almond extract. Spread evenly in ungreased 15½ by 10½ by 1 inch pan. Smooth batter to edges. Bake in moderate oven (350°) for 25 to 30 minutes, or until cake springs back when lightly touched with finger. Invert and cool cake in pan for 8 to 10 minutes. Loosen edges with wet, sharp knife. Carefully turn pan upside down on towel dusted with powdered sugar. Guard cake as it comes from pan so it does not break. Beginning at long side, roll up cake in towel, jelly-roll fashion. Cool on cake rack. Unroll cake, remove towel, and spread with Apricot-Almond Filling.

Re-roll cake. Chill at least 6 to 8 hours. Just before serving, frost with whipped cream and garnish with apricot slices, if desired. Makes 8 to 10 servings.

APRICOT-ALMOND FILLING

1 envelope unflavored gelatin
¼ cup cold water
¼ cup apricot syrup
    sieved
1 cup drained canned apricots

2 tablespoons lemon juice
¼ teaspoon almond extract
⅛ teaspoon salt
½ cup whipping cream
½ cup powdered sugar
¼ cup chopped blanched almonds

Soften gelatine in cold water. Heat apricot syrup to boiling. Add gelatine, remove from heat, and stir until gelatine is dissolved. Combine with sieved apricots, lemon juice, almond extract, and salt. Chill until slightly congealed. Beat until fluffy. Whip cream and blend in powdered sugar. Fold whipped cream and almonds into gelatine mixture. Add few drops yellow food coloring, if desired. Serves 8.

LEMON-PIE DESSERT

5 tablespoons cornstarch
    Pinch of salt
1 cup sugar
3 eggs, separated

1 cup boiling water
6 tablespoons lemon juice
1 tablespoon grated lemon rind
1 tablespoon butter or margarine
1 cup heavy cream, whipped

Combine cornstarch with salt and sugar. Beat egg yolks and add dry ingredients. Pour in boiling water, add lemon juice and rind and butter or margarine. Cook over slow heat, stirring constantly until thick and smooth. Fold in stiffly beaten egg whites. Cool; fold in whipped cream. Pour into mold lined with split ladyfingers. Chill overnight. Serve with whiped cream. Yield: 6 portions.

LEMON-Y CHEESECAKE

2 envelopes unflavored gelatin
½ cup cold water
4 packages (3-oz. size) cream cheese
¼ cup lemon juice
½ teaspoon vanilla

¼ teaspoon salt
¾ cup sugar
1 tablespoon grated lemon rind
3 cups dairy sour cream
2 egg whites
Nut-Crumb Topping

Soften gelatin in cold water. Dissolve over hot water. Blend cream cheese with lemon juice, vanilla, salt, and sugar. Beat until creamy and fluffy. Stir in lemon rind and dissolve gelatin. Fold in sour cream. Beat egg whites until stiff peaks form and fold into lemon-sour cream mixture. Prepare Nut-Crumb Topping. Press one-half in bottom of buttered 9-inch spring-form pan. Chill. Spoon in cheesecake mixture. Top with remaining crumbs. Chill overnight. Place pan on warm, wet towel for 4 to 5 minutes. Loosen sides carefully and remove to serving plate. Makes 10 to 12 servings.

NUT-CRUMB TOPPING:

Combine 1½ cups fine graham cracker crumbs, ½ teaspoon nutmeg, ¼ cup finely chopped pecans, ¼ cup powdered sugar, and ⅓ cup melted butter. Use as directed.

LIME MERINGUETTES

3 eggs, separated
¼ teaspoon cream of tartar
⅛ teaspoon salt

1 cup sugar
4 tablespoons lime juice
1½ teaspoons lime rind
1 cup heavy cream, whipped

Beat egg whites until foamy; add cream of tartar and salt; beat until stiff but not dry. Add ¾ cup of the sugar gradually, beating until very stiff. Cover baking sheet with heavy brown paper. Pile meringue into

6 rounds about 3 inches in diameter. Make a 2-inch depression in the center. Bake in a very slow oven (275° F.) 1 hour. For the filling, beat the egg yolks; add remaining ¼ cup sugar and the lime juice. Cook over boiling water, stirring constantly until thickened. Add grated lime rind. Remove from heat; chill. Fold into whipped cream. Fill meringue shells. Chill 6 to 12 hours in refrigerator. Yield: 6 servings.

MARSHMALLOW DIXIE PARFAIT

⅔ cup uncooked white rice
1⅓ cups water
1 teaspoon salt
2 cups milk
¼ cup sugar
⅔ cup marshmallow cream

1½ teaspoons vanilla
¼ cup chopped pecans
12 well drained green maraschino cherries, chopped
½ to ⅓ cup marshmallow cream

Put rice, water and 1 teaspoon salt into a 2-quart saucepan. Bring to a vigorous boil over a high heat. Turn heat down low. Cover with lid and simmer 14 minutes. Stir in 1½ cups of milk. Cover and cook over low heat 40 minutes or until milk is absorbed. Stir occasionally. Do not allow to boil. Add remaining milk and sugar. Cool.

Measure ⅔ cup marshmallow cream in a wet measuring cup. Stir in vanilla, pecans and cherries. Cover and store in a refrigerator until time to serve.

To serve, thin remaining marshmallow cream with one or two teaspoons of water. Alternate layers of the rice mixture and marshmallow sauce in parfait glasses. You may wish to top the dessert with additional marshmallow sauce. Garnish with whole green cherries.

MAY APPLES

Apples, pared and cored.

Syrup:

5 cups sugar
6 cups water

1½ teaspoon green color
1 teaspoon mint flavoring
3 tablespoons lemon juice

FILLING:

½ cup chopped raw carrots   ½ cup diced celery
                                French dressing to moisten

Mix ingredients for syrup and bring to the boiling point in a pan
sufficiently wide to hold the desired number of apples. Put the prepared apples into the hot syrup, and let them cook slowly. Some apples
hold their shape better, when stewed, than other varieties; select the
best cooking apples available. Turn the apples over in the syrup frequently with a wooden spoon that they may absorb the color evenly.
When cooked completely tender, lift apples from syrup and let cool.
Fill apples with carrot salad and decorate each with a candied mint
leaf and a piece of candied orange peel cut to simulate an apple stem.

MIAMI TRIAD ICE

3 cups ganulated sugar   Grated rind 1 orange
3 cups water   Grated rind 1 lemon
Juice 3 oranges   1 No. 2 can crushed pineapple
Juice 3 lemons

Boil the sugar and water together five minutes and cool. Add the
strained fruit juice, grated rind and pineapple. Pour into two refrigerator pans and freeze with the temperature control set at the lowest
point. This takes several hours to freeze but requires no stirring, therefore it is quickly and easily made.

MINTED PEARS

6 fresh pears   2 tablespoons powdered sugar
3 tablespoons green crème de   ½ pint heavy cream
   menthe   6 sprigs fresh mint

Whip cream and add crème de menthe. Set in refrigerator for 1
hour. Slice pears and mix with sugar. To serve, mix whipped minted
cream and pears, and serve with sprig of mint on top. Makes about 6
servings.

MOCHA ROLL DE LUXE

¼ cup enriched flour	½ teaspoon salt
1 cup confectioners' sugar	5 eggs
3 tablespoons cocoa	1 teaspoon vanilla

Sift the flour and measure it, add confectioners' suar, cocoa and salt and sift again. Separate egg yolks from whites and beat thoroughly until thick and lemon-colored. The sifted dry ingredients and vanilla go in now and are beaten until well-blended. Then beat egg whites until they're stiff but not dry. Fold in egg-yolk mixture, blend it well. Line a greased jelly roll pan (10 by 15 inches) with waxed paper and grease again, pour in the batter. This is baked in a moderate oven 375° for 15 to 20 minutes. With a sharp knife loosen edges and turn it out on a towel sprinkled with confectioners' sugar. Then remove paper, cut off crisp edges of cake. Cake is rolled up and allowed to stand 1 minute. Then it's unrolled to cool. Spread it with whipped-cream filling and roll it like a jelly roll. A chocolate butter frosting that's fluffed up with strong coffee goes over all. Makes 8 to 10 servings.

WHIPPED-CREAM FILLING

Whip 1½ cups heavy cream until stiff; fold in 2 tablespoons confectioners' sugar and ¼ teaspoon vanilla.

NECTAR CREAM PUFFS

PUFFS:

1¼ cups water	1⅓ cups sifted all-purpose flour
½ cup butter or margarine	4 eggs

FILLING:

1½ cups apricot whole fruit nectar	3 tablespoons cornstarch
1 cup sugar	1 cup whipping cream
⅛ teaspoon salt	½ teaspoon lemon extract

Puffs: Combine water and butter and heat to boiling. Add flour all at once, stirring briskly. Continue cooking and stirring about 2 or 3 minutes or until dough forms a ball on spoon and leaves sides of kettle clean. Remove from heat and cool slightly. Add eggs one at a time, beating well after each addition. Continue beating until batter is smooth. Form into mounds about one inch across and 1½ inches high on greased cookie sheet, using a pastry bag or spoon. (Space about 2 inches apart). Bake in hot oven (400° F.) about 40 minutes; cool. Fill centers with nectar filling.

Filling: Combine 1 cup nectar and sugar and bring to boil. Blend remaining ½ cup nectar, salt and cornstarch. Add to hot nectar and cook and stir about 2 minutes until thick and clear; cool. Whip cream; fold in cool nectar mixture and lemon extract. Makes approximately 12 small puffs.

NECTAR LEMON CREAM

1 lemon	1½ cups pear whole fruit nectar
⅔ cup sugar	1 cup table cream
Few grains salt	

Rinse lemon, and slice thin. Remove seeds, and chop lemon slices. Add sugar and let stand about 30 minutes. Blend in remaining ingredients. Pour into refrigerator tray, place in freezing compartment with control set at lowest temperature and freeze until firm. Remove to chilled bowl, and beat with rotary beater until smooth and fluffy. Return to freezing compartment and freeze to desired consistency. Reset temperature control to normal. Makes about 1½ pints.

OLD VIRGINIA COBBLER

Cut ½ lemon into thin slices; simmer in ½ cup water until tender, about 5 minutes. Drain water and reserve.

Combine ¾ cups sugar, 2 tablespoons flour, ¼ teaspoon nutmeg in saucepan; blend in reserved lemon water. Cook until thickened, stirring constantly. Add 3 cups apples, pared and sliced, 2 tablespoons butter and the lemon slices.

Sift together 1 cup sifted enriched flour, ¼ teaspoon salt. Cut in ⅓ cup shortening until particles are the size of small peas. Sprinkle 2 to 3 tablespoons cold water over mixture, tossing lightly with fork until dough is moist enough to hold together. Form into a ball. Roll out on floured pastry cloth or board to 10x6 inch rectangle. Cut with pastry wheel or knife into triangles or diamonds.

Pour hot apple filling into well greased 10x6x2-inch pan or 9-inch glass piepan. Arrange pastry over filling.

Bake in moderately hot oven (400° F.) 35 to 45 minutes. Serve with plain or whipped cream.

Makes 10x6x2-inch cobbler. Serves 6.

ORANGE PUDDING PALM BEACH

4 egg whites   2 tablespoons orange marmalade
2 tablespoons sugar   Grated rind 1 orange

Beat the egg whites stiff, add the sugar, marmalade and grated rind. Grease the top of a double boiler, put in the mixture and steam forty-five minutes. Pour out and serve at once with the following sauce.

SAUCE:

Yolks 4 eggs   1 tablespoon orange juice
2 tablespoons sugar   1 cup heavy cream

Put all the ingredients into a bowl and beat until thick.

ORANGE SHORTCAKE

2 oranges

Grate the rind of one orange and then peel both and remove the sections.

EGG PASTE:

Use two well-beaten yolks of eggs, two-thirds cup sugar and the grated orange rind, well mixed.

BUTTER SAUCE:

Two-thirds cup milk, one-half cup sugar and two tablespoons butter. Cook together until slightly thickened.

ORANGE PASTRY:

¼ cup shortening
1 cup pastry flour

½ teaspoon salt
½ teaspoon orange rind
¼ cup orange juice

Cut the shortening into the dry ingredients with a pastry cutter. Reserve one-fourth of the mixture and add enough orange juice to the remainder to make the particles hold together, using no more juice than necessary. Roll out about six inches in diameter and sprinkle a little of the reserved mixture over it, about one-third; fold the pastry over and roll it again; repeat this process until all the reserved mixture has been used. Then roll thin and cut into the desired size, allowing two for each serving. Bake.

To complete the shortcake, spread the egg paste on each layer of pastry; place orange sections on bottom layer, add second layer of pastry and add orange sections on that too. Pour the butter sauce over all and top with whipped cream. These amounts serve six.

PEACH-LIME BAVARIAN CREAM

1 tablespoon gelatin
¼ cup cold water
¼ cup lime juice

¾ cup mashed cooked peaches
⅓ cup honey
1 cup whipping cream, whipped

Soften gelatin in cold water, dissolve over hot water. Add lime juice, peaches and honey. Cool and when the mixture begins to thicken, whip. Fold in whipped cream, turn into mold and chill until firm. 6 servings.

PEACH PLEASE

1 cup vanilla wafer crumbs
¼ cup melted butter
1 tablespoon unflavored gelatin
¼ cup cold water
¼ cup soft butter

½ cup powdered sugar
2 egg yolks, beaten
16 marshmallows, quartered
2 cups drained peach slices
　　(fresh or frozen)
2 egg whites, stiffly beaten

Line 8-inch-square or 11x7-inch baking dish with foil. Combine crumbs and butter and pat one-half of crumbs in bottom of dish. Soften gelatin in cold water. Cream butter and powdered sugar and beat in egg yolks. Cook mixture over low heat until thick, stirring constantly. Remove from heat. Dissolve softened gelatin in hot mixture. Cool. Spoon peach filling over crumb layer and top with remaining crumbs. Freeze. To serve, cut in squares and garnish with whipped cream, peach slices, and maraschino cherry. Makes 6 to 8 servings.

PECAN SHELLS

2 tablespoons butter
½ cup brown sugar
1 slightly beaten egg

¼ cup very finely chopped pecans
⅓ cup cake flour
¼ teaspoon vanilla
Few grains salt

Cream butter; add sugar. Add egg and beat thoroughly. Add very finely choped pecans (to get them very fine, you can crush them with a rolling pin after chopping). Add remaining ingredients. Mix well. *Make and bake one cooky at a time,* because you have to work very fast. The pretty, crisp fuffly pecan shells are worth every bit of the trouble they take!

Put 2 level tablespoons of the cooky batter on a very well-greased cooky sheet. Spread very thin with spoon. Bake in moderate oven (350°) 8 to 10 minutes. Remove from sheet immediately. Hold cooky on palm of hand a few seconds till firm enough to shape. Then shape it over the bottom of a custard cup or glass. Each one you make will look just a little different. Prepare to hear the guests oh and ah, because the pecan shells are as pretty as a picture. This recipe makes 6 big pecan shells.

RAISIN CHEESE CAKE

1 cup matzo meal	4 eggs
½ cup melted butter or margarine	1 cup granulated sugar
½ cup confectioners' sugar	¼ teaspoon salt
1 cup seedless raisins	½ teaspoon vanilla extract
1 large lemon	1 cup heavy cream
1 pound cottage cheese	¼ cup sifted potato flour

Mix matzo meal with melted butter and confectioners' sugar. Pat crumbs onto bottom and sides of greased 9-inch spring form pan, saving a few for top of cake. Rinse and drain raisins. Grate rind from lemon and squeeze juice. Force cottage cheese through sieve. Separate eggs and beat yolks very thick, then gradually beat in ½ cup sugar. Mix in all other ingredients except egg whites and sugar very thoroughly. Beat egg whites until stiff, then gradually beat in remaining ½ cup sugar. Fold into cheese batter. Pour into pan and top with remaining crumbs. Bake in very slow oven (250° F.) one hour and 45 minutes. Leave in oven until cake is cool and it won't fall!

RASPBERRY ICE

1 cup water	3 tablespoons cold water
2 cups sugar	2 cups raspberry juice
1½ tablespoons gelatin,	Grated rind 1 lemon
softened in	½ cup lemon juice

Place the water and sugar in a saucepan, bring to the boiling point, stirring constantly, and allow to boil five minutes. Remove from the heat; add the gelatin. Stir the mixture until it is thoroughly dissolved. Add the raspberry juice, lemon rind and juice. Cool and freeze, using a hand freezer or the tray of an automatic refrigerator.

RICH CHOCO-CREAM FILLING

For Coffee Cream Puffs

2 cups coffee cream	⅓ cup flour
2 squares unsweetened chocolate	½ teaspoon salt
⅔ cup sugar	6 egg yolks, slightly beaten
	1 teaspoon vanilla

Heat cream and chocolate in heavy saucepan to scalding. Combine sugar, flour, and salt. Add hot mixture gradually to dry mixture, stirring until smooth. Return to heat and cook slowly until mixture thickens, stirring constantly. Blend egg yolks carefully into chocolate mixture and cook for two or three minutes more. Remove from heat and add vanilla. Cool and chill. Use as directed.

SHERRIED FIG-NUT DELIGHT

1 envelope unflavored gelatin	⅓ cup sherry wine
2 tablespoons cold water	1 cup finely cut fig cookies
½ cup boiling water	(use scissors)
½ cup sugar	½ cup chopped walnuts
Dash of salt	2 egg whites, stiffly beaten
1 teaspoon grated lemon peel	½ cup heavy cream, whipped

Soften gelatin in the cold water 5 minutes; disolve in the boiling water. Add sugar and salt; stir to dissolve sugar. Add lemon peel and wine. Cool, then chill. When mixture begins to thicken, stir in fig cookies and nuts; fold in beaten egg whites and cream, blending gently but thoroughly. Spoon into dessert dishes or a serving bowl; chill until firm. Serve plain or with whipped or "pour" cream. Serves 6.

SHERRY CHEESE CAKE DE LUXE

CRUST:

1½ cups graham crackers, crushed   ½ cup butter, melted

FILLING:

2 pkgs. (8 oz. each) cream
cheese
1 cup sugar

1 teaspoon lemon juice
¼ cup sherry
3 eggs

TOPPING:

½ pint sour cream

2 tablespoons powdered sugar
1 tablespoon sherry

Crush graham crackers until very fine; add melted butter and mix well. Line the bottom and sides of an 8-inch spring form pan or a deep (at least 2½ inches) baking dish with crumb-butter mixture. Combine cheese, sugar, lemon juice, the ¼-cup sherry, and eggs and beat until smooth. Pour into crumb crust and bake in slow oven (300° F.) for 40 to 45 minutes or until cheese mixture is firm. Remove from oven and cover with the sour cream, powdered sugar and 1 tablespoon sherry, well mixed. Return to the oven, and bake for another 10 minutes. For full flavor, refrigerate overnight before serving. Serves 10 to 12 generously.

ANGEL PUFFS WITH APRICOT CREAM SAUCE

Sift together two cups of flour, two teaspoons of baking powder and one-half teaspoon salt. Cream one-half cup shortening and add gradually one cup sugar. Add the dry ingredients to the mixture alternately with one-half cup milk. Fold in the whites of four eggs beaten stiff. Flavor with two teaspoons lemon juice. Fill buttered custard cups two-thirds full with the mixture; cover the tops with heavy waxed paper tied securely in place; and steam for forty minutes. Remove from the molds and serve with Apricot Cream Sauce.

APRICOT CREAM SAUCE:

Blend four egg yolks, slightly beaten, with one-half cup granulated sugar, one-half cup juice from cooked dried apricots and the grated rind of a lemon. Cook, stirring constantly, over hot water until the sauce thickens. Chill thoroughly and fold in two cups cream whipped stiff. This amount of sauce makes generous allowance for serving and may be reduced as desired.

STRAWBERRY BLITZ TORTE

1⅓ cups sifted cake flour
1¼ teaspoons double-acting
    baking powder
½ cup butter or other shortening
½ cup sugar

4 egg yolks, unbeaten
5 tablespoons milk
4 egg whites
1 cup sugar
1 quart strawberries, crushed
    and sweetened

Sift flour once, measure, add baking powder, and sift together 3 times. Cream butter thoroughly, add sugar gradually, and cream together until light and fluffy. Add egg yolks, one at a time, beating very thoroughly after each. Add flour, alternately with milk, a small amount at a time, beating after each addition until smooth. Spread in two greased 9-inch layer pans. Beat egg whites until foamy throughout. Add sugar, 2 tablespoons at a time, beating after each addition until sugar is thoroughly blended. After all sugar is added, continue beating until mixture will stand in peaks. Spread in equal amounts on top of each layer. Bake in slow oven (325° F.) 25 minutes, then increase heat to moderate (350° F.) and bake 30 minutes longer. Spread with crushed sweetened strawberries.

STRAWBERRY TARTS

1 quart strawberries
½ cup water
1 tablespoon arrowroot

½ cup sugar
1 egg-white
⅓ cup chopped nut meats
6 medium-sized pastry cases

Bake the cases by placing round pieces of pastry over inverted muffin pans. Wash and hull the berries, crush one cup, add sugar and water. Heat and thicken the juice by adding the arrowroot, moistened with a little cold water, and bring to the boiling point. Reserve about six spoons of the thickened liquid for a glaze to be put on the top of the filling of the tarts. Pour the rest over the whole berries—if some are large, cut in halves—and chill. Beat to a froth the egg-white and dip the edge of each pastry case in this and then in the chopped nut meats spread on a saucer. Pistachio nut meats give the green bits in with the other pieces, furnishing an attractive color and flavor. Just before serving fill these cases with the berries and add the glaze. One and one-half tablespoons cornstarch will thicken in place of the arrowroot but does not give so clear a syrup.

SUPER BAKED ALASKA

1 package devil's food cake mix	1 quart coffee ice cream
8 egg whites, beaten till foamy	½ cup sugar

Bake devil's food cake mix in 2 round 9-inch layer pans, according to package directions. Reserve 1 cake for future dessert. Earlier in day, line an 8-inch layer pan with aluminum foil so that edges of foil stick up over edge of pan. Let ice cream get soft enough to spoon easily and pack into the foil-lined pan. Freeze until hard. Beat egg whites, then gradually add sugar and continue beating until meringue stands in peaks. Place hard-frozen ice cream on cake, making sure that there is about a half-inch rim of cake all around. Cover all cake and ice cream with meringue. Brown meringue in hot oven (450° .F) about 5 minutes. Makes 6 to 8 servings.

UPSIDE-DOWN BAKED NUT PUDDING

1 cup enriched flour	milk and half water
2 teaspoons baking powder	2 tablespoons salad oil or
½ teaspoon salt	melted shortening
¾ cup sugar	½ cup walnuts, coarsely chopped
3 tablespoons cocoa	1¼ cups light brown sugar
1 teaspoon vanilla	¼ cup cocoa
½ cup milk, or half evaporated	2 cups hot water

Sift flour, measure; add baking powder, salt, sugar and the 3 table-spoons of cocoa and sift together into mixing bowl. Add vanilla to milk, then add this—with salad oil or shortening and chopped nuts—to the dry ingredients. Stir until well blended. Turn into square pan (8x8x2 inches). Mix the brown sugar and the ¼ cup cocoa. Sprinkle this mixture over batter. Pour the hot water over entire surface. Bake in moderate oven 350° for 40 to 45 minutes. So you won't be surprised— the baking process produces a delicious rich chocolate sauce in the bottom of the pan. Spoon out while warm into serving dishes, sauce side up. Pluperfect with whipped cream.

WINTER PARTY MERINGUE

MERINGUE SHELL:

3 egg whites
⅛ teaspoon salt

½ teaspoon cream of tartar
½ teaspoon vinegar
¾ cup granulated sugar

RAISIN NECTAR FILLING:

1 cup light or dark seedless raisins
1½ cups apricot whole fruit nectar
⅓ cup granulated sugar

2 tablespoons cornstarch
Few grains salt
3 egg yolks
1 tablespoon lemon juice
½ cup whipping cream

Meringue Shell: Beat egg whites with salt until foamy. Add cream of tartar and vinegar, and beat until stiff. Gradually beat in sugar. On double sheet of brown paper draw a 9-inch circle. Spread meringue mixture evenly over circle, then build up edges with pastry tube or spoon. Bake in very slow oven (225° F.) 1¾ hours. Cool. Remove from paper carefully with spatula. Fill with Raisin Nectar Filling. Chill several hours before serving.

Raisin Nectar Filling: Rinse and drain raisins, add nectar and heat to boiling. Blend sugar, cornstarch and salt, and stir into hot raisin mixture. Cook and stir until mixture boils thoroughly and is thickened. Beat egg yolks and stir a little of hot mixture into them. Combine with remaining hot mixture and cook and stir a few minutes longer, until very thick. Remove from heat and blend in lemon junce. Cool. Fold in whipped cream and turn into cooled meringue shell. Chill several hours. Cut into small wedges to serve. Makes 6 to 8 servings.

DUTCH ZWIEBACK DESSERT

CUSTARD FILLING:

2 cups milk	½ cup sugar
3 egg yolks	1 tablespoon cornstarch

CRUMB MIXTURE AND TOPPING:

1 package zwieback, rolled into fine crumbs	½ cup melted butter or margarine
½ cup chopped nut meats	1 teaspoon cinnamon
½ cup sugar	¼ teaspoon salt
	3 egg whites

Combine custard ingredients in the top of the double boiler and cook together until thickened. Cool. Mix together zwieback crumbs, nut meats, sugar, butter, cinnamon, and salt. Pat into an 8-inch square pan, reserving a few crumbs for the top. Pour custard into pan. Top with egg whites which have been beaten until stiff. Sprinkle with crumbs. Bake in a moderate oven (350°) for 30 minutes. Serve the following day. Makes 9 servings.

DESSERT ACCOMPANIMENTS

It's worth the weary traveler's time to come out of his way to visit Grandma Anderson's in December. He'll find Belle Anderson Ebner out in the little factory turning out trays of fabulous homemade candy, sheets and sheets of Grandma Anderson famous Dutch Cookies, sauces to be bottled for Christmas, orders being filled for customers' Christmas boxes.

There isn't a single, modern streamlined item in Mrs. Ebner's Christmas preparation. It's a one-woman operation and since Mrs. Ebner never sleeps anyway and treats her insomnia with her own collection of well over three hundred old and valuable cook books, she is just as apt to be working at three in the morning as at three in the afternoon.

Her Christmas breads are a rite. Her candy is the result of a professional Fanny Farmers Candy course many years ago, and her cookie skill is straight from Grandma Anderson as are most of the recipes.

Her French Cocoa Balls, her Candied Walnuts, her Brazil Nut Fudge, her Pecan Pralines . . . these are all made with the richest butter, the finest ingredients obtainable. Mrs. Ebner says you never made a good product out of a bad product . . . and that's why the Anderson Hotel storeroom boasts the finest labels that can possibly be purchased.

Through all this preparation runs one vital and necessary ingredient. Love! Mrs. Ebner loves to cook and most particularly does she love this season of the year.

Our serving hours are short in winter at Hotel Anderson, but even if you miss us at mealtime Mrs. Ebner's dazzling counters of Christmas and holiday foods are ready for you any hour of the day.

CANDIES AND CONFECTIONS
ALMOND CRUNCH

½ lb. finely chopped blanched   1 cup butter
    almonds   1 cup sugar
                                    ½ lb. semi-sweet chocolate

Toast nuts. Combine butter and sugar and stir over a low heat until sugar melts. Add half the nuts and cook to 310° F. Pour into buttered pan and cool. Heat chocolate in double boiler until of soft consistency. Remove and stir until melted. Spread over top and sprinkle with almonds. Cool and turn upside down and pour more chocolate and nuts on uncovered side. Break in about 1 to 1½-inch irregular pieces.

BAKED NUT CANDY

1 egg white   ½ cup firmly packed brown sugar
¼ teaspoon salt   ½ teaspoon vanilla
                                    1 cup nuts, finely chopped

Beat egg whites until foamy. Add salt. Beat in sugar gradually and continue beating until mixture is stiff. Fold in vanilla and nuts. Drop by spoonfuls on an oiled cookie sheet. Bake at 225° for one hour. Remove from pan at once. Yield: 24 pieces.

BUTTERSCOTCH CANDY

3 cups brown sugar   2 tablespoons corn syrup
5 tablespoons butter   1½ teaspoons vanilla
4 tablespoons water   ¼ teaspoon salt
                                    2 tablespoons cream

Cook sugar, butter, water and syrup together in saucepan until a little dropped in cold water forms a soft ball. Add salt and cream and cook until a little dropped in cold water hardens instantly. Remove from fire, add vanilla and turn into a shallow buttered pan. Mark into squares when cool enough.

CANDIED WALNUTS

1½ cups granulated sugar
½ cup sour cream

1 teaspoon vanilla
2½ cups walnut halves

Bring sugar and sour cream to a boil in a heavy saucepan, stirring constantly. Cook to the soft-ball stage (236° F. to 238° F.). Remove from heat. Add vanilla; beat until mixture begins to thicken. Add nuts; stir until well coated. Turn out on greased cookie sheet; separate in individual pieces. Makes about 1⅛ pounds nuts.

JOHANNA'S BRAZIL NUT FUDGE

4½ cups sugar
1 large can evaporated milk
3 5-oz. plain chocolate bars
2 6-oz. pkgs. chopped
    semisweet chocolate

8-oz. jar marshmallow whip
1½ teaspoons salt
1 cup Brazil nut pieces
1 teaspoon vanilla extract

Bring sugar and milk together to boiling point, then cook over medium heat 4½ minutes (clock it exactly), stirring occasionally.

Break chocolate bars into pieces, mix with chopped semisweet chocolate, marshmallow whip and salt in a large bowl. Pour hot sugar-milk mixture over, one-half at a time, mixing thoroughly after each addition.

Let stand until cool, add nuts and vanilla extract and pour into a large, buttered pan (about 8" x 12"). Cool in refrigerator and cut into pieces. Makes lots and keeps beautifully.

CHOCOLATE "PHILLY" FUDGE

1 3-oz. pkg. Philadelphia Brand
    Cream Cheese
2 cups sifted confectioners' sugar

2 1-ounce squares unsweetened
    chocolate, melted
¼ teaspoon vanilla
Dash of salt
½ cup chopped pecans

Place the cream cheese in a bowl and cream it until soft and smooth. Slowly blend the sugar into it. Add the melted chocolate. Mix well. Add vanilla, salt and chopped pecans and mix until well blended. Press into a well greased shallow pan. Place in refrigerator until firm (about 15 minutes). Cut into squares. (For slightly softer fudge blend in 1 teaspoon of cream.)

MAPLE "PHILLY" FUDGE

Follow directions for the chocolate "Philly" fudge except use 2¾ cups of sugar and add ¼ teaspoon of maple flavoring instead of the chocolate and vanilla.

ALMOND "PHILLY" FUDGE

Follow directions for the chocolate "Philly" fudge except use 2¾ cups of sugar, add ¼ teaspoon of almond flavoring instead of the chocolate and vanilla, and use ½ cup chopped almonds instead of pecans.

COCONUT "PHILLY" FUDGE

Follow directions for the chocolate "Philly" fudge except use 3¼ cups sugar, add ½ cup shredded coconut instead of the chocolate, and leave out the pecans.

PEANUT BUTTER "PHILLY" FUDGE

Follow directions for the chocolate "Philly" Fudge except use 2¾ cups of sugar, add 2 tablespoons peanut butter instead of the chocolate, and use ¼ cup chopped salted peanuts instead of pecans.

CHOCOLATE FUDGE

2 cups sugar
2 tablespoons corn syrup
⅛ teaspoon salt
¾ cup cream or milk

2 tablespoons butter
2 squares chocolate cut in thin pieces
1 teaspoon vanilla

Cook sugar, syrup, salt and milk very slowly. Cook without stirring until mixture forms soft ball in cold water. Remove from fire, add butter and cool. Add vanilla. When quite cool work and beat until fudge is thick and creamy. Pour one-half inch thick in buttered pan or plate. Cut in squares.

PEANUT BUTTER FUDGE

Omit butter and add 4 tablespoons peanut butter when beating fudge.

COLD METHOD FUDGE

1 egg, well beaten	1 teaspoon vanilla
3 tablespoons cream	¼ teaspoon salt
2 tablespoons soft butter	1 pound powdered sugar

Four squares of chocolate melted in double boiler with 1 tablespoon butter. Cream powdered sugar with 2 tablespoons soft but not melted butter. Add cream and beaten egg. Pour in melted chocolate. Stir, beat and mix ingredients until smooth and thick enough to work into desired shapes or cut into squares. Add more powdered sugar if not stiff enough. Place walnut meat on each piece. Cool in refrigerator for several hours.

SOUR CREAM FUDGE

4½ cups brown sugar	2 cups sour cream
¼ teaspoon salt	½ teaspoon vanilla
	½ cup nut meats, chopped

Combine sugar, salt, and cream; cook to soft ball stage (236° F.). Cool to lukewarm, add vanilla. Beat until thick and creamy. Add nut meats. Pour into well-buttered shallow pan.

WHITE NUT FUDGE

2 cups sugar	2 tablespoons butter
¼ teaspoon salt	1 cup milk
2 tablespoons white corn syrup	1 teaspoon vanilla
	¾ cup coarsely chopped nut meats

Combine sugar, salt, corn syrup, butter, and milk in saucepan, blending well. Cook slowly to soft boil stage, (234°) stirring occasionally to prevent scorching. Remove from heat; allow to stand undisturbed until bottom of saucepan is lukewarm to the hand. Add vanilla and nut meats. Beat mixture until it becomes creamy and loses its gloss —almost holds shape. Pour into well-buttered (8 x 8 x 2″) pan. Cut into 1″ squares while still warm. Makes about 1 pound of candy.

CHOCOLATE CREAM PISTACHIO BALLS

½ pound chocolate bits	¼ cup heavy cream
2 tablespoons strong coffee	½ cup ground pistachio nuts
½ cup butter	(may substitute pecans
2 egg yolks	instead, if desired)

Melt chocolate over hot water. Blend in coffee. Cool. Cream butter. Add egg yolks and cream, and gradually add the chocolate mixture. Set bowl in larger bowl filled with ice cubes. Beat until mixture is firm enough to roll into small balls. Roll in nuts, chill until firm. Yield: 34 balls.

COCONUT CREAMS

2 teaspoons butter	½ cup milk
1½ cups sugar	⅓ cup shredded coconut
	½ teaspoon vanilla

Melt butter in saucepan. Add sugar and milk. Heat to boiling point, boil 12 minutes. Remove from range; add coconut and vanilla. Beat until creamy. Pour into buttered pan. Cool. Cut into squares. Makes 12 pieces.

ENGLISH TOFFEE

1 cup sugar
1 cup butter or margarine
1 tablespoon corn syrup

3 tablespoons water
¾ cup chopped almonds or
   peanuts
1 small chocolate bar, cut fine

Cook sugar, butter or margarine, corn syrup and water until a few drops tested in cold water crack (290° F. on candy thermometer).

While syrup cooks, chop nuts fine and sprinkle almost all of them over bottom of piepan. Pour hot syrup over nuts, sprinkle with finely chopped chocolate bar, and top it off with the remaining almonds or peanuts.

When toffee is cool, break into about 15 good chewing chunks.

FRENCH COCOA BALLS

½ cup cocoa
1½ cups powdered sugar
½ teaspoon salt

1 cup chopped filberts
½ cup sweetened condensed
   milk
1 teaspoon vanilla

Mix cocoa, powdered sugar, and salt thoroughly. Add filberts, milk, and vanilla and mix well. Form into 1-inch balls and chill.

MIX TOGETHER

2 tablespoons cocoa

2 tablespoons powdered sugar

Roll the balls in this mixture. Store in the refrigerator or a covered container. Makes 4 dozen.

NUT GLACE

3 cups sugar

½ teaspoon cream of tartar

Dissolve in a saucepan with one cup water. After it heats, stir until sugar is entirely dissolved. Wipe away any crystals from the sides and then allow the syrup to cook without stirring until it threads crisply when dropped from a spoon. Pick the sort of nuts you wish to glacé, almonds, Brazil, walnuts, or pecans. Using a long, sharp pin, pierce the nuts one at a time and dip in the glacé. Place on a buttered dish. It is necessary to work fast because the glacé hardens rapidly. Fruit sections, such as grapes, oranges, and dates may be treated in the same way.

BILOXI INN PECAN PRALINES

Into a saucepan put 4 tablespoons water and 2 tablespoons evaporated milk, 1 level tablespoon butter, 4 cups brown sugar, ½ teaspoon salt. Stir and mix well and then melt over a slow fire and allow to boil, stirring all the time. Add 2 cups broken pecans. When candy begins to thicken remove from the fire and stir constantly while cooling. After it is fairly cool add ½ teaspoon vanilla extract. Do not allow to harden but while the candy is still pourable, drop with a large spoon on oiled paper, making patties 3 or 4 inches in diameter.

TOASTED NUTS

Heat ½ cup butter or olive oil. Put in enough nut meats to cover bottom of pan. Stir until delicately browned. Remove with skimmer and drain on paper toweling. Do not cook too long as nut meats will darken when removed from fat.

ALTERNATE METHOD

Dip nut meats in warm butter or olive oil and brown in 400° oven. Stir so they will not burn. Sprinkle nuts while still hot with salt.

VANILLA CARAMELS

2 cups sugar	1 teaspoon Vanilla Extract,
½ cup corn syrup	Special
½ cup milk	4 tablespoons butter
	1 cup cream or condensed milk

Cook the ingredients, except the Vanilla Extract, Special, to the stiff-ball stage or 246°. Remove from the fire, add the Vanilla Extract, Special, and pour into a buttered pan. When it is cold, turn it out of the pan and cut into squares.

WHITE TAFFY

2 cups granulated sugar
½ cup water
1 teaspoon glycerin

2½ tablespoons vinegar
1 teaspoon Vanilla Extract, Special

Boil the sugar, water, glycerin, and vinegar to the hard-ball stage (260°). Add Vanilla Extract, Special. Pour onto a greased platter. When cool enough to handle, pull until very white, stretch into a long rope and cut into short pieces.

FROSTINGS, FILLINGS, DESSERT SAUCES

BANANA CREAM FLUFF

1 ripe banana, riced or mashed
Juice of ½ lemon
1½ tablespoons confectioners' sugar

1 egg white, stiffly beaten
Dash of salt
4 tablespoons cream, whipped

Combine riced banana with lemon juice and sugar. Beat salt into egg white and fold into first mixture. Chill thoroughly. Beat chilled cream until it thickens and fold into banana mixture. Especially good on a steamed chocolate pudding, or chocolate cake. Yield: 1 cup.

BANANA LEMON FILLING

In top of double boiler, combine 6 tablespoons cornstarch, ¼ cup sugar, ¾ cup water. Cook over rapidly boiling water, stirring constantly until thickened and clear. Add gradually 1 egg yolk, beaten. Return to double boiler. Add and stir in ½ cup sugar. Cook, stirring constantly, 2 minutes longer. Remove from heat.

Add and mix well 2 tablespoons lemon juice, 1 tablespoon grated lemon rind, 1 tablespoon margarine. Cool. Spread ½ of filling on bottom layer. Add 1 small banana, thinly sliced. Spread remaining filling over banana slices.

BASIC RECIPE FOR "PHILLY" FROSTING

1 3-oz. pkg. Philadelphia Brand Cream Cheese	1 tablespoon milk 2 cups confectioners' sugar

Your favorite flavoring according to directions. Blend the cream cheese and the milk. Add the sugar gradually, blending it in well. Then add your selected flavoring according to directions and mix again.

VANILLA FROSTING

To the basic recipe above, add ½ teaspoon of vanilla. Enough to frost and fill a 2-layer, 8-inch cake.

MAPLE "PHILLY" FROSTING

Basic recipe. Add ¼ teaspoon maple flavoring. A flavor variation pretty sure to delight your family and guests.

COCONUT "PHILLY" FROSTING

Basic recipe but add ¼ teaspoon of vanilla and ½ cup of shredded coconut.

LEMON "PHILLY" FROSTING

Basic recipe but instead of the milk use 1 tablespoon of lemon juice and 1 teaspoon of grated lemon rind.

ORANGE "PHILLY" FROSTING

Basic recipe but instead of the milk use 1 tablespoon of orange juice and ½ teaspoon of grated orange rind.

STRAWBERRY "PHILLY" FROSTING

Basic recipe except use 2½ cups sugar, but leave out milk. After sugar is blended into cream cheese add 1 tablespoon Kraft Pure Strawberry Preserves, a dash of salt and 4 drops red food coloring.

MARASCHINO CHERRY "PHILLY" FROSTING

Basic recipe but instead of the milk use 1 tablespoon of marachino cherry juice and 1 tablespoon of chopped maraschino cherries.

DATE NUT "PHILLY" FROSTING

Basic recipe except use 2½ cups sugar. After sugar is blended in add ¼ cup chopped dates, ¼ cup chopped pecans and ¼ teaspoon vanilla.

CINNAMON "PHILLY" FROSTING

Basic recipe. Add ½ teaspoon of cinnamon. This is particularly good on plain layer or cup cakes or for frosted cookies.

PINEAPPLE "PHILLY" FROSTING

Basic recipe except use 2½ cups sugar, but instead of milk use 1 tablespoon crushed pineapple with juice and a dash of salt.

CHOCOLATE "PHILLY" FROSTING

Basic recipe except use 2½ cups sugar. After sugar is blended in add 1 square of unsweetened chocolate, melted and slightly cooled, 1 teaspoon of vanilla and a dash of salt.

BLACK WALNUT "PHILLY" FROSTING

Basic recipe. Add ¼ teaspoon of black walnut flavoring. Here is a surprise. Try it.

CHOCOLATE MALTED "PHILLY" FROSTING

Basic recipe except use 2½ cups sugar sifted with ¼ cup Kraft Instant Sweetened Chocolate Flavored Malted Milk. Add ½ teaspoon vanilla and a dash of salt.

ALMOND "PHILLY" FROSTING

Basic recipe. Add ½ teaspoon of almond flavoring. Wonderful for frosting a jelly roll, studded with shreds of blanched almonds.

FRESH LIME "PHILLY" FROSTING

Basic recipe but instead of the milk use one tablespoon of lime juice. Add 2 teaspoons of grated lime rind and a dash of salt.

PEPPERMINT STICK "PHILLY" FROSTING

Basic recipe except use 2½ cups sugar. Add 1 tablespoon of crushed peppermint stick candy. The youngsters will love it.

MINT "PHILLY" FROSTING

Basic recipe. Add 1 tablespoon of chopped green maraschino cherries, ¼ teaspoon of mint flavoring and a dash of salt.

MOCHA "PHILLY" FROSTING

Basic recipe. Add 2 teaspoons of coffee powder (instant). A lot of people are very fond of this.

BOILED FROSTING

In saucepan, combine 2 cups sugar and 1 cup water. Cook over direct heat, without stirring, to thread stage (238° F.). Remove from heat.

Beat until stiff 2 egg whites. Add syrup gradually, beating constantly. Add 1 teaspoon vanilla extract. Beat until thick.

Add ¼ teaspoon Cream of Tartar Baking Powder. Beat until thick and of good spreading consistency.

BRANDY SAUCE

1 cup hot water	⅛ teaspoon salt
⅓ cup sugar	1 tablespoon butter
½ tablespoon cornstarch	1 tablespoon brandy

Add hot water slowly to combined sugar, cornstarch, and salt in a saucepan. Stir constantly and cook until clear. Add butter and brandy. Serve hot over mince pie or steamed pudding. Yield: 1 cup.

CARAMEL FROSTING

In saucepan, over low heat, melt slowly ¼ cup granulated sugar. Stir until light golden brown. Add gradually, stirring constantly, ⅓ cup boiling water. Boil to soft ball stage (234° F.). Remove from heat; cool. Cream thoroughly 1½ tablespoons margarine, 1¾ cups sifted confectioners' sugar. Add gradually, mixing well, cooled syrup, and 1 to 2 tablespoons cream. Mix until smooth. Add and mix in a drop or two of red food coloring, if desired.

CHOCOLATE MALLOW SAUCE

⅓ cup water
1 square (1 ounce) unsweetened
    chocolate
2 dozen marshmallows

Dash salt
½ teaspoon vanilla
Vanilla or peppermint ice
    cream, 1 quart

Combine water, chocolate, marshmallows and salt in top of double boiler. Place over boiling water. Cover and cook for 5 minutes. Remove from heat; add vanilla, stir until well blended; cool. Serve over ice cream. Makes 6 servings.

COFFEE CREAM ICING

Cream ½ cup margarine. Add and mix in well 3 cups sifted confectioners' sugar, 5 teaspoons Instant Coffee, 4 teaspoons cocoa. Add gradually and blend well 4 tablespoons light cream, ½ teaspoon vanilla extract. Beat until smooth and of good spreading consistency.

COFFEE CREAM SAUCE

Stir ¼ cup sugar over low heat until it forms a golden brown syrup. Remove from heat. Gradually add ¼ cup strong coffee. Return to heat and boil until smooth. Cool slightly and fold into ½ pint heavy cream, whipped.

COFFEE WALNUT SAUCE

1 cup sugar
1½ cups strong coffee
2 tablespoons cornstarch

3 tablespoons cold coffee
2 tablespoons butter
⅓ teaspoon salt
½ cup broken walnut meats

Melt sugar slowly, in heavy skillet, stirring often. Add 1½ cups coffee, slowly and carefully (much steam will rise). Stir constantly. Dissolve cornstarch in cold coffee, stir into warm mixture and continue stirring over low heat until sauce boils and thickens. Add butter, salt and walnuts. Serve warm on ice cream. Makes about 2 cups.

CREAM CHEESE TOPPING FOR PIE

1 3-ounce package cream cheese   1 cup whipping cream
                                       Few grains of salt

    Soften cream cheese with a fork and fold into whipped cream. Add salt. Put mixture through a pastry tube, or spread on top of apple, mince, strawberry, blackberry, cherry, or other fruit pie. If desired, add ¼ cup confectioners' sugar and a bit of vanilla to the cheese mixture.

CREAMY CHOCOLATE ICING

    Cream ¼ cup margarine. Add and mix in well 2¼ cups sifted confectioners' sugar. Add gradually and blend well 2 squares unsweetened chocolate, melted, 3 tablespoons cream, ½ teaspoon vanilla extract. Beat until smooth and of good spreading consistency.

CREAMY WINE SAUCE

1 cup sugar   ¼ cup sherry, port, or other wine
½ cup butter   ⅛ teaspoon salt
4 egg yolks, well beaten   1 cup cream, heated

    Cream sugar and butter together and add well beaten egg yolks. Stir in wine and add salt and hot cream. Beat well. Cook in the top of a double boiler, stirring constantly, until sauce thickens. Do not overcook. Yield: About 2 cups.

FLUFFY COFFEE FROSTING

1½ cups vegetable shortening   ¼ cup cold coffee
 1 cup granulated sugar   1 teaspoon vanilla
 ½ teaspoon salt   2 eggs

In a small mixing bowl, combine all ingredients. Beat at high speed of electric mixer or with sturdy rotary beater about 10 minutes, until smooth and fluffy.

While the proportion of shortening may seem high, it is correct. Properly made, this frosting resembles that used in French pastries.

FLUFFY FRUIT FROSTING

1 cup dark or golden raisins
¼ cup candied cherries
⅓ cup walnuts
½ cup granulated sugar

¼ cup light corn syrup
2 tablespons water
2 egg whites
Dash salt
1 teaspoon vanilla extract

Rinse raisins, cover with boiling water and let stand 5 minutes. Drain and dry thoroughly. Chop. Chop cherries and walnuts. Combine sugar, syrup and water and stir over low heat until sugar is dissolved. Boil until syrup spins an 8-inch thread (242° F.). Beat egg whites with salt, and pour syrup slowly over them continuing to beat. Blend in vanilla, and beat until stiff. Set aside about ⅓ of frosting for top of cake. Fold raisins, cherries, and nuts into remaining frosting. Spread between layers and on sides. Spread top with plain frosting. Makes enough for top and sides of 2 (9 inch) layers.

FLAMING ICE CREAM SAUCE

1 small round of sponge cake
Scoop of vanilla ice cream
½ brandied peach cubed
½ brandied apricot cubed

4 brandied sliced, pitted cherries
½ teaspoon Curaçao liqueur
Sugar to taste
1 tablespoon brandy

Place sponge cake or any other kind of cake cut to size with a large round cutter on a dessert plate, top with ice cream. Heat the combined brandied fruits in a small frying or saucepan. Add Curaçao, sprinkle with sugar, stir gently but do not allow to boil; simply heat. Pour some slightly warm brandy over this mixture and touch with a match. It is preferable to put the brandy sauce on at the table and light as the flame does not last more than a few moments. If a longer flame is wanted, add 1 tablespoon pure grain alcohol. Never use any other kind of alcohol for a substitute. Adding the alcohol merely lengthens the time of burning and, of course, is entirely consumed by the flame. Variations to the above can be made by using any kind of canned fruit.

HARD SAUCE

STANDARD HARD SAUCE

⅓ cup butter
1 cup confectioners' sugar

½ teaspoon vanilla
Dash of nutmeg

Cream butter thoroughly, add sugar gradually, beating well. Add flavoring and nutmeg. Serve on baked or steamed pudding.

QUEEN'S HARD SAUCE

Substitute 2 tablespoons liqueur or fruit flavored cordial for the vanilla.

BRANDY HARD SAUCE

Substitute 2 tablespoons brandy for vanilla.

CHERRY HARD SAUCE

Substitute 2 tablespoons cherry syrup for vanilla. Add ½ cup drained chopped cherries.

APRICOT HARD SAUCE

Beat in ½ cup strained apricot pulp with the sugar. Omit vanilla. A teaspoon of apricot brandy may be added, in which case a little more sugar will be needed.

Cocoa Hard Sauce

Work 2 tablespoons or more of cocoa in with the confectioners' sugar. Flavor sauce with vanilla, rum, brandy, or orange.

HONEY BUTTER SAUCE

2 tablespoons butter	8 marshmallows
1 cup honey	⅛ teaspoon salt
1½ tablespoons cornstarch	1 teaspoon grated orange rind
1 cup water	or vanilla

Add butter to warm honey with cornstarch and water paste and cook gently until clear. Add quartered marshmallows, salt, and flavoring. Heat gently until marshmallows have melted. Fold them into other ingredients. Serve warm on ice cream or steamed puddings. Yield: 2 cups.

LEMON SAUCE

½ cup sugar	Rind of ½ lemon, grated
1 tablespoon cornstarch	1 cup boiling water
⅛ teaspoon salt	⅛ teaspoon nutmeg (optional)
Juice of ½ lemon	1 tablespoon butter or margarine

Mix sugar, cornstarch and salt. Add lemon juice, rind and boiling water. Cook until thickened and clear. Add nutmeg and butter. Serve hot, over puddings and other desserts. Yield: 1½ cups.

VARIATIONS OF LEMON SAUCE

Fluffy Sauce

Just before taking sauce from heat, quickly stir in the slightly beaten yolk of an egg and fold in the stiff beaten white.

Orange-Lemon Sauce

Use orange juice, fresh or canned, in place of water.

Pineapple-Lemon Sauce

Use pineapple juice in place of water.

Lemon Whipped Cream Sauce

Fold equal parts of the lemon sauce and whipped cream together.

Lime Sauce

Use juice and rind of 1 lime in place of lemon juice and rind. Omit nutmeg.

Sugarless Lemon Sauce

Use ¾ cup corn syrup in place of sugar, and only ½ cup water.

MARSHMALLOW FROSTING

In top of double boiler, combine 2 egg whites, unbeaten, 1½ cups sugar, 6 tablespoons water, 6 marshmallows, quartered. Cook over rapidly boiling water, beating with rotary egg beater about 10 minutes or until mixture stands in peaks. Remove top of double boiler from heat. Add 1 teaspoon vanilla extract, ¼ teaspoon cream of tartar baking powder. Beat about 5 minutes or until thick and of good spreading consistency.

MARASCHINO SAUCE

⅓ cup sugar
2 tablespoons cornstarch
⅔ cup boiling water

¼ cup halved maraschino cherries
½ cup maraschino syrup
1 tablespoon butter

Blend sugar and cornstarch, gradually add the boiling water, stirring constantly. Boil for 5 minutes, then add cherries, syrup and butter. Serve hot or cold. Yield: about 1½ cups.

OLD-FASHIONED CHOCOLATE FROSTING

In top of double boiler, combine 3 tablespoons cornstarch, ¼ teaspoon salt, 2 cups confectioners' sugar, sifted, 2 tablespoons margarine, 4 squares unsweetened chocolate, shaved or cut up. Add and stir in ½ cup milk, 2 egg yolks, well beaten. Cook over rapidly boiling water, stirring constantly until thick and smooth. Remove from heat. Add and mix in well 1½ teaspoons vanilla extract. Divide frosting in half. Spread one half between layers of cake. To the other half, add gradually 1½ cups sifted confectioners' sugar, 1 to 2 tablespoons cream. Beat until smooth and of good spreading consistency.

ORANGE COCONUT SAUCE

Melt ¼ pound butter. Add 1 tablespoon flour, 1 tablespoon brown sugar, 1 teaspoonful confectioners' sugar. Add gradually ¼ cup sherry wine, ⅛ cup concentrated orange juice, ½ cup coconut honey, ⅓ cup pineapple juice. Cook until smooth.

ORANGE CREAM FILLING

In top of double boiler, combine ¼ cup sugar, 1½ tablespoons flour, ⅛ teaspoon salt, 2 teaspoons grated orange rind, ½ cup orange juice, 1 egg yolk, 1 tablespoon margarine. Cook over rapidly boiling water, stirring constantly, until thick and smooth. Remove from heat. Add and stir in 1 teaspoon lemon juice. Cool to room temperature.

ORANGE-HONEY BUTTER

¼ pound butter
4 tablespoons honey

3 tablespoons frozen orange juice
6 tablespoons confectioners' sugar

Cream butter. Alternately add honey and orange juice, blending thoroughly. Stir in sugar a little at a time. Blend until smooth and creamy. Serve over hot waffles or pancakes or use as a sauce with hot gingerbread.

ORANGE ICING

Cream ⅓ cup margarine. Add and mix in well 2¼ cups sifted confectioners' sugar. Grated rind of 1 orange, 2 tablespoons orange juice and pulp. Beat until smooth and of good spreading consistency.

PINEAPPLE SAUCE

3 tablespoons sugar	1¼ cups canned unsweetened
1 tablespoon cornstarch	pineapple juice
Dash of salt	1 teaspoon lemon juice
	¼ cup drained crushed pineapple

Mix together sugar, cornstarch and salt in saucepan. Add pineapple juice gradually. Bring to boiling temperature and cook about 5 minutes, or until thickened, stirring constantly. Add lemon juice and pineapple. Makes about 1½ cups sauce.

PINEAPPLE MINT SAUCE

Flavor Pineapple Sauce with 1 to 3 drops of oil of peppermint. Add enough green food coloring to tint the sauce a delicate green. *Important:* If juice from sweetened canned pineapple is used, reduce sugar 1 to 2 tablespoons, depending upon the sweetness of the juice. Diced canned pineapple may be used in place of crushed pineapple.

PLUM PUDDING SAUCE

Mix together 1 cup sugar, 1 tablespoon instant tapioca, and a generous sprinkle of salt in the top pan of the chafing dish over the water jacket. Then slowly pour in 1½ cups hot water, stirring all the while. While this mixture is heating whip well 1 egg and stir it into the sugar mixture. Continue cooking for 5 minutes, stirring all the while. After that time, lower the flame and stir in 1½ tablespoons butter or margarine, and 2 oz. rum. Into the sauce, place a warmed plum pudding, sprinkle it with sugar, and pour ¼ cup warmed rum over all. Flame it, and serve as soon as the fire flickers out. (For meat, eggs.)

RUM SAUCE

4 tablespoons butter	½ cup cream
1 cup brown sugar	⅛ teaspoon salt
2 egg yolks, well beaten	3 tablespoons rum

Cream butter and sugar together; add egg yolks, cream and salt. Cook over boiling water until creamy. Remove from heat, cool, then add rum. Yield: 1 cup.

SEA FOAM FROSTING

In saucepan, combine ½ cup brown sugar, 1 cup sugar, 1 teaspoon instant coffee, 6 tablespoons water, ¼ teaspoon cream of tartar. Cook over direct heat, without stirring, to thread stage (238° F.). Remove from heat. Beat until stiff 2 egg whites. Add syrup gradually, beating constantly. Add and beat until thick ⅛ teaspoon Cream of Tartar Baking Powder. Beat until thick and of good spreading consistency.

7-MINUTE FROSTING

In top of double boiler, combine 1 egg white, unbeaten, 1 cup sugar, 3 tablespoons cold water.

Cook over rapidly boiling water, beating with rotary egg beater until mixture stands in peaks. Remove top of double boiler from heat. Add ½ teaspoon vanilla extract, ¼ teaspoon Cream of Tartar Baking Powder. Beat until thick and of good spreading consistency.

SPARKLING AMBER GLAZE

Stir together 1 cup sugar, ¼ teaspoon each of cream of tartar and salt, 2 teaspoons lemon juice, ½ cup water. Cook to 300° F. (About 8 minutes). Brush on top of fruit cake.

SPICED HARD SAUCE

¼ cup butter
1 cup confectioners' sugar

1 teaspoon vanilla
¼ teaspoon cinnamon
¼ teaspoon nutmeg

Allow the butter to soften at room temperature. Cream and add the sugar gradually until the mixture is light and fluffy. Season with the vanilla, cinnamon and nutmeg. More of the spices may be added if desired.

THIN BITTER CHOCOLATE ICING

In top of double boiler, melt 4 squares unsweetened chocolate. Remove from heat. Cool slightly. Boil together for 5 minutes to make a thin syrup ⅓ cup sugar, ½ cup water. Slowly pour thin syrup into melted chocolate, beating constantly. When slightly thick, spread thinly on Chocolate Roll.

TROPICAL BANANA SAUCE

2 cups crushed banana, ripe
1 cup brown sugar
½ cup sherry wine

Dash salt
1 teaspoon lemon juice
½ cup coconut syrup

Simmer for 10 minutes. Cool and strain. Fold into 2 cups unsweetened whipped cream.

ZABAIONE SAUCE

4 egg yolks

1 cup sherry wine
⅓ cup sugar

Beat egg yolks until thick, add sugar gradually and beat for 2 minutes. Place over hot, not boiling water, and continue to beat while adding sherry gradually. Keep beating until wine has been added and sauce is light and fluffy. Serve warm or chilled. Yield: 1½ cups approximately.

CAKES

There was always a mile high sunshine cake in Grandma Anderson's pantry in her house across from the Hotel, and there was always a towering filled angel food at the Hotel for the unexpected guest and the small granddaughters to nibble on.

On New Year's Eve, extra rich, extra black devil's food cake was a custom, its filling laced with rum and its frosting loaded with pecans and almonds and cashews. This was a cake! Pound cake came with Christmas and it kept forever. The fruit cakes were marvels of jeweled cookery, the Pennsylvania Dutch cakes were made and packed for special customers as unexpected gifts from Grandma Anderson.

She held with the theory that sugar is the greatest energy builder in the world and she looked with great disdain at thin men. If you weighed under 150 pounds you were "poorly" in her eyes and needed special attention immediately. Liking food as she did, Grandma was a woman of ample proportions and great dignity and humor. Her biggest worry was me because I wouldn't eat, couldn't top the scales at more than one hundred pounds and besides had a high disdain for food, plain, fancy or otherwise. I ate because I had to.

How she would marvel at a cook book coming from my hands . . . not one but three! How she would laugh at my frequent dieting bouts, my constant struggle against her wonderful cakes.

Miss Ann developed a recipe called Cedric Adams' Chocolate Cake named after a beloved Minneapolis Journal columnist who first told the world about the Hotel Anderson in his column. It was a signal for greater business, for new customers being added to the old and eventually caused the first book to be born. The cake appears often and is a tall, luscious concoction of chocolate, marshmallow and spices. The recipe is in our first book but you will find other favorites here.

ADJUSTMENTS FOR HIGH ALTITUDE BAKING

	3000 ft.	5000 ft.	7000 ft.
Reduce Baking Powder			
For each teaspoon, decrease....	⅛ tsp.	⅛-½ tsp.	¼-½ tsp.
Reduce Sugar		No	Usually no	
For each cup, decrease.........	change	change	1-2 tbsps.
Reduce Lard			
For each cup, decrease.........	1-2 tbsp.	2 tbsp.	2-3 tbsp.
Increase Liquid			
For each cup, add...........	1-2 tbsp.	2-3 tbsp.	3-4 tbsp.
Increase Baking Temperature.....	6-10° F.	10-15° F.	15-25° F.

Decrease Baking Time 5 to 10 minutes when recipes have been tested at sea level.

Note: When two amounts are given, try the smaller adjustment first, then if cake still needs improvement, use the larger adjustment the next time you make the cake.

EGG NOG TORTE

ANGEL FOOD CAKE

1 cup sifted cake flour	¼ teaspoon salt
1¾ cups sugar	1½ cups egg whites
1½ teaspoons cream of tartar	½ teaspoon almond extract
	¾ teaspoon vanilla extract

Mix flour and ¾ cup sugar and sift 3 times. Sift 1 cup sugar 3 times. Sprinkle cream of tartar and salt over egg whites (removed from refrigerator long enough to reach room temperature) and beat with a flat whip until soft peaks are formed. Add 1 cup sugar gradually by sprinkling a little at a time over egg whites and beat until soft peaks are formed. Fold in extracts. Add flour-sugar mixture gradually by sifting a little at a time over meringue and folding gently after each addition. Stop folding as soon as no flecks of flour can be seen. Pour batter into an ungreased angel food pan (top diameter, 10 inches).

With a spatula, cut through batter several times, using circular motion, to prevent large holes in cake. Bake in a preheated oven. Invert pan 1 hour before removing cake from pan. Cool thoroughly on wire cooling rack. Cut into 2 layers horizontally. Put layers together and cover top and side of cake with Rum Filling. Chill in refrigerator until firm (about 4 hours).

RUM FILLING

1 tablespoon gelatin	⅓ cup Jamaica rum
¼ cup cold water	¾ cup chopped, toasted, salted,
¾ cup butter	almond nut meats (3 ounces)
1 cup sifted confectioners' sugar	¼ teaspoon salt
4 eggs, separated	1 cup heavy cream, chilled and
	whipped

Soak gelatin in cold water 5 minutes, dissolve over hot water. Cream butter well, add sugar gradually and continue creaming until mixture is light and fluffy; add unbeaten egg yolks, one at a time, beating well after each addition. Add rum and nut meats and mix. Gradually fold in slightly cooled gelatin. Add salt to egg whites and beat with a rotary beater until a peak of egg white will stand upright when beater is pulled out; fold into butter mixture; fold in whipped cream. Chill until thickened (about 1 hour). Yield: 16 servings.

FRUIT CAKE KNOW-HOW

THE BAKING PANS

Suitable for use are tube or loaf pans, coffee cans, ring molds or casseroles. To prepare, grease well, then line smoothly with heavy brown wrapping paper; let it extend up along sides to protect cake edges from over-baking; grease and flour well. Paper-lined muffin cups may be used.

THE MIXING

For ease in mixing, use a flat pan to coat the fruit and nutmeats with the dry ingredients before adding to the creamed mixture.

THE BAKING

For a deliciously moist fruit cake, place a shallow pan of water on the lowest rack of the oven and let steam work its magic while the cake bakes. If the cake seems to brown too fast, cover with heavy paper to finish baking.

THE STORAGE

To cool, remove cake from pan, place on rack and pull paper down from sides. When completely cooled replace paper and wrap in plio-film or cellophane. Overwrap with aluminum foil, molding it to the cake. Store in tightly covered container in cool place.

FRUIT CAKE GLAZE

1 cup sugar	2 teaspoons lemon juice
¼ teaspoon cream of tartar	½ cup water
¼ teaspoon salt	(some red coloring may be used if desired)

Stir all ingredients together. Cook to 300° F. (about 8 minutes) Brush on top of Fruit Cakes before or after decorating.

ANGEL FRUIT CAKE

Drain eight slices of canned pineapple from the juice, cut into pieces, and put into a syrup made by boiling two cups of sugar in one cup of water five minutes; let cook slowly to 219° F.; drain, and spread on a wire rack to cool overnight. Cut a portion into small pieces, slice thin and measure one-half cup. Slice candied orange peel and candied citron into very small, thin pieces, and measure one-half cup, making one cup of fruits altogether; rub with two tablespoonfuls of flour, to separate the pieces, so that they will not stick together, and shake in a wire strainer to sift off all excess flour.

Sift together one and one-fourth cup sugar, one and one-fourth cup flour, one-fourth teaspoon salt, one teaspoon nutmeg, one-sixteenth teaspoon allspice, one sixteenth teaspoon cloves, one-sixteenth teaspoon cinnamon and one teaspoon baking powder. Beat one and three-fourths cup egg-whites until frothy, add one teaspoon cream of tartar, beat until barely stiff, fold in the sifted dry ingredients, and finally the prepared fruits. Bake at 350° F. about thirty-five minutes. Invert on a wire cake cooler and let cool in the pan; loosen the cake with a spatula, turn out of the pan, and cover with the following frosting:

Mix together two and one-half cups sugar, one-fourth teaspoon salt, one teaspoon white corn syrup and three-fourths cup milk; cook to 234° F. (soft ball stage), cool to lukewarm temperature, beat until creamy, knead thoroughly, melt over hot water until soft enough to pour on the cake. Decorate with candied pineapple, cherries and citron.

APPLESAUCE RAISIN SPICE CAKE

½ cup shortening	1½ teaspoons ground cinnamon
1 cup sugar	1 teaspoon ground allspice
⅓ cup seedless raisins	1 teaspoon ground nutmeg
1 egg	¼ teaspoon ground cloves
1 cup unsweetened applesauce	½ teaspoon salt
1¾ cups sifted flour	1 teaspoon baking soda
	½ cup broken walnut meats

Cream shortening until fluffy. Add sugar gradually and continue creaming. Stir in raisins. Beat egg until light and lemon-colored; add and mix well. Add applesauce. Sift together the sifted and measured flour, the spices, salt and baking soda; add and mix well. Stir in walnuts. Pour into two greased and floured 8-inch layer cake pans. Bake in moderate oven (350° F.) 35 to 45 minutes until cake springs back when touched lightly. Put layers together with this very quick and easy cream cheese frosting.

DREAMY CREAM CHEESE FROSTING

1 package (3 ounces) cream
    cheese
1 tablespoon lemon juice

½ teaspoon lemon extract
1 egg white, slightly beaten
1½ to 2 cups confectioners' sugar

Blend softened cream cheese with lemon juice, lemon extract and egg white. Add sugar gradually, blending well, until of spreading consistency (size of egg determines amount of sugar). Chopped raisins or walnuts or both may be added. Makes filling and frosting for an 8-inch, two-layer cake.

BRAZIL NUT FUDGE CAKE

2 squares (2 oz.) unsweetened
    chocolate
1 cup boiling water, divided
1 cup sugar
2 tablespoons salad oil
1 egg

1½ cups sifted flour
1 teaspoon baking soda
1 teaspoon baking powder
½ teaspoon salt
1 teaspoon vanilla
1 cup shaved Brazil nuts

Melt chocolate over hot water. Add ½ cup boiling water; stir until custard-like in consistency. Remove from heat. Add sugar and salad oil; mix well. Beat egg; add. Mix and sift dry ingredients; stir in. Add vanilla. Add remaining boiling water, and fold in shaved Brazil nuts. Bake in greased 8″ square cake pan (350° F.) 45 to 50 minutes. Cool on cake rack. Split into two layers. Fill and frost.

MOCHA FROSTING

Cream ⅓ cup butter or margarine; add 1½ cups confectioners' sugar (10X) while continuing to cream. Melt 1½ squares (1½ oz.) unsweetened chocolate over hot water; add. Add 1½ cups confectioners' sugar and enough strong cold coffee to make frosting fluffy and easy to spread. Makes enough to fill and frost 8″ layer cake.

BUTTERSCOTCH LOAF

2 cups flour	1 egg
1 teaspoon baking powder	1 cup brown sugar
¾ teaspoon soda	2 tablespoons melted butter
½ teaspoon salt	1 cup sour milk
	¾ cup dates, chopped

Sift together the flour, baking powder, soda and salt. Beat the egg and to it add the brown sugar and melted butter. Add the dry ingredients to the egg mixture alternately with the milk; stir in the dates. Pour into a buttered loaf pan and bake. Temperature 350° F. Time: 50 minutes.

CHOCOLATE COCONUT CAKE

Preparation: Have shortening at room temperature. Cut circles of waxed paper to fit bottoms of two 9-inch layer pans. Grease paper and sides of pans. Set oven for moderate, 350° F. Sift flour once, then measure into sifter 2 cups cake flour, 1 teaspoon baking powder, ¾ teaspoon salt, 1 teaspoon soda, ½ cup cocoa, 1½ cups sugar. Measure into mixing bowl ½ cup vegetable shortening. Measure into cup ½ cup water, 1 teaspoon vanilla. Have ready 3 eggs and ¾ cup sour milk or buttermilk.

Mixing: Stir shortening just to soften. Sift in dry ingredients, add water with vanilla, and eggs. Mix (by hand or at low speed of electric mixer) until all the flour is dampened, then beat 1 minute. Add sour milk or buttermilk, blend, beat 2 minutes. Count only the actual beating time, or allow 150 full strokes per minute. Scrape both bowl and beater often.

Baking: Turn batter into pans, bake 30 minutes, or until done. (Toothpick inserted near center comes out clean and top of layer springs back when touched leaving no imprint.) Turn layers out on rack to cool. Cover with 7-minute frosting, sprinkle with coconut.

CHOCOLATE-FLAKE COCONUT CAKE

2 cups sifted all-purpose flour
2½ teaspoons double-acting
   baking powder
½ cup shortening
½ teaspoon salt
1 teaspoon almond extract
1 cup granulated sugar

2 egg yolks, unbeaten
1 cup less 2 tbsp. milk
1 cup chilled semi-sweet
   chocolate pieces, finely
   chopped
2 egg whites
1 cup flaked coconut
1 cup heavy cream, whipped

1. Early in the day make, cool, refrigerate Creamy Custard Filling, recipe below.

2. Start heating oven to 350° F. Grease and flour two 8″ layer-cake pans. Sift flour with baking powder three times.

3. In large electric-mixer bowl, with mixer at medium speed, mix shortening, salt, and almond extract until light and fluffy. Gradually add sugar, beating well. Add egg yolks; blend well.

4. With mixer at low speed, add flour mixture alternately with milk, beating after each addition just until well blended. Then stir in chocolate.

5. Now beat egg whites till stiff; then gently fold into batter. Turn batter into prepared pans; sprinkle each pan of batter with ½ cup coconut. Bake 35 minutes or till cakes spring back when lightly touched with finger. Cool 5 minutes in pans; then turn out of pans, and finish cooling.

6. On cake plate, arrange layers with bottoms together and Creamy Custard Filling between. Generously frost side of cake with whipped cream. Refrigerate till served.

CREAMY CUSTARD FILLING

In top of double boiler, mix ⅓ cup granulated sugar, 2 tablespoons flour, and ⅛ teaspoon salt. Slightly beat 1 egg; gradually add ⅔ cup scalded milk; then slowly stir into sugar mixture. Cook over boiling water 8 minutes, stirring constantly. Cool, stirring occasionally; add ¼ teaspoon almond and ¼ teaspoon vanilla extracts; fold in ⅓ cup heavy cream, whipped. Refrigerate till needed.

For three-layer cake, make Creamy Custard Filling, doubling all ingredients, but using only 1 egg, then a second set of cake layers as in steps 2 through 5. Increase heavy cream for whipping to 1½ cups. (Fourth cake layer may be split and filled with whipped cream for dessert next day, or it may be frozen.)

CINNAMON-RAISIN CAKE

½ cup lard	1 tablespoon cinnamon
1¾ cups sifted cake flour	1 teaspoon vanilla
⅞ cup sugar	½ cup milk
2 teaspoons baking powder	2 eggs
½ teaspoon salt	½ cup raisins

Line two 8-inch cake pans with waxed paper. Cream together lard and ½ cup flour. Reserve ¼ cup flour for raisins. Add remaining flour, sugar, baking powder, salt, cinnamon, vanilla and ⅓ cup milk. Beat until smooth and fluffy. Add remaining milk. Beat again until thoroughly combined. Add eggs, one at a time, beating well after each addition. Combine remaining flour and raisins and stir into batter. Pour into cake pans and bake in a moderate oven (375° F.) for 20 to 25 minutes. Cool and frost with Butter Cream Frosting.

BUTTER CREAM FROSTING

¼ cup butter or margarine	1 teaspoon vanilla
3 cups sifted confectioners' sugar	3 tablespoons milk
Dash of salt	

Cream butter or margarine and add confectioners' sugar and salt. Mix well. Add vanilla and milk and beat until fluffy.

COCONUT MARSHMALLOW LAYER CAKE

Cream ½ cup butter; add 1 cup sugar, a little at a time, beating until light; add beaten yolks of 2 eggs, 1 teaspoon lemon juice and 1 teaspoon vanilla extract. Add 2 cups pastry flour, sifted with ¼ teaspoon salt and 3 teaspoons baking powder, alternately with ⅔ cup milk. Fold in stiffly beaten whites of 2 eggs. Bake in 3 greased 8-inch layer cake pans in moderate oven at 400° F. about 20 minutes. Put together with Coconut Marshmallow Filling and Frosting.

DOUBLE CHOCOLATE DELIGHT

Sift together 2 cups sifted all-purpose flour and 1 teaspoon salt. Set aside.

Add 1¾ cups sugar gradually to ½ cup shortening, creaming well. Blend in 2 unbeaten eggs; beat well. Combine ½ cup cocoa and 1 cup hot coffee; stir to dissolve cocoa. Add to creamed mixture. Add the dry ingredients gradually; blend thoroughly. Dissolve 1 teaspoon soda in ½ cup boiling water. Add to batter, mixing thoroughly. Pour into two 8- or 9-inch round layer pans, well greased and lightly floured on the bottoms. Bake in moderate oven (375°) 30 to 35 minutes. Cool and frost.

CHOCOLATE FROSTING

Melt ¼ cup butter or margarine and 4 squares (4 oz.) unsweetened chocolate over boiling water. Combine 3 cups sifted confectioners' sugar, ⅛ teaspoon salt and ⅓ cup hot milk; beat until smooth. Blend in the hot chocolate mixture; beat until of spreading consistency. Stir in 1 teaspoon vanilla. If necessary, thin with a few drops of milk. Makes two 8- or 9-inch round layers.

DREAM CAKE

1½ cups apricot whole fruit
    nectar
½ cup sugar
⅛ teaspoon salt
6 egg yolks
1 envelope (1 tablespoon)
    plain gelatin

¼ cup cold water
1 cup whipping cream
¼ cup chopped maraschino
    cherries
½ cup coconut flakes
½ cup slivered blanched almonds
    angel food cake (page 206)

Heat nectar with sugar and salt. Beat egg yolks well. Stir a little of hot nectar into yolks, then stir yolk mixture into nectar. Place over boiling water, and cook, stirring constantly, until mixture coats spoon (about 10 to 15 minutes). Soften gelatin in cold water, and dissolve in hot nectar. Cool until mixture begins to thicken. Whip cream until stiff and fold into gelatin. Fold in well-drained cherries, coconut and about ⅔ of the almonds. Chill a few minutes longer until almost set. Meanwhile cut cake crosswise into 3 layers and put together with a thick layer of apricot cream between layers and on top. Decorate top with a circlet of slivered almonds and additional coconut and halved cherries. Serves 12 generously.

NEW ORLEANS BLACK CHOCOLATE CAKE

1¼ cups sifted all-purpose flour
1 teaspoon salt
⅓ cup margarine
1 cup sugar

2 egg yolks
2 squares chocolate, melted and
    cooled
1 cup sour milk
1 teaspoon baking soda

Sift together flour and salt. Cream margarine until soft and fluffy. Gradually add sugar, beating until light. Beat in egg yolks. Blend in melted chocolate. Add flour mixture alternately with sour milk, to which the soda is added. Beat well after each addition. Pour into greased eight-inch-square cake pan. Bake in moderate oven (350° F.) for about 35 minutes. Ice with caramel icing or seven-minute frosting.

NO-BAKE FRUITCAKE

Combine ½ cup softened butter or margarine and ½ cup strained honey; add ½ teaspoon cinnamon, ⅛ teaspoon nutmeg and ¾ teaspoon salt; mix well. Add 1 cup seedless raisins, ¾ cup each finely chopped dried apricots, figs and dates; 3-ounce can (½ cup) each of ready-to-use candied orange peel, lemon peel, citron, pineapple and candied cherries; ¾ cup finely chopped walnuts, 1 teaspoon grated lemon rind, 1 tablespoon lemon juice, 4 tablespoons orange juice or sherry. Mix all together will. Add 2 cups finely rolled graham or soda crackers or crisp rice cereal and mix thoroughly until well blended. Line loaf pan (approximately 9 x 5 inches) with waxed paper or aluminum foil and press the fruitcake mixture firmly into it. Cover with waxed paper or foil and let ripen for several days in refrigerator before serving; or it can be kept for weeks. Makes a 3-pound cake.

ORANGE PICNIC CAKES

1⅓ cups cake flour	1 egg
2 teaspoons baking powder	¼ cup butter, melted
½ teaspoon salt	¼ cup evaporated milk
¾ cup sugar	¼ cup orange juice
	1 teaspoon grated orange rind

Sift into a bowl the flour, baking powder, salt and sugar. Mix the egg, unbeaten, with the butter, milk and orange juice and rind; stir lightly into the dry ingredients. Beat until the batter is smooth; place in paper baking cups in muffin tins and bake. Temperature: 375° F. Time: about 20 minutes.

HACIENDA BLACK WALNUT CAKE

2½ cups sifted cake flour	1 cup milk
2½ teaspoons baking powder	1 teaspoon vanilla extract
½ teaspoon salt	1 cup black walnuts, finely
½ cup lard	chopped
1½ cups sugar	4 egg whites

Line bottom of two 9-inch layer cake pans with waxed paper. Sift flour, baking powder and salt together. Cream lard and sugar. Add sifted dry ingredients alternately with milk. Beat 2 minutes. Add vanilla and finely chopped nuts. Beat egg whites until stiff but not dry. Fold into batter. Pour batter into cake pans. Bake in moderate oven (350° F.) for 30 minutes. Cool and cover with Hacienda Icing.

HACIENDA ICING

2 egg whites	⅛ teaspoon black walnut extract
1 tablespoon lemon juice	4 cups sifted confectioners' sugar

Beat egg whites until stiff but not dry. Add lemon juice, black walnut extract and confectioners' sugar. Beat until smooth.

(From "The Hacienda Hotel"—Las Vegas, Nevada)

PARTY PETITS FOURS

Prepare batter for a 10-inch tube angel cake. Pour batter into ungreased by 9 by 13-inch pan. Bake in moderate oven (350°) for 25 to 30 minutes. Remove from oven and invert. Do not remove cake from pan until it is cold. With serrated knife cut cake into 2-inch diamonds or bars; using two forks, pull out ball-shaped pieces. Frost small cakes with Fluffy Frosting or Glossy Chocolate Frosting.

FLUFFY FROSTING

¾ cup sugar	2 egg whites, beaten to soft peak
Dash of salt	stage
⅛ teaspoon cream of tartar	½ teaspoon vanilla
¼ cup water	

Combine sugar, salt, cream of tartar, and water in heavy saucepan. Stir over low heat until sugar dissolves. Cover until syrup boils to dissolve sugar crystals on sides of pan. Uncover and cook without stirring, to 260° (a small amount of syrup forms a hard ball when dropped in cold water). Add syrup gradually to egg whites, beating constantly until mixture holds its shape. Blend in vanilla. To frost, hold cake shapes with a fork and spread with frosting. Sprinkle with coconut. Makes enough to frost 16 to 20 Petits Fours.

GLOSSY CHOCOLATE

⅓ cup powdered sugar
⅓ cup butter

2 tablespoons water
2 tablespoons cocoa
2 cups sifted powdered sugar

Combine first four ingredients in small, heavy saucepan. Stirring constantly, simmer about 1 minute. Remove from heat. Stir in 2 cups powdered sugar. Beat until smooth. Spread evenly over angel cake diamonds or bars. Top each with an almond. Makes enough to frost 20 Petits Fours.

PENNSYLVANIA DUTCH APPLE BREAD

1 cup milk
¼ cup sugar
2 teaspoons salt
¼ cup shortening
¼ cup warm water
1 package or cake yeast, active
   dry or compressed

1 egg
½ teaspoon cinnamon
2½ cups sifted flour
6 medium apples
2 tablespoons melted butter
   or margarine
3 tablespoons sugar
1 teaspoon nutmeg

Scald milk. Stir in sugar; salt and shortening. Cool to lukewarm. Measure water into a large mixing bowl (warm, not hot, water for active dry yeast; lukewarm water for compressed yeast). Sprinkle or crumble in yeast. Stir until dissolved. Stir in lukewarm milk mixture. Beat in egg. Stir in cinnamon and flour to make a soft dough. Turn out on a lightly floured board and knead until smooth and elastic. Place dough in an oiled bowl. Cover and let rise until doubled in bulk. Punch down; knead a few moments and divide dough in half. Pat into 2 oiled 8-inch layer pans. Peel and core apples. Slice in very thin slices. Arrange in rows on top of dough. Brush with butter and sprinkle with combined sugar and nutmeg. Let rise 15 minutes. Bake in a moderate oven (350° F.) 45 minutes to 1 hour. Makes two 8-inch apple cakes.

PENNSYLVANIA DUTCH MYSTERY CAKE

1¼ cups sifted cake flour
1 teaspoon double-acting
baking powder
½ teaspoon salt
¾ cup sugar
¼ cup shortening
½ cup milk
1 teaspoon vanilla
1 egg

1 9-inch unbaked pie shell
¼ cup butter or margarine
½ cup firmly packed brown
sugar
2 tablespoons light corn syrup
3 tablespoons water
¾ cup drained canned crushed
pineapple
3 tablespoons chopped nuts

Sift together flour, baking powder, salt and sugar. Place shortening in a mixing bowl. Sift in flour mixture. Add milk and vanilla and mix until all flour is dampened. Then beat 2 minutes with low speed of an electric mixer, or beat 300 strokes by hand. Scrape bowl and spoon or beater often. Add egg and beat 1 minute, or 150 strokes. Pour batter into pie shell. Combine butter, brown sugar and corn syrup in a saucepan. Place over low heat. Cook and stir constantly until mixture comes to a boil. Add water and bring again to a boil. Boil 1 to 2 minutes. Remove from heat. Stir in pineapple. Cool to lukewarm and pour gently over cake batter. Sprinkle with chopped nuts. Bake in a moderate oven (350° F.) 50 to 55 minutes or until done. Cake is best when served warm. Makes one 9-inch cake.

Cut in pie-shaped wedges. Serve with whipped cream.

POPPY SEED CAKE

½ cup poppy seeds
1 cup milk
2½ cups sifted enriched flour
2½ teaspoons baking powder

½ teaspoon salt
⅔ cup lard
1¼ cups sugar
4 egg whites
1 teaspoon vanilla

Add poppy seeds to milk and soak in refrigerator overnight. Line two 9-inch layer cake pans with waxed paper. Sift together flour, baking powder and salt. Cream lard, gradually add ¾ cup sugar and continue creaming until light and fluffy. Add sifted dry ingredients alternately with poppy seed mixture. Beat egg whites until frothy. Add remaining ½ cup sugar gradually to egg whites, beating until stiff. Fold beaten egg white-sugar mixture into batter. Add vanilla. Pour into cake pans and bake in a moderate oven (350° F.) for 25 to 30 minutes. Cool, spread Custard Filling between layers and Chocolate Frosting, page 214, on top and sides.

CUSTARD FILLING

6 tablespoons flour
1 cup sugar
¼ teaspoon salt

4 egg yolks, beaten
2 cups milk
½ teaspoon vanilla
⅔ cup chopped pecans, if desired

Mix together flour, sugar and salt. Stir in eggs and milk. Cook, stirring constantly, until thickened. Add vanilla, cool. Stir in nuts.

PRALINE CRUNCH CAKE

Sift together into mixing bowl 2 cups sifted all-purpose flour, 1¼ cups sugar, 2 teaspoons double-acting baking powder, 1 teaspoon salt and 2 teaspoons instant coffee.

Add ¾ cup milk, ½ cup shortening, 2 tablespoons molasses. Beat for 1½ minutes. (With electric mixer, blend at lowest speed, then beat at a low speed. By hand, beat 225 strokes with a spoon.) Add ¼ cup milk, 2 unbeaten eggs, 1 teaspoon vanilla. Beat for 1½ minutes.

Turn into 13x9x2″ or 12x8x2″ pan, well greased and lightly floured on the bottom only.

Bake in moderate oven (350°) 35 to 45 minutes. Cool and frost with Butter Cream Frosting. Top with Praline Crunch.

BUTTER CREAM FROSTING

Blend together 2 tablespoons butter and 1½ cups sifted confectioners' sugar. Combine 2 tablespoons cream and 1 teaspoon instant coffee. Add to sugar-butter mixture, a few drops at a time, until of spreading consistency. Add ½ teaspoon vanilla.

PRALINE CRUNCH

Cut 2 tablespoons butter into ¼ cup all-purpose flour and 2 tablespoons brown sugar to make a crumb mixture. Add ¼ cup chopped pecans. Place in a small pan. Bake at 350° for 15 minutes. Cool; break into small pieces.

REGAL CHOCOLATE CAKE

4 cups sifted cake flour	2½ cups sugar
1½ teaspoons soda	4 squares (4 ounces) chocolate
1 teaspoon baking powder	1½ cups boiling water
1 teaspoon salt	4 eggs
1 cup lard	2 teaspoons vanilla
	⅔ cup sour milk

Line bottom of three 9-inch cake pans with waxed paper. Sift together flour, soda, baking powder and salt. Cream lard and sugar well. Melt chocolate in boiling water. Cook, stirring constantly, until thick. Cool and add to creamed mixture. Add eggs and vanilla. Beat. Add sifted dry ingredients alternately with sour milk. Pour batter into cake pans. Bake in a moderate oven (350° F.) for 30 to 35 minutes. Cool. Frost with Princess Icing. Melt 1 package (4 ounces) of chocolate chips or 4 squares (4 ounces) of chocolate over hot water. Pour over and around top edge of cake.

PRINCESS ICING

2 cups sugar	4 egg whites
⅔ cup water	1 teaspoon vanilla
½ teaspoon cream of tartar	3 or 4 drops peppermint extract

Boil water, sugar and cream of tartar slowly in a covered saucepan for 3 minutes. Remove cover, insert candy thermometer and continue boiling slowly until syrup reaches 242° F. or spins a 6 to 8-inch thread. Beat egg whites until stiff enough to form peaks. Pour hot syrup very slowly in a thin stream into egg whites, beating constantly. Add vanilla and beat until frosting holds its shape.

WHITE FRUIT CAKE

1½ cups pineapple chunks
1 cup cubed citron
1 cup halved candied cherries
1 cup each cut-up candied
   lemon and orange rind
1 cup golden seedless raisins

1½ cups slivered blanched
   almonds
4 cups sifted all-purpose flour
2 teaspoons each baking
   powder, salt
¾ cup shortening
¼ cup butter or margarine
2 cups sugar

Prepare baking pan; makes a 5½ lb. cake in spring form pan with tube center, or 10-inch angel food cake pan.

Combine fruits and almonds with sifted dry ingredients.

Cream together shortening, butter or margarine and sugar until fluffy.

Stir in combined fruit, nut meats and sifted dry ingredients alternately with milk to make a stiff batter.

Fold in stiffly beaten whites. Spoon batter into pan.

Bake in slow oven (300° F.) about 2½ hours or until top is firm to light touch.

FILLED PRUNE SPICE CAKE

2¼ cups cake flour
3 teaspoons baking powder
½ teaspoon salt
1¼ teaspoon cinnamon
¼ teaspoon nutmeg
¼ teaspoon cloves

½ cup shortening
1 cup light corn sirup
2 eggs, unbeaten
½ cup milk
1 cup whipping cream
4 large cooked prunes

Sift together flour, baking powder, salt, cinnamon, nutmeg and cloves. Cream shortening, add corn sirup; add ½ cup of the flour mixture and beat well. Add eggs, one at a time, beating well after each. Add remaining flour alternately with milk, beating well after each addition. Place in 2 well-buttered, 8-inch layer pans and bake in moderate oven, 375°F. for 30 minutes (or more). Cool and spread Prune Filling between layers; cover top with whipped cream, flavored with vanilla. Garnish with 8 half prunes.

PRUNE FILLING

3½ tablespoons cornstarch
1 cup prune juice
¼ teaspoon salt

2 tablespoons light corn sirup
1 cup cooked prunes, chopped
2 teaspoons lemon juice
¾ teaspoon lemon rind

Place cornstarch in top of double boiler. Add prune juice gradually and salt. Cook over direct heat until thickened. Add corn sirup and prunes; cook over hot water 12 minutes. Cool, add lemon juice and rind.

FLORIDA LIME CAKE

Preparation: Let eggs stand at room temperature an hour or two before using. Use ungreased 9-inch tube pan. Start oven for moderate heat (375°F.) Sift flour once before measuing. Sift sugar also. (All measurements are level.)

1 cup plus 2 tablespoons sifted
    cake flour
5 eggs yolks, unbeaten
2 tablespoons water
1 cup sifted granulated sugar

1 tablespoon lime juice
1 teaspoon grated lime rind
5 egg whites
¼ teaspoon salt
¼ teaspoon cream of tartar

Sift flour once, measure, and sift 4 times more.

Place egg yolks and water in deep 1-quart mixing bowl and beat with rotary egg beater until very thick and light (about 4 minutes). Add ½ cup of the sugar gradually, beating constantly with rotary beater (about 1 minute). Add lime juice and rind and beat 1 minute longer.

Add flour all at once and fold in with spoon until just blended. Use 50 complete fold-over strokes.

Beat egg whites, and salt with flat wire whisk or rotary egg beater until egg whites are still enough to hold up in soft peaks, but are still moist and glossy. Add cream of tartar.

Add remaining ½ cup sugar in 4 additions by sprinkling 2 tablespoons at a time over egg whites and beating 25 strokes or turns each time. Fold in egg-yolk mixture, using 25 fold-over strokes.

Turn batter into pan. Bake in moderate oven (375° F.) 30 to 35 minutes.

Remove cake from oven, invert pan on cake rack, and let stand 1 hour or until cake is cool. To remove cake, loosen from sides of pan with spatula and around tube with slender knife, gently drawing cake from pan at the same time.

Decorate top of cake by sifting confectioners' sugar through lace paper doily. Cut cake in wedges and serve with chilled Lime Cream Sauce.

LIME CREAM SAUCE

5 tablespoons cake flour	¾ cup water
¾ cups sugar	2 teaspoons butter
Dash of salt	2 egg whites, stiffly beaten
2 slightly beaten egg yolks	¼ cup sugar
¼ cup lime juice	½ teaspoon grated lime rind

FRENCH PASTRY CHOCOLATE CAKE

STEP 1

½ cup cocoa   ¾ cup boiling water
Dissolve cocoa in water and
    cool.

STEP 2

1 cup sour cream   ½ teaspoon baking soda
Dissolve baking soda in cream

STEP 3

½ cup butter   2 cups sugar
Cream sugar and butter.

STEP 4

2 cups cake flour (measured after
    flour has been sifted twice)

STEP 5

3 egg whites beaten stiff   1 teaspoon vanilla

Combine ingredients of steps 1 and 2. Alternately add flour and
cocoa mixture to creamed butter and sugar. Beat together in electric
mixer or with a rotary beater until fluffy. Fold in egg whites and
vanilla. Pour into 10 x 14″ pan. Bake at 350° for 30 minutes.

CHOCOLATE TOPPING

½ cup butter
¼ teaspoon salt
5 teaspoons cream

1 teaspoonful vanilla
3 squares chocolate
3 cups powdered sugar, sifted
1 egg white, beaten

Heat butter and chocolate over hot water until melted. Stir until
smooth. Take off stove. Add salt, sugar and cream, beating until
smooth. Stir in beaten egg white and flavoring. Beat until cool enough
to spread.

GEORGIA FRUIT CAKE

½ pound butter
1 cup sugar
5 eggs
2½ cups cake flour
½ cup crushed pineapple
1 tablespoon vanilla extract
¾ pound candied pineapple,
    cut in pieces

¾ pound candied cherries, cut
    in pieces
1 pound white raisins
½ pound pecans, chopped
½ pound Brazil nuts, chopped
¼ pound black walnuts,
    chopped
¼ pound English walnuts,
    chopped

Cream butter until light. Add sugar gradually and cream well. Add
eggs one at a time, beating hard after each addition. Gradually add

the cake flour and mix well. Stir in the crushed pineapple and vanilla. Add the fruit and nuts and mix well.

Bake in two fruit cake and loaf pans (10¼ x 3⅝ x 2⅝) which have been greased and lined with waxed paper. Place a pan of water in the oven below the fruit cakes while they are baking. Yield: two 3-lb. fruit cakes.

GOLDEN REFRIGERATOR PARTY CAKE

4 teaspoons plain gelatin
1 (12-ounce) can apricot whole fruit nectar
½ cup sugar

2 eggs
1 tablespoon lemon juice
¼ teaspoon salt
1 cup whipping cream
2 dozen small ladyfingers

Soften gelatin in ¼ cup nectar. Heat remaining nectar with ¼ cup sugar. Separate eggs and beat yolks lightly. Stir a little of hot nectar into yolks, then combine with remaining hot nectar. Place over hot water, and cook and stir until mixture coats spoon. Add softened gelatin, and stir until it is dissolved. Remove from heat and stir in lemon juice. Cool until mixture thickens slightly. Beat egg whites with salt until stiff, and gradually beat in remaining ¼ cup sugar. With same beater whip cream until stiff. Fold egg whites and cream into gelatin mixture. Line 2-quart mold with split ladyfingers. Fill mold with layers of gelatin mixture and remaining ladyfingers. Chill several hours or overnight. Unmold to serve. Makes 8 servings.

GOLDEN SPICE LOAF

¾ cup dark or golden raisins
⅓ cup shortening
¾ cup brown sugar (packed)
1 egg
1½ cups sifted all-purpose flour
1 teaspoon baking powder

½ teaspoon soda
¾ teaspoon salt
1 teaspoon cinnamon
½ teaspoon cloves
¼ teaspoon nutmeg
½ cup buttermilk or sour milk

Rinse and drain raisins. Cream shortening and sugar together thoroughly. Add egg and beat well. Sift together flour, baking powder, soda, salt and spices. Blend into creamed mixture alternately with buttermilk. Stir in raisins. Turn into greased pan 8-inches square. Bake in moderate oven (350° F.) about 50 minutes. Cool in pan. Frost if desired. Makes 1 (8-inch) square cake.

GYPSY SPICE CAKE

3 cups sifted cake flour	1 cup lard
1 teaspoon baking powder	2 cups sugar
¾ teaspoon salt	5 eggs
1¼ teaspoons nutmeg	1½ teaspoons vanilla extract
1½ teaspoons cinnamon	½ teaspoon lemon extract
3 tablespoons cocoa	1 cup buttermilk
	¾ teaspoon baking soda

Line bottom of three 9-inch layer cake pans with waxed paper. Sift flour, baking powder, salt, nutmeg, cinnamon and cocoa together. Cream lard and sugar, add eggs, vanilla and lemon extract. Beat. Add dry ingredients alternately with buttermilk to which soda has been added. Bake in moderate (350° F.) oven for 35 to 40 minutes. Cool and cover with Gypsy Spice Frosting.

GYPSY SPICE FROSTING

¾ cup butter	3 tablespoons cocoa
2 egg yolks	2 teaspoons cinnamon
6 cups sifted confectioners' sugar	2 tablespoons hot strong coffee

Cream butter and add egg yolks. Beat. Add confectioners' sugar, cocoa and cinnamon alternately with coffee. Beat until smooth.

OLD HOMESTEAD CAKE

2½ cups sifted cake flour	1½ cups sugar
2½ teaspoons baking powder	3 eggs
1 teaspoon salt	1 teaspoon vanilla
¾ cup lard	¾ cup milk
	1 cup Spanish peanuts ground

Line bottom of two 9-inch layer cake pans with waxed paper. Sift together flour, baking powder and salt. Cream lard with sugar until light and fluffy. Add eggs and beat. Add vanilla. Add sifted dry ingredients alternately with milk. Add ground peanuts. Pour batter into cake pans. Bake in a moderate oven (375° F.) for 25 minutes. Cool. Frost with Peanut Butter Frosting.

PEANUT BUTTER FROSTING

1 egg white	6 tablespoons cream
5 cups sifted confectioners' sugar	1 teaspoon vanilla
	½ cup peanut butter

Beat egg white until stiff but not dry. Add confectioners' sugar and cream alternately. Beat well. Add vanilla. Add peanut butter and beat smooth.

HONEY POUND CAKE

1⅔ cups cake flour	½ cup honey
1 teaspoon baking powder	½ cup sugar
1 cup butter	6 egg yolks
	4 egg whites

Reserve one-half a cup of flour and mix with the baking powder. Sift flour three times. Cream butter well. Add honey and beat until fluffy (three minutes). Add sugar and beat until fluffy (three minutes). Beat yolks until lemon-colored, add to mixture and blend well (three minutes). Beat whites until stiff but not dry. Add them alternately with the flour and stir until the batter is smooth. Then add the half-cup of flour containing the baking powder. Pour into a well-greased loaf pan, lining the bottom with waxed paper. Bake at 325° F. for one hour and ten minutes.

JUBILEE CAKE

2 pounds dried prunes, cooked	1 cup sugar
½ cup prune liquid	2 eggs
1 cup sugar	1 teaspoon vanilla extract
½ teaspoon cardamon seeds	4 cups sifted all-purpose flour
1 teaspoon vanilla extract	2 teaspoons baking powder
¼ teaspoon salt	¼ teaspoon salt
1 cup butter	¼ cup milk

Best to make up prune filling first. Wash prunes. (If you use bulk or untenderized ones, soak fruit for 2 hours. With packaged tenderized prunes, soaking is not necessary.) Cover fruit with water and cook slowly for about 45 minutes or until tender when tested with a fork. Drain prunes, saving the liquid. Cool, remove pits, put prunes through a food grinder or cut them into fine pieces with scissors.

Now add prune liquid, sugar and cardamon seeds, split in half, to prunes and cook until filling is about as thick as jam. Cool, add vanilla extract (many Icelanders use wine, rum or whiskey) and salt. Set aside until all cake layers are baked.

Now comes the cake-making time. Work or cream butter until soft. Add sugar gradually and continue mixing until very creamy. Beat eggs slightly, then stir eggs and vanilla extract into creamed sugar. Sift flour, baking powder, salt together. Add alternately with milk to butter mixture. The dough should be firm but not stiff. We suggest you chill dough in the refrigerator so it will handle more easily.

Start your oven at 350° F. or moderate.

When dough has chilled enough to be manageable, divide into 7 equal portions. Roll out each portion very thin on a lightly floured bread board to fit an 8" cake pan. Turn cake pan upside down, place dough on ungreased top of pan and trim the edges tidily. Bake 20 minutes or until edges turn a delicate brown. Remove from oven and slide cake off bottom of pan with the help of a spatula and cool on a wire rack until all 7 layers are baked. Of course, bake as many layers at a time as you have 8" cake pans and oven space. The baked layers should not be more than ¼" in thickness and will be very hard.

When all 7 layers of dough have been rolled and baked and cooled, spread a generous amount of prune filling between the layers and pat with the palm of your hand to make the many thin layers of cake blend with the fruity filling.

Wrap our handsome holiday cake rather tightly in a dry cloth so moisture from the filling mellows the cake, then let it stand at least overnight before cutting. Better yet, let it age several days.

MAHALA'S GINGER POUNDCAKE

1 cup butter or margarine	1 teaspoon baking powder
1 cup sugar	1 teaspoon baking soda
1 cup light corn syrup	1 teaspoon grated nutmeg
3⅓ cups sifted cake flour	1½ tablespoons ginger
¾ teaspoon salt	½ cup light cream
	4 eggs

Work butter or margarine until creamy, then gradually work in the sugar. Add syrup and beat thoroughly.

Sift dry ingredients together 3 times, then beat in alternately with cream, to butter-sugar mixture.

Separate eggs and beat yolks until thick as mayonnaise, stir into batter. Finally, beat egg whites until they stand in peaks and mix or fold gently into cake.

Pour into a greased, paper-lined 10″ tube cake pan and bake 1 hour or until a toothpick comes out dry when tested in center of cake.

Equally good served plain or with lemon-flavored confectioner's sugar icing.

Start your oven at 325° F. or slow.

MILK CHOCOLATE QUEEN'S CAKE

Melt 1 bar (¼ lb.) sweet chocolate or 3 squares (3 oz.) semi-sweet chocolate in 2 tablespoons water in top of double boiler over hot water.

Sift together 2¼ cups sifted all-purpose flour and 1 teaspoon salt. Cream ½ cup butter or margarine. Add gradually 1¼ cups sugar, creaming well. Add 3 unbeaten eggs, one at a time, beating well after each. Stir in 1 teaspoon vanilla and the melted chocolate; mix well. Dissolve 1 teaspoon soda in 1 cup buttermilk or sour milk. Or combine 1 cup sweet milk and 2 tablespoons vinegar; let stand 5 minutes. Add alternately with the dry ingredients to creamed mixture, beginning and ending with dry ingredients. Blend thoroughly after each addition. (With electric mixer use a low speed..)

Turn into two 8-inch round layer pans, well greased and lightly floured on the bottoms. Bake in moderate oven (350°) 40 to 45 minutes. Cool and frost.

Mocha Frosting

Cream ⅓ cup butter or margarine. Stir in ¼ cup cocoa, 1 teaspoon instant coffee, 1 teaspoon vanilla and ¼ teaspoon salt. Blend in 1 pound (4 to 4½ cups) sifted confectioners' sugar and 7 to 8 tablespoons hot milk until of spreading consistency. If necessary, thin with a few drops more milk.

COOKIES

Along toward the end of Indian summer Belle Anderson Ebner begins to look moodily out the window for the first flock of south bound ducks. She knows the first snow flake cannot be far behind. And even if the snow arrives in September, as it has on rare occasions, Mrs. Ebner knows that Christmas is on the way.

There is a kind of secret signal between Mrs. Ebner and the elements. It means the glazed fruits are placed in special old-fashioned hand-turned wooden bowls to soak up the fine bonded bourbons, the imported rums, the delicate, light sweet sherries. The wooden bowls were originally part of Grandma Anderson's dowry. They belonged to her Grandmother, and they seemed to have a very special magic. There was never fruit cake like hers until Belle Ebner found the recipe and faithfully followed it down to the last Brazil nut.

Imagine, if you can, a fruit cake created from jumbo pecan halves from Mississippi's choicest groves, almonds from Barcelona, whole Brazil nuts, plump whole red and green cherries and pineapple glazed to an incredible richness blended together with an old-fashioned butter batter and laced with the finest bonded bourbon obtainable. Aged in liquor-soaked casks to be brought triumphantly to your Christmas table with a flourish! So wonderfully flavored it can be served as a steamed Holiday Pudding with brandied hard sauce. And the final secret? Put together with care and love!

And the cookies. Mrs. Ebner is an artist extraordinary. She collects cookie recipes as feverishly and relentlessly as some women collect diamonds! It's one of the reasons the world still beats a path to Hotel Anderson's doors—the vast trays of exquisite cookies, the little crystal dishes of holiday conserves, the wonderful varied breads and rolls . . . the little unexpected, beautifully executed touches that make even a simple meal a gourmet's delight!

In this chapter you will find some of Belle's marvelous and favorite cookie recipes, how we wish we could have included them all!

Cookies Are for Christmas and Children!

This was the most difficult chapter of the book to prepare. We have, literally, tons of cookie recipes. Hard ones, soft ones, old-fashioned ones, new ones, frosted ones, drop cookies, sheet cookies, pan cookies, filled cookies, foreign ones, native ones, simple ones, complicated ones . . . more cookie recipes than we know what to do with.

Which ones to include? That was the problem. It took us months to decide. We did the cookie chapter over and over again. In 1955 it was complete. In 1956 it had eight more recipes; in 1957 we had to delete, and the day before the book went to the Publishers we were still in an uproar of indecision.

Here, then, is the chapter. We think, we hope, it is the best cookie chapter in captivity. We hope you'll find a cookie for every occasion or an occasion for every cookie. We hope you'll find cookies for every member of your family, and we hope there are recipes here that even a very small child can bake.

We think cookies are for children and Christmas in that order. We start baking Christmas cookies early in December, and if there is a wanderer on the road unfortunate enough not to be at his own home and hearth on Christmas Eve—if he finds himself at Grandma Andersons' Hotel Anderson and Dutch Kitchens—he also finds a stocking full of Christmas cookies on his door when he awakens. Or some of Grandma Anderson's Pennsylvania Dutch Black Fruit Cake!

You can almost eat your way around the world in this cookie chapter. They are from all corners of the world, from all countries and we hope we have saved the very best for you.

Try them all at some time or other. And if you don't keep a cookie jar you'll want to, after you read this chapter. We believe in cookie jars as an important piece of Americana and we hope that you do too!

BLACK WALNUT WONDERS

1 cup sugar	2 cups flour
½ cup melted butter	1 teaspoonful soda
2 eggs	3 tablespoonfuls cocoa
½ cup milk (or more)	1 cup black walnuts, chopped
	1 cup raisins

Sift together flour, soda, cocoa. Cream sugar in melted butter, beat in eggs one at a time. Add sifted dry ingredients alternately with milk. Add chopped black walnuts, raisins. Drop from spoon (teaspoon or dessert spoon) on buttered baking sheet and cook for thirty minutes in moderate oven (350° F.). Ice each cookie with the following butter icing:

2½ cups confectioners' sugar	2 tablespoons butter
2½ tablespoonfuls cocoa	5 tablespoons cream
	1 teaspoonful vanilla

Mix sugar and cocoa. Cream butter, add sugar and cocoa gradually, creaming well and moistening with cream to achieve the correct consistency to spread. Add flavoring. If mixture becomes too thin, thicken by addition of a little more sugar. Yield: 4 to 4½ dozen cookies.

CARNIVAL COOKIES

1 cup lard	½ teaspoon soda
1½ cups brown sugar	2 eggs
3 cups enriched flour, sifted	2 teaspoons vanilla
½ teaspoon salt	2 cups Spanish peanuts
	Sugar

Cream lard and brown sugar. Sift flour, salt and soda together. Add eggs, vanilla and sifted dry ingredients. Stir in peanuts. Shape into balls about the size of a walnut. Place about 2 inches apart on ungreased cookie sheet. Flatten with a water glass wrapped in a damp towel. Sprinkle with granulated sugar. Bake in a moderate oven (350° F.) 12 to 15 minutes. Yield: 5½ dozen.

CELEBRATION COOKIES

¾ cup dark or golden raisins	1 teaspoon vanilla
1 cup butter or margarine	2 or 3 drops almond extract
½ cup sugar	2 cups sifted all-purpose flour
1 egg yolk	½ teaspoon salt

Rinse and drain raisins. Cream butter and sugar together. Add egg yolk and flavorings and blend well. Sift flour with salt, and blend into creamed mixture. Stir in raisins. Drop by small teaspoonfuls onto greased baking sheet. Bake in hot oven (400° F.) 10 to 12 minutes. Allow to cool 2 or 3 minutes. With broad spatula remove carefully to wire rack to cool. Makes about 4 dozen cookies.

BUTTER CHEWS

BUTTERSCOTCH CRUST

⅓ cup butter

½ cup brown sugar, packed
1 cup sifted all-purpose flour

Cream butter and brown sugar, mixing until light and fluffy. Stir in flour. Mix until blended. Pat in bottom of 8″ square oiled cake pan. Bake at 375° F. for 15 minutes. While Butterscotch Crust is baking prepare Crunch Topping.

CRUNCH TOPPING

1 egg
⅔ cup brown sugar, packed
1 teaspoon vanilla
⅔ chopped walnuts

½ cup shredded coconut
2 tablespoons sifted all-purpose
flour
Dash salt

Beat egg and add brown sugar, mixing until smooth. Add vanilla. Combine walnuts, coconut, flour and salt. Add to brown sugar mixture, mixing until well blended.

Spread on top of Butterscotch Crust. Continue baking 15 minutes longer. Makes 16 2-inch squares.

CHOCOLATE-FUDGE COOKIES

3½ cups sifted flour
2 teaspoons baking powder
¼ teaspoon baking soda
½ teaspoon salt
1 teaspoon mace

1 cup butter or other shortening
2 cups sugar
4 egg yolks
2 ounces unsweetened chocolate,
melted and cooled
¼ cup milk

Mix and sift flour, baking powder, soda, salt and mace. Cream butter or other shortening well, add sugar gradually and continue creaming until light and fluffy; add well-beaten egg yolks and chocolate and mix well. Add sifted dry ingredients alternately with milk, mixing just enough after each addition to combine ingredients. Roll thin on floured pastry cover and cut with a floured 2-inch round cooky cutter. Bake on baking sheets in a preheated oven. Cool. Frost half of cookies with Rum Frosting; cover with remaining cookies. Store in covered container.

RUM FROSTING

3 tablespoons melted butter	2 tablespoons cream
3 cups sifted confectioners' sugar	3 tablespoons plus 1 teaspoon rum

Mix all ingredients. Approximate Yield: 8 dozen double cookies. Temperature: 400° F. Time: about 7 minutes.

"DUTCH BREAD CRUMB COOKIES"

1½ cups flour	1 cup sugar
1 teaspoon soda	1 egg
¼ teaspoon salt	1 teaspoon vanilla
¼ teaspoon nutmeg	1¼ cups dry bread crumbs
¼ teaspoon cinnamon	½ cup boiling water
½ cup shortening	¾ cup chopped nut meats
	1 cup seedless raisins

Sift the flour, soda, salt, nutmeg and cinnamon together. Cream the shortening and add sugar; cream thoroughly. Add egg and flavoring and beat well; then add the bread crumbs and the boiling water alternately with the flour mixture. Stir in the nut meats and raisins last. Drop from tablespoon onto a greased baking sheet and bake. Temperature: 400° F. Time: 15 minutes.

BROWNIES

½ cup butter or margarine
1 cup sugar
2 eggs
2 squares chocolate, melted

½ teaspoon vanilla
⅞ cup flour (1 minus 2 tablespoons)
½ cup chopped nuts

ICING

½ square chocolate, melted
1 teaspoon butter, melted

½ cup confectioners' sugar
1 tablespoon water
¼ teaspoon vanilla

Cream butter until soft; gradually beat in sugar, then eggs, chocolate and vanilla; stir in flour and nuts; turn into greased, shallow 9-inch pan and bake in a moderate (350° F.) oven for 25 minutes. Combine remaining ingredients and mix until smooth and thick enough to spread. Ice brownies when cool and cut into 1½-inch squares before removing from pan. Yield: 3 dozen small.

CHRISTMAS SHEERS

1 pound shelled almonds
4 1-oz. squares unsweetened chocolate
2 cups and 2 tablespoons sugar

1 teaspoon cinnamon
¼ teaspoon cloves
¼ teaspoon salt
3 eggs

Grind the almonds and the unsweetened chocolate fine through your food chopper.

Mix thoroughly with remaining ingredients. Sprinkle bread board with mixture of half flour, half sugar and pat on small pieces of dough about ¼″ thick. Cut into stars, crescents, circles (any shape your heart desires), transfer to greased baking sheet and let stand in a cool place overnight.

Next day start your oven at 325° F. or slow and bake cookies 15 minutes. Cool slightly before removing from pan. Makes 3 dozen.

When cold, glaze sparingly with the following: Mix ¾ cup confectioners' sugar with 2 tablespoons milk and ¼ teaspoon almond extract.

CHOCOLATE INDIANS (DATE BROWNIES)

⅓ cup butter or margarine,
    softened
1 cup sugar
3 eggs, well beaten
2 squares unsweetened chocolate,
    melted

1 teaspoon baking powder
½ teaspoon salt
¾ cups sifted flour
1 teaspoon vanilla
½ cup finely chopped dates

Cream the butter and sugar together and add eggs. Beat until well blended. Add melted chocolate and baking powder, salt and flour which have been sifted together. Add vanilla and chopped dates and when thoroughly mixed turn into a greased pan, 8 inches square. Bake in moderate oven (350°) 40 minutes, or until done. Cut into squares while still warm. Yield: 1½ to 2 dozen.

CHOCOLATE MINT STICKS

½ cup shortening
2 squares chocolate
2 eggs

1 cup sugar
½ teaspoon peppermint extract
½ cup sifted all-purpose flour
½ cup shredded almonds

Melt shortening and chocolate together. Cool. Beat eggs, add sugar and beat well. Add shortening, chocolate and peppermint extract and stir until thoroughly blended. Add flour and nuts. Mix well. Pour into oiled 8″ x 8″ pan and bake at 350° about 30 minutes. Cool. Frost with the following:

2 tablespoons butter
1 tablespoon cream

1 cup sifted confectioners' sugar
1 teaspoon peppermint extract

Cream butter until soft. Add cream, confections' sugar and extract. Beat well. Spread. Mint sticks may be cut into strips about ¾″ x 2″. Makes 40 pieces.

CHOCOLATE-SPICE SQUARES

1½ cups sifted flour
½ teaspoon baking soda
1½ teaspoons cinnamon
¾ teaspoons cloves
½ teaspoon nutmeg
¼ teaspoon salt
¼ cup butter
1¼ cups brown sugar, sifted and
    packed (7½ ounces)

2 eggs
2 ounces unsweetened chocolate,
    grated
1 tablespoon grated orange rind
¼ cup cut, candied citron
1 cup chopped nut meats
½ cup light molasses
⅓ cup orange juice
Chocolate Butter Frosting

Mix and sift flour, soda, spices and salt. Cream butter well, add sugar gradually and continue creaming until light and fluffy. Add well-beaten eggs, chocolate, orange rind, citron and nut meats and mix. Combine molasses and orange juice. Add sifted dry ingredients alternately with molasses mixture to butter mixture, mixing just enough after each addition to combine ingredients. Spread batter in a greased pan (8 x 12 inches). Bake in a preheated oven. Cool. Frost with Chocolate Butter Frosting. Cut into squares. Store in covered container.

CHOCOLATE BUTTER FROSTING

¼ cup butter
⅛ teaspoon salt
2 ounces unsweetened chocolate,
    melted and cooled

½ teaspoon vanilla extract
2 cups sifted confectioners' sugar
About 3 tablespoons milk

Cream butter well, add salt, chocolate and extract and mix. Add confectioners' sugar alternately with milk, beating well after each addition. Yield: 2 dozen. Temperature: 350° F. Time: about 40 minutes.

CHOCOLATE WALNUT SQUARES

½ cup butter or margarine   ½ cup sifted all-purpose flour
¼ cup white sugar   ½ cup rolled oats
¼ cup brown sugar, firmly packed   3 small plain chocolate bars
½ teaspoon vanilla extract   1 teaspoon butter
1 egg yolk   ½ cup chopped walnuts

Work butter or margarine until creamy, then gradually work in both kinds of sugar. Add vanilla extract and egg yolk. Then beat until light. Next, stir in the flour and rolled oats thoroughly.

Spread mixture in a greased 8″ x 8″ pan and bake 20 minutes at 350° F. or until nicely browned. Remove from the oven and let stand 10 minutes.

Meanwhile, melt chocolate and butter over hot water. When smooth, spread over cookies and sprinkle with nuts. Cut into squares while still warm. Makes about 18.

CHRISTMAS WREATH COOKIES

1¾ cups enriched all-purpose flour   ¾ teaspoon vanilla
1½ teaspoons baking powder   ¼ teaspoon almond flavoring
½ teaspoon salt   ¼ cup blanched almonds, finely
½ cup shortening   chopped
1 cup sugar   1 egg white
1 egg   Green crystalline sugar
    Red cinnamon candies

Sift flour; measure; add baking powder and salt; sift again. Cream shortening; add sugar gradually and continue beating until fluffy. Add egg, vanilla and almond flavoring; beat thoroughly. Add almonds; blend well. Stir in flour mixture; mix thoroughly and chill 3 hours. Divide dough in half; roll out ⅛-inch thick between sheets of waxed paper. Cut with a leaf-shaped cooky cutter or make a cardboard leaf pattern and cut around it with a sharp knife. Join leaves together in groups of 2 or 3 on an ungreased cooky sheet; brush surfaces with egg white slightly beaten. Sprinkle green sugar on top; place 3 or 4 cinnamon candies at the base of the leaves. Bake in moderate oven 375° for 8 to 10 minutes. Cool on cake rack. Makes approximately 3 dozen 3-inch leaves.

CRISP CHRISTMAS COOKIES

2 cups butter	1 egg yolk
1 cup sugar	4 cups sifted all-purpose flour
1 whole egg	1 tablespoon almond extract

Work butter until creamy, then gradually work in the sugar. Beat in egg and egg yolk and half of the flour. Add almond extract and remaining flour and beat very thoroughly.

Next, line a loaf pan with waxed paper, place cookie dough in pan, smooth it down into the shape of the pan and chill in the refrigerator overnight.

To bake, cut dough into paper-thin slices with a sharp knife, brush tops with the leftover egg white that has been beaten, then decorate with chopped almonds and sugar. Bake in a 350° F. oven 8 to 10 minutes or until golden. Makes 6 dozen.

CRUSTY TOP DATE BARS

1½ cups fresh dates	1 cup sugar
¼ cup margarine	1 cup sifted flour
⅔ cup peanut butter	¼ teaspoon salt
2 eggs	1 teaspoon baking powder
	½ cup chopped roasted peanuts

TOPPING

¼ cup sugar	2 tablespoons cream
	¼ teaspoon cinnamon

Pit dates and cut into small pieces. Cream margarine and peanut butter thoroughly. Beat eggs until light. Add sugar to peanut butter mixture, alternately with sifted flour, salt, and baking powder. Add dates and nuts and stir until blended. Pour into waxed paper lined pan, 10 by 10 inches. Smooth top with spatula. Blend topping ingredients and spread over dough. Bake about 30 minutes at 350° F. Cool and cut into strips. Yield: 30 bars.

DANISH COOKIES

½ cup milk
1 cake compressed yeast
3 tablespoons sugar

2 cups flour
½ teaspoon salt
3 egg yolks
1 cup butter, melted

FILLING

3 egg whites
¾ cup sugar

¾ cup nut meats, chopped
½ teaspoon vanilla

Heat the milk to lukewarm, crumble the yeast cake into it and add the sugar. Allow the yeast to soften about five minutes. Add one cup of the flour with the salt, add the egg yolks, the butter, and the remainder of the flour. If dough is too soft to handle, add a little more flour but not too much, as some flour will be worked in when the dough is being rolled out. Toss the dough onto a lightly floured board and roll about one-fourth an inch thick. Cut in triangles, put one teaspoon of filling on each and fold corners over one another to the center. Place on baking sheets and allow to rise for one hour. Bake in a hot oven.

GLAZED GINGER COOKIES

1 cup molasses
1 cup shortening, melted
1 cup hot water
1 cup sugar

1½ teaspoons soda
1 teaspoon ginger
1 teaspoon cinnamon
5 cups flour

Mix liquid ingredients. Sift dry ingredients together and add. Spread very thin (14 inch) on greased baking sheet and bake about 15 minutes at 375° F.

ICING

1 cup confectioners' sugar	½ teaspoon vanilla
¼ teaspoon salt	4 tablespoons cream

Mix ingredients until smooth. Spread icing while cookies are still warm. When frosting sets, cut in 2-inch squares. These cookies will keep well stored in air tight container. Yield: 5 dozen cookies.

GRANDMA GUENTHER'S PRIZE-WINNING CHERRY BALLS

Sift together 2 tablespoons cocoa and 1 cup of powdered sugar. Stir in ¼ cup bourbon that has been combined with 2 tablespoons light corn syrup. Add 2½ cups of crushed vanilla wafers and 1 cup of broken pecans and mix thoroughly. Roll the mixture around a cherry (you will need an 8-ounce bottle of maraschino cherries with stems), dredge with powdered sugar mixed with 1 teaspoon of cocoa. Place on dish with stem sides up.

HEDGEHOGS

2 cups shelled walnuts	2 cups shredded coconut
1 cup dates	1 cup brown sugar, firmly packed
	2 eggs, beaten

Grind walnuts and dates in food chopper. Mix in 1½ cups coconut and remaining ingredients thoroughly.

Scoop up a spoonful of the mixture and shape into a roll as thick as a frankfurter and half as long. Roll each Hedgehog in coconut, place on a greased baking sheet and bake 10 to 12 minutes. Makes 40. Start your oven at 350° F. or moderate.

MAGIC MOCHA CIRCLES

¾ cup butter or margarine

1 cup sugar

1 egg

2 cups sifted all-purpose flour

¾ cup cocoa

½ teaspoon salt

1 teaspoon baking powder

½ teaspoon baking soda

¼ cup cold, double-strength coffee

Chocolate rum wafers

Cream butter or margarine and add sugar. Cream until light and fluffy. Add unbeaten egg and beat thoroughly. Mix and sift flour, cocoa, salt, baking powder and baking soda. Add dry ingredients alternately with coffee to creamed mixture. Wrap dough in waxed paper and chill several hours. Roll out on floured board at least ⅛-inch thick. Cut in small circles with cooky cutter. Put 1 chocolate rum wafer between 2 cookies. Bake in moderate oven, 350° F., 8 minutes. Cool and frost, if desired, with tinted confectioners' sugar frosting. Makes about 2 dozen.

NEAPOLITAN REFRIGERATOR COOKIES

Spiced Dough

3 cups sifted flour

½ teaspoon cinnamon

½ teaspoon cloves

1 teaspoon baking soda

¼ teaspoon salt

1 cup chopped nut meats

1 cup butter

1½ cups brown sugar, sifted

  packed (9 ounces)

2 eggs

Mix and sift flour, spices, soda and salt; add nut meats and mix. Cream butter well, add sugar gradually and continue creaming until light and fluffy; add well-beaten eggs and mix. Add flour mixture gradually and mix. Pack ½ of dough in a pan (10 by 3½ by 2¾ inches). Chill in refrigerator until firm (about 2 hours).

RAISIN DOUGH

2 cups sifted flour
¼ teaspoon baking soda
½ teaspoon salt
½ cup butter
¾ cup sugar

¾ cup seedless raisins, ground
12 candied cherries, cut into thirds
1 egg
1 teaspoon vanilla extract
½ teaspoon almond extract
2 tablespoons water

Mix and sift flour, soda and salt. Cream butter well, add sugar gradually and continue creaming until light and fluffy. Add raisins and cherries and mix well; add well-beaten egg and mix. Add extracts to water. Add sifted dry ingredients alternately with flavored water to butter mixture, mixing just enough after each addition to combine ingredients. Cover spiced dough in pan with raisin dough, pack and chill until firm (about 2 hours). Press remaining spiced dough on top, cover and chill thoroughly. Remove dough carefully from pan, cut slices crosswise, ⅜ inch thick, then cut each slice crosswise into 3 parts. Bake in a preheated oven. Store in covered container. Approximate yield: 7 dozen. Temperature: 400° F. Time: about 9 minutes.

NUT-FUDGE BARS

¼ cup shortening
2 squares unsweetened chocolate
½ cup water
1 cup sugar
1 teaspoon vanilla
1 egg

1 cup enriched all-purpose flour
½ teaspoon salt
½ teaspoon baking powder
½ teaspoon baking soda
¼ cup sour milk or buttermilk
¼ cup chopped walnuts

Melt shortening and chocolate in saucepan over low heat; add water and sugar; stir until well blended; cool to room temperature; add vanilla and unbeaten egg, beat well. Sift flour, measure; add salt, baking powder and soda; sift again. Stir into chocolate mixture alternately with milk; beat vigorously about 1 minute until smooth. Pour into greased square pan (9 x 9 x 2 inches). Sprinkle nuts over top. Bake in moderate oven 350° for 30 to 35 minutes. Sprinkle with granulated sugar. Cool in pan. Cut into 18 bars.

NUT FINGERS

½ cup shortening
1 cup sugar
1 egg, unbeaten

2 cups flour, sifted
2 teaspoons baking powder
1 cup milk
1 teaspoon vanilla

Cream shortening, add sugar gradually, and cream until light and fluffy. Add egg and beat well. Sift flour and baking powder together. Add to creamed mixture alternately with milk. Add vanilla. Bake in 9 x 12 inch greased paper-lined cake pan at 350° for 30 minutes. Yield: 3 dozen.

FROSTING FOR NUT FINGERS

1 tablespoon shortening
2 cups confectioners' sugar
1 egg white, beaten until stiff

1 teaspoon vanilla
3 tablespoons boiling water
Chopped nuts

Cream shortening and add sugar gradually. When about one cup has been added, add beaten egg white. Add remaining sugar and vanilla. Add water to make a paste about consistency of thick buttermilk. Frost baked batter with this icing and sprinkle thickly with nut meats. Cut into strips about 1 inch wide and 3 inches long.

OLD-FASHIONED "BILLY GOATS"

¾ cup butter
1½ cups light brown sugar
3 eggs, beaten
1 cup nut meats, chopped
½ pound raisins or chopped
    dates

1 teaspoon vanilla
4 cups flour
¼ teaspoon salt
1 teaspoon cinnamon
1 teaspoon cloves
1 teaspoon soda
2 tablespoons buttermilk

Cream the butter and the sugar together and add the beaten eggs. Stir in the nut meats, the raisins or dates and the vanilla. Sift together the flour, salt, cinnamon and cloves, and add alternately with the soda dissolved in the buttermilk. Drop by spoonfuls on a buttered pan and bake about twenty minutes in a moderate oven.

ORANGE CRUMBLES

¼ cup shortening
½ cup sugar
1 egg
1 cup minus 2 tablespoons sifted flour
⅛ teaspoon baking soda

½ teaspoon baking powder
¼ teaspoon salt
¼ cup orange juice
⅓ cup orange juice
1 tablespoon grated orange peel
1 cup crushed cornflakes

Cream shortening and sugar together and beat in egg. Sift dry ingredients together and add alternately with ¼ cup orange juice. Spread in greased 8 x 12″ pan. Cook dates with ½ cup orange juice, stirring to prevent scorching, until they form a thick smooth paste. Cool slightly and add grated orange peel. Spread over dough and cover with cornflakes. Bake in 375° oven for 20 to 25 minutes or until slightly browned. Cool in pan and cut in squares. Yield: 24 2-inch square cookies.

PECAN KISSES

2 cups sifted flour
1 cup sugar
1 pound pecan nut meats; ground (4 cups)

1 cup soft butter
2 teaspoons rum
Confectioners' sugar

Mix and sift flour and sugar; add nut meats and mix. Add remaining ingredients and mix well. Using about 1 tablespoon for each, shape into balls. Bake on baking sheets in a preheated oven. Cool; sprinkle with confectioners' sugar. Store in airtight container. Approximate yield: 5⅓ dozen. Temperature: 300° F. Time: about 25 minutes.

PECAN SPICE BARS

3 egg yolks
1 cup dark brown sugar
⅔ cup sifted flour
1 teaspoon baking powder
⅛ teaspoon salt

1 teaspon cinnamon
½ teaspoon cloves
1 teaspoon vanilla
3 egg whites, beaten stiff
½ cup broken pecans

Beat egg yolks until thick and lemon colored. Add sugar and beat well. Sift flour with baking powder, salt and spices, and add to mixture. Stir well; fold in vanilla, stiffly beaten egg whites and nuts. Pour into greased, waxed paper lined square pan and bake for 25 minutes, in moderate oven, 350° F. Cool for 5 minutes, cut into thin bars and roll in spicy sugar (⅓ cup confectioners' sugar mixed with ¼ teaspoon cloves). Yield: 16 bars.

PRUNE SQUARES

1 cup whole dried prunes
3 eggs
1 cup sugar

1 cup flour
1 teaspoon baking powder
⅛ teaspoon salt
¾ cup chopped nuts

Wash the prunes and soak 3 to 4 hours. Drain and cut into fine pieces. Beat eggs; add sugar gradually. Add sifted dry ingredients; mix well. Stir in prunes and nuts and turn into a shallow greased pan. Bake at 350° F. for ½ hour. Cut in squares and ice or dust with confectioners' sugar. Yield: 12.

RAISIN SNAPS

⅔ cups golden raisins
⅔ cup sugar
¼ cup shortening
½ teaspoon baking soda
½ teaspoon salt

½ teaspoon cinnamon
1 teaspoon ginger
½ teaspoon vanilla
1 large egg
½ cup molasses
1½ cups sifted all-purpose flour

Rinse, dry and chop raisins. Cream next seven ingredients until fluffy. Beat in egg and molasses. Add raisins and flour, mix well. Drop from teaspoon onto ungreased baking sheets. Bake in moderately hot oven (375° F.) 12 to 15 minutes. Remove *immediately;* cool; store in a tightly-covered container. Makes about 3 dozen cookies.

RASPBERRY TEAS

½ cup butter	1 egg yolk
½ cup shortening	1 teaspoon vanilla
½ cup confectioners' sugar	2¼ cups flour
½ cup granulated sugar	½ cup finely chopped walnuts
⅛ teaspoon salt	Raspberry jam

Cream butter, shortening, sugars, and salt until light and fluffy. Add egg yolk and vanilla; mix well. Add flour and blend. Divide dough into two parts. Place half in refrigerator and chill for several hours. Divide other half into 48 pieces. Roll into balls in palms of hands. Roll in nuts. Then roll chilled dough ⅛-inch thick on a well floured pastry cloth. Cut out with 2-inch serrated cooky cutter. Place on ungreased cooky sheets. Add ¼ teaspoon jam to center of each flat cooky. Place balls on jam, and press gently. Make an indentation in center of each ball with a thimble. Place ¼ teaspoon jam in center of each ball. Bake in a moderate oven (350° F.) for about 15 minutes, or until delicately browned. Yield: 48 cookies.

SCOTCH TEAS

½ cup margarine	2 cups rolled oats
1 cup brown sugar	½ teaspoon salt
	1 teaspoon baking powder

Melt margarine and stir in sugar. When well blended add oatmeal, salt and baking powder, mixed together. Spread in greased 8-inch square pan. Bake in moderate (350° F.) oven for 30 minutes. Cool about 5 minutes and cut in squares. Remove from pan as soon as cookies are cool enough to hold together. Yield: 12 cookies.

SNOW CAPS

2 cups sugar
1 cup less 2 tablespoons milk
2 tablespoons butter or
   margarine

1 teaspoon almond extract
1 can moist coconut
Melted chopped semi-sweet
   chocolate

Cook sugar and milk together over a low heat, stirring constantly until sugar melts. Then continue cooking, without stirring, until a few drops of syrup tested in cold water form a soft ball that holds a shape (243° F. on candy thermometer.)

Remove from heat, add butter or margarine and almond flavoring. Cool until lukewarm, then beat hard until candy thickens and loses its shine. Add coconut and beat again until stiff enough to shape a peak.

Drop candy in irregular peaks from tip of teaspoon onto a buttered platter. When cool, dip base of peaks into melted chocolate, then let cool on a piece of waxed paper until chocolate hardens. Makes about 2 dozen little Snow Caps.

SOUR CREAM OATMEAL COOKIES

1¼ cups sifted flour
1 teaspoon baking powder
¼ teaspoon soda
¼ teaspoon salt
¼ teaspoon nutmeg
1 teaspoon cinnamon
¼ cup butter

1 cup firmly packed light
   brown sugar
1 egg
1 teaspoon vanilla
½ cup dairy sour cream
½ cup chopped raisins
½ cup chopped nuts
⅔ cup quick cooking oatmeal

Sift dry ingredients together. Cream butter and sugar, add egg and blend. Add vanilla. Add sifted dry ingredients alternately with sour cream. Lastly fold in raisins, nuts, and oatmeal. Drop by teaspoonfuls onto a greased cooky sheet and bake in a 425° oven for 8-10 minutes. Remove from cooky sheet and cool on cake racks. Yield: 4-5 dozen cookies.

UNBAKED BROWNIES

2 squares unsweetened chocolate
1 can (1⅓ cups) sweetened
   condensed milk

2 cups vanilla wafer crumbs
   (⅓ pound)
1 cup finely chopped walnuts

Melt chocolate in top of double boiler. Add sweetened condensed milk and stir over rapidly boiling water for 5 minutes until thick. Remove from heat. Add vanilla wafer crumbs and ½ cup nuts. Butter a shallow pan and sprinkle with ¼ cup nuts. Place chocolate mixture in pan and spread evenly, using a knife dipped in hot water. Sprinkle top with remaining nuts. Chill in refrigerator for six hours, or overnight. Yield: 16 or more.

ALMONDETTES

3 cups blanched almonds
3 cups confectioners' sugar
1 cup sifted all-purpose flour

2 eggs
Juice of 1 lemon
Grated rind of 1 lemon

Grind almonds fine through food chopper. Mix thoroughly with remaining ingredients. Then divide dough into 6 parts.

Now roll one portion of dough thin on a board that has been sprinkled with confectioners' sugar, spread with apricot or raspberry jam. Roll out second portion same size as the first and place over jam-covered dough. Cut in squares, strips or circles and let dry overnight on a tray. Repeat with remaining dough.

Next morning start your oven at 350° F. or moderate and bake cookis about 10 minutes. Cookies should be pale and soft. While they are still hot, cover with a glaze of ½ cup confectioners' sugar mixed smooth with 3 teaspoons cold water. Makes 2½ dozen very elegant confections.

PIES

PIE CRUST SUCCESS HINTS

1. Keep pastry cold if you want it flaky.

2. Handle and roll as little as possible, and as gently as a baby!

3. Roll lightly, using as little flour as possible. Roll from the center of the dough out and up, not back and forth. Let the rolling pin do the work.

4. If you can, use pastry cloths over the board and rolling pin. These hold the rolled pastry and lessen the amount of flour and rolling needed. Lift the crust occasionally during rolling to prevent sticking.

5. Try making unbaked pie shell the day before filling and baking. Pastry will be more crisp.

6. Fruit pies may be served hot or cold. They're juicier hot, but firmer and more easily cut when cold.

7. Soaking of lower crust of all filled pies can be cut down by baking pie in hot oven (450° F.) for 10 minutes and then lowering temperature to moderate (350° F.) for the remainder of the baking period.

8. In using lower crust for juicy pies pour over bottom crust one-half cup of corn flakes before pouring in filling.

9. Inserting small paper cone in top crust of pie will eliminate most running over.

10. Sealing edges of pie with clean cloth strips will guarantee to keep juice in.

ALMOND-FRUIT MERINGUE

This one's easy! You'll have dainty individual meringues you can fill a dozen different ways—with fruits, rich chocolate sauce, ice cream, or sherbet, to mention only a few.

Prepare the basic meringue for the Lime Meringuettes, (page 165) but change the shape and the flavor.

Substitute ½ cup brown sugar for ½ cup of the white sugar.

Omit the lime juice and rind and fold ¼ teaspoon of almond extract and ¼ cup slivered almonds into the stiffly beaten egg whites and sugar.

Drop heaping tablespoonfuls of the meringue onto a buttered baking sheet. Makes 12 to 14 plump meringues or 2 dozen dainty ones. Hollow out centers with back of spoon.

Bake in slow oven (275°) for 45 minutes, then turn off heat and let meringues cool in oven.

Fill with fresh fruit and top with ice cream, whipped cream, or sherbet.

APPLE CIDER PIE

2½ cups (1 can) sliced applies
⅔ cup light brown sugar
½ teaspoon cinnamon
½ teaspoon nutmeg
2 teaspoons grated orange rind

½ cup coarsely chopped blanched almonds
1 package lemon flavored gelatin
1½ cups hot apple juice
½ cup heavy cream
1 9" baked pastry shell

Dice apples; cook with sugar, cinnamon and nutmeg until apples look slightly transparent. Add grated orange rind. Cool; add almonds. Dissolve gelatin in hot apple juice; cool until slightly thickened. Fold in apple mixture. Pour into baked pastry shell and chill until firm. Whip cream, use as a garnish on the pie.

APPLE DATE PIE WITH CHEESE CRUST

Pastry
6 to 8 tart apples
6 dates, pitted

½ cup brown sugar
½ lemon
¼ teaspoon salt

2 tablespoons butter

Prepare favorite pastry recipe, using two tablespoons snappy cheese for two tablespoons of the shortening. Divide, roll out half for bottom crust and line a glass baking plate. Peel apples, remove core and blossom end and slice. Slice the dates. Arrange apples in plate, also dates. Add sugar, juice and rind of lemon and salt. Dot with butter. Roll out remaining crust and cover. Pierce and bake at 375° F. for 45 minutes.

APPLE STRUDEL PIE (for variation)

1 recipe double-crust pastry
½ cup grated bread crumbs
3 tablespoons melted butter
4 tablespoons sugar

½ cup raisins
6 finely cut, juicy apples
1 cup sugar
Cinnamon

Line 9-inch pie pan with pastry. Mix crumbs, butter and sugar together and spread in pie crust. Sprinkle raisins over crumb mixture, then add apples. Add sugar and dash of cinnamon. Place top crust and seal well. Bake in moderate over (350° F.) for one hour.

APRICOT NECTAR MERINGUE PIE

1 can Apricot Nectar
½ cup granulated sugar
¼ teaspoon salt
3 tablespoons cornstarch
2 tablespoons butter

2 tablespoons lemon juice
2 eggs
Baked pastry shell, 8-inch
4 tablespoons sugar for meringue (preferably powdered sugar)

Combine nectar, sugar, salt, cornstarch, butter and lemon juice in a saucepan and stir until well blended. Cook and stir until mixture boils and thickens. Remove from the fire, add beaten egg yolks and stir to blend. Return to fire and cook and stir about two minutes. Pour into baked pastry shell. Cover top with meringue made from egg whites and four tablespoons sugar. Bake about fifteen minutes in a moderate oven (350° F.) Serves 4 to 6.

APRICOT TANG PIE

1¼ cups graham cracker crumbs
⅓ cup melted margarine
1 No. 2½-can apricot halves
1½ teaspoon gelatin
¼ cup apricot juice

1 3-oz. pkg. Philadelphia
    Brand Cream Cheese
¼ cup sugar
1 6-oz. can evaporated milk,
    chilled icy cold
2 tablespoons lemon juice

Mix the crumbs and margarine; press into a 9-inch pie pan. Chill.
Drain the apricot halves and set aside 7 halves for garnish. Save the
juice. Cut the remaining halves into small pieces. Soften the gelatin
in the ¼ cup of apricot juice and dissolve over hot water.

Place the cream cheese in a bowl and cream it until soft and smooth.
Slowly blend the sugar into it. Add the dissolved gelatin.

Whip the chilled milk with a cold rotary beater until fluffy. Add
the lemon juice and whip until stiff. Add the cheese mixture slowly
and continue mixing until thoroughly blended. Fold in the cut-up
apricots. Pour into the chilled crust. Garnish the top with the 7 apricot
halves. Chill in the refrigerator until firm.

BANANA CREAM PIE

1 baked pie shell, 9 inch
⅓ cup sugar
½ cups sifted enriched flour
¼ teaspoon salt

3 cups milk
2 slighty beaten egg yolks
1½ teaspoons vanilla
1 tablespoon butter
2 ripe bananas cut in thin slices

Mix sugar, flour, and salt in top of double boiler; add milk gradually stirring until smooth. Cook over boiling water for about 15
minutes, stirring constantly. Mix small portion with egg yolks, return
to double boiler and cook 2 minutes longer. Remove from heat, add
vanilla, and butter; cool. Place sliced bananas in bottom of cooled shell,
add filling. Beat egg whites until stiff but not dry; gradually add 4
tablespoons sugar. Beat until stiff and glossy; spread over cream mixture, making sure to spread way to the edge to anchor meringue.

Bake in slow oven (325° F.) for 20 to 25 minutes or until meringue is delicately browned. 8 servings.

Note: Whipped cream and sliced bananas may also be used as a topping.

BANANA SPLIT PIE

1 cup flour	⅓ cup Homogenized Spry
½ teaspoon salt	3 to 4 tablespoons cold water

Sift together flour and salt. Cut in Spry until particles are the size of small peas. Sprinkle cold water over mixture, tossing lightly with fork until dough is moist enough to hold together. Form into ball.

Roll out on floured board to circle 1½ inches larger than inverted 8-inch tin. Fit loosely into pie pan. Fold edge to form standing rim; flute. Prick crust with fork. Bake in hot oven 450° F. 10 to 12 minutes. Cool.

BANANA FILLING:

½ cup butter	2 bananas
1½ cups sifted confectioner's sugar	1 tablespoon lemon juice
2 eggs	1 square (1 ounce) grated chocolate
1 teaspoon vanilla	¼ cup walnuts

Cream butter and confectioners' sugar. Add 2 eggs, one at a time, beating 3 minutes after each addition. Blend in 1 teaspoon of vanilla. Slice 2 bananas and sprinkle with lemon juice. Reserve 12 slices for garnish. Fold in 1 square of grated chocolate and bananas into sugar mixture.

Turn into cooled baked shell and garnish with ¼ cup chopped walnuts and banana slices. Chill 5 hours before serving, and serve the same day it is made.

POLLY'S BRAZIL NUT PIE

1 envelope unflavored gelatin
¼ cup cold water
3 eggs, separated
½ cup sugar
⅛ teaspoon salt

1½ cups scalded milk
2 teaspoons rum flavoring
½ teaspoon vanilla
¼ cup chopped maraschino cherries
1 10-inch Brazil nut pie crust

Soften gelatin in cold water. Beat egg yolks slightly in top of double boiler; add ¼ cup of the sugar and salt. Gradually stir in scalded milk. Cook, stirring constantly, over hot water until mixture coats a metal spoon. Add softened gelatin, rum flavoring and vanilla and stir until dissolved. Chill until the mixture is slightly thicker than the consistency of unbeaten egg white. Beat egg whites until stiff; gradually beat in remaining ¼ cup sugar. Fold custard into egg whites. Add cherries. Turn into 10-inch Brazil nut pie crust. Chill until firm. If desired, garnish with whipped cream, shaved Brazil nuts, shaved chocolate and pieces of maraschino cherries. Makes 1 ten-inch pie.

BRAZIL NUT PIE CRUST

1½ cups ground Brazil nuts   3 tablespoons sugar

Mix the Brazil nuts with sugar in a 10-inch pie plate. Press the mixture against the bottom and sides and rim of the pie plate. Use as is, or if a toasted flavor is desired bake in a moderately hot oven (400° F.) 8 minutes, or until lightly browned. Cool, and fill with filling.

CALIFORNIA WALNUT PIE

¼ cup butter or margarine
2 tablespoons flour
½ cup dark corn syrup
⅓ cup sherry

1 cup sugar
3 eggs, well beaten
1 cup coarsely broken walnuts
1 9-inch unbaked pie shell

Melt butter and stir in flour; add corn syrup, wine and sugar; cook, stirring constantly, until mixture boils. Gradually stir hot mixture into eggs; add walnuts. Pour into pie shell. Bake in a moderately hot oven (375° F.) about 45 minutes, or until firm. Serve warm or cold, topped with whipped cream to which 1 tablespoon of sherry has been added.

CHEESE PASTRY SHELL

1 cup flour
¼ teaspoon salt
⅓ cup lard

⅓ cup natural American cheese,
    grated
2 to 3 tablespoons cold water

Mix flour and salt, cut in lard, add cheese, mix evenly. Sprinkle a little water over dry ingredients, toss lightly with fork until whole mixture is uniformly dampened. Press into a ball. Roll out thin on a slightly-floured board. Fit loosely in a pie pan. Prick bottom and sides with a fork. Bake in a hot oven (450° F.) 9 to 10 minutes.

CHOCOLATE CHIP CUSTARD PIE

4 egg yolks, beaten
½ cup sugar
2 cups milk, scalded
1 tablespoon gelatin
¼ cup cold water
1 teaspoon vanilla

1 graham cracker crust
½ cup semi-sweet chocolate,
    chipped
¼ teaspoon cream of tartar
4 egg whites
½ cup sugar

Beat egg yolks and sugar, add milk, cook in double boiler until thick. Add gelatin softened in water, add vanilla. Cool. Pour into crust. Sprinkle with chocolate. Add cream of tartar to egg whites and beat stiffly. Add sugar. Continue beating until very stiff. Spread over chocolate. Chill 1 hour. Makes a 10-inch pie.

CHOCOLATE-CHIP WALNUT PIE

1 unbaked 9" pie shell, made
    from favorite pastry or
    piecrust mix
3 eggs
⅛ teaspoon salt
1 teaspoon vanilla extract
½ cup granulated sugar

1¼ cups white corn syrup
1 cup semisweet-chocolate
    pieces
⅔ cup walnut halves
Green Grapes or orange
    sections
½ cup heavy cream, whipped
    Walnut halves

Early in afternoon:

1. Make 9" pie shell with fluted, rolled, or other favorite edge. Set aside.

2. Start heating oven to 375° F.

3. In medium-size bowl, beat eggs slightly with fork; add salt, vanilla extract, sugar, corn syrup, beating just till well blended. Stir in ⅔ cup walnut halves and semisweet-chocolate pieces.

4. Pour mixture into unbaked pie shell, and bake 45 minutes or until top is evenly puffed up and starts to crack.

At dinnertime:

1. Cut warm pie into 6 to 8 wedges. Then, on large serving plate, arrange wedges in a circle, with green grapes or orange sections heaped in the center.

2. Top each wedge with whipped-cream dollop and walnut.

To do ahead:

1. This chocolate-chip pie freezes well. So if it's more convenient, make and cool it. Then all or part of it may be freezer-wrapped and frozen for later use.

2. To serve, unwrap pie; thaw at room temperature; or heat un-wrapped, unthawed pie at 350° F. about 15 minutes.

CHOCOLATE LAYER PIE

2 ounces sweet chocolate,
grated
9-inch pastry shell, baked
1½ cups milk
4 egg yolks, beaten
1 tablespoon gelatin

⅓ cup cold water
4 egg whites, well beaten
⅔ cup sugar
¼ teaspoon salt
1 teaspoon vanilla
⅛ teaspoon nutmeg
1 cup cream, whipped

Sprinkle half the chocolate over bottom of hot pastry shell. Scald milk in double boiler. Combine small amount of milk with egg yolks and return to double boiler; continue cooking until custard coats spoon. Add gelatin softened in water; chill. Combine egg whites, sugar, and salt. Fold into mixture; add flavorings. Pour filling into baked pastry shell. Place in refrigerator until set. Before serving spread with whipped cream and sprinkle with remaining chocolate. Makes 10-inch pie.

CHOCOLATE LIME SHERBET PIE

Chocolate Wafer Crust

1 quart Lime Sherbet
Semisweet chocolate, chopped

To make Chocolate Wafer Crust: Combine 1½ cups chocolate wafer crumbs (about 20 wafers) with ⅓ cup melted butter. Press firmly into a greased 9-inch pie pan. Chill thoroughly. Spread the lime sherbet in crumb crust. Top with chopped semisweet chocolate. Place in freezing compartment of refrigerator or home freezer and freeze until firm. Serves 6.

CHOCOLATE PEPPERMINT PIE

2 cups crushed chocolate
cookies

½ cup melted butter

CRUST

Blend crushed cookies with melted butter. Press on bottom and sides of 9-inch pie plate. Chill.

FILLING:

1 envelope unflavored gelatin
¼ cup cold water
3 egg whites
⅓ cup sugar

1 cup heavy cream, whipped
½ cup plus 2 tablespoons crushed peppermint-stick candy

Dissolve gelatin in cold water. Place over boiling water; stir until dissolved. Cool. Beat egg whites until stiff, but not dry; gradually beat in sugar. Fold in cooled dissolved gelatin. Stir in whipped cream and ½ cup of the crushed peppermint candy. Turn into chocolate crumb crust. Chill until firm. Before serving, sprinkle top with remaining 2 tablespoons peppermint candy.

CINNAMON-APPLE-MINCE PIE

Unbaked pastry shell, 9-inch
4 tablespoons flour
6 tablespoons sugar
⅛ teaspoon salt
1 tablespoon butter or margarine

5 tablespoons water
1 tablespoon red cinnamon candies
3 to 4 medium tart apples
2 cups moist mincemeat

Prepare pastry shell and make a fluted edge. Sprinkle 2 tablespoons of the flour over bottom of pastry shell. Combine remaining 2 tablespoons flour with sugar and salt in small bowl. Cut in butter or margarine to a granular consistency. Heat water in small saucepan to boiling; remove from heat; add cinnamon candies, stir until dissolved; set aside for topping. Pare, quarter and core apples, cut quarters into slices about ½-inch thick. Spread mincemeat evenly in pastry shell; cover with apple slices, overlapping the slices closely in 2 circles and covering mincemeat completely. Sprinkle sugar-flour mixture evenly over apples and spoon cinnamon sirup over all, moistening as much of sugar mixture as possible. Bake on lower rack in hot oven 425° for 15 minutes; then reduce heat to 375° and continue baking for 40 to 50 minutes. Makes 8 servings.

COCONUT CREAM PIE

½ cup sugar
5 tablespoons flour
⅛ teaspoon salt

1½ cups milk, scalded
3 egg yolks, well beaten
1 teaspoon vanilla
1 cup coconut, shredded

Combine first 3 ingredients, then add milk, cook over low fire until thickened. Add egg yolks, cook 2 minutes. Remove from fire, cool, add vanilla and coconut. Pour into baked pie shell. Cover with meringue.

MERINGUE

4 tablespoons sugar
2 egg whites, well beaten

⅛ teaspoon salt
½ teaspoon vanilla

Add sugar gradually to egg whites, beating constantly. Add salt and vanilla. Pile lightly on pie, bringing it over crust. Brown in a moderate oven (350° F.) 9 or 10 minutes. Makes a 9-inch pie.

COFFEE PECAN PIE

3 eggs, beaten
¾ cup unsulphured molasses
¾ cup white corn syrup
½ cup double-strength coffee
2 tablespoons melted butter

¼ teaspoon salt
1 teaspoon vanilla
1 cup chopped pecan meats
4 tablespoons all-purpose flour
1 8-inch unbaked pie shell

Preheat oven to 375° F. Combine eggs, molasses, corn syrup, coffee, melted butter, salt and vanilla. Mix thoroughly. Combine pecans and flour, add to liquid mixture and pour into unbaked pie shell. Bake 40 to 45 minutes in moderate oven, 375° F., or until firm. Cool before cutting. Garnish with whipped cream, if desired. Portions should be smaller than average. Makes 7 servings.

COTTAGE CHEESE APPLE PIE

1½ cups apples, sliced thin
¼ cup sugar
¼ teaspoon cinnamon
¼ teaspoon nutmeg
Pastry
½ cup sugar

⅛ teaspoon salt
2 eggs, slightly beaten
½ cup cream and ¾ cup milk,
   scalded together
1 teaspoon vanilla
1 cup cottage cheese

Combine apples, sugar, and spices. Pour into pastry lined pie tin. Bake in a hot oven (425° F.) 15 minutes. Meanwhile add sugar and salt to eggs, combine with hot milk and cream. Continue baking in a moderate oven (325° to 350° F.) 40 minutes, or until mixture sets and is a delicate brown. 9-inch pie.

CRANBERRY PIE

Cook together for ten minutes three cups of cranberries, one cup and one-half of sugar, and one cup of water; let the mixture cool, then pour into a deep pie plate lined with pastry. Cut the pastry rolled for the upper crust into bands three-fourths an inch wide and brush over the edge of the under crust with cold water; lay the bands over the filling parallel one to another, then lay bands across the pie, at right angles to these, lattice fashion. Cut the bands at the edge of the under paste and press them upon it. Bake in a hot oven until the crust is browned.

CRANBERRY WHIP PIE

1 baked pie shell, 9 inch
1 can cranberry sauce or jelly
   (1½ cups) or 1½ cups
   homemade sauce or jelly
1 tablespoon gelatin

¼ cup cold water
1 tablespoon lemon juice
1 teaspoon orange rind
3 egg whites
¼ cup sugar

Heat cranberries and beat until they are smooth and free from lumps.

Add 1 tablespoon gelatin which has been dissolved in ¼ cup cold water. Allow to stand until it begins to thicken.

Add lemon juice and orange rind.

Beat egg whites adding sugar gradually, beating until stiff but not dry.

Fold egg whites into cranberry mixture.

Note: Be sure pastry shell is thoroughly cold before putting cranberry mixture into it. Chill.

DATE CREAM PIE

½ cup sugar
¼ cup cornstarch
1 teaspoon salt
2 cups thick sour cream
2 eggs, slightly beaten

2 cups dates, quartered
¼ cup pecan meats, chopped
1 teaspoon lemon juice
9-inch baked pie shell
Whipped cream

Combine sugar, cornstarch, and salt. Add cream. Cook in double boiler, stirring constantly, until thickened. Add eggs, then dates and pecan meats, stir well, cool. Add lemon juice, pour into pie shell. Cool. Top with whipped cream. 9-inch pie.

DRIED APRICOT PIE

2½ cups Homemade Pastry Mix
   (See recipe page 269).

4 to 6 tablespoons water
Apricot Filling

Make Apricot Filling (see below). Add water to Homemade Pastry Mix, a small amount at a time, mixing quickly and evenly with a fork until dough just holds in a ball. Divide pastry almost in half, using smaller portion for top crust. Roll pastry to about ⅛-inch thickness. Invert a 9-inch pie plate or pan over pastry and cut around pie plate allowing a margin of about ¼-inch. Cut slits or design in top pastry to allow for escape of steam. Put top pastry aside. Roll remaining pastry about ⅛-inch thick and line a 9-inch pie plate or pan, allowing about ½-inch of crust to extend over edge. Pour Apricot

Filling into pastry lined pan. Place top pastry over filling, folding lower crust over edge of top crust. Crimp edges. Bake in a hot oven (400° F.) for 30 to 35 minutes.

APRICOT FILLING

12 ounces dried apricots	2 tablespoons cornstarch
3 cups water	¼ teaspoon salt
¾ cup sugar	1 tablespoon butter

Cover apricots with 3 cups water, bring to a boil, and simmer 25 minutes. Drain apricots and measure liquid to make 1 cup, adding water if necessary. Mix sugar, cornstarch and salt in saucepan. Add liquid. Mix well and boil, stirring constantly, 3 minutes or until thick and clear. Fold in apricots and butter. Cool.

DUTCH APPLE PIE

PASTRY

2½ cups flour	¾ cup shortening
½ teaspoon salt	⅓ cup (approx.) cold water

FILLING

2 cups tart apples sliced	2 tablespoons butter
½ cups sugar	1 tablespoon milk
	1 teaspoon light brown sugar

Sift flour and salt. Cut in shortening with finger tips or pastry blender, keeping out a small portion of shortening for rolling out the pastry. Add just enough water so pastry will form a ball by no means sticky. Roll out and line an 8-inch pie tin.

For Filling; sprinkle apples with sugar and dot well with butter. Add a little lemon juice if desired. Fill the pie, cover with pastry, brush with brown sugar dissolved in milk, and bake 40 to 50 minutes at 425°.

EGGNOG PIE IN GRAHAM CRACKER SHELL

1 cup rich milk	¼ cup cold water
¼ teaspoon nutmeg	½ cup coconut or nut meats
3 egg yolks	1 teaspoon vanilla
½ cup sugar	3 egg whites
⅛ teaspoon salt	1 graham cracker crust
1 tablespoon gelatin	½ cup cream, whipped
	Semisweet chocolate, grated

Heat milk in double boiler, add nutmeg. Beat egg yolks, sugar, and salt together, add to milk, stirring constantly. Cook until mixture coats the spoon. Soak gelatin in water, add to custard, cool. Add coconut and flavoring. Fold in well-beaten egg whites. Put in pie crust, chill. Top with whipped cream and chocolate. 9-inch pie.

FLAKY PIE CRUST

¾ cup shortening	¾ teaspoon salt
2¼ cups sifted all-purpose flour	3 to 5 tablespoons ice water

Sift flour and salt together. Cut in shortening with dough blender or 2 knives until particles are size of small peas; chill.

Sprinkle water, few drops at a time, over mixture, working it in lightly with a fork until all particles are moistened and in small lumps.

Pour onto piece of waxed paper; fold paper over. Press into firm ball.

Divide into halves; roll each half to ⅛ inch thickness.

Sufficient dough for a double crust 9-inch pie.

HOTEL ANDERSON'S FAMOUS KENTUCKY
FUDGE PIE

1 cup Pillsbury's flour	⅓ cup lard
½ teaspoon salt	2 or 3 tablespoons of cold water

METHOD

Sift together the flour and salt. Cut in lard. Sprinkle cold water over the mixture, tossing lightly with fork until dough is moist enough to hold together. Form into a ball. Roll out on floured cloth to eleven-inch circle. Fit loosely into 8 inch plate, fold edge to form rim. Flute and prick crust with fork. Bake in hot oven. Cool.

FILLING

½ cup butter
¾ cup sugar
2 squares chocolate, melted
    and cooled

1 teaspoon vanilla
2 eggs

Cream butter and gradually add the sugar. Cream well. Blend in chocolate, melted and cooled, and 1 teaspoon vanilla. Add 2 eggs, one at a time. Beat 5 minutes with electric mixer at medium speed, after each egg. Turn into cooled baked shell. Chill 4 hours. Topped with whipped cream and shaved nuts.

GLAZED APPLE PIE

CRUST

2 cups flour
1 teaspoon salt

⅔ cup vegetable shortening
⅓ cup margarine
5½ tablespoons cold water

Blend flour, salt, and shortenings and enough cold water to hold mixture together. Roll out pastry and line a 8-inch pie plate. Roll out top crust.

FILLING

6 to 7 cups sliced tart apples
1 cup granulated sugar
1 teaspoon cinnamon

⅓ orange juice
¼ cup confectioners' sugar
2 teaspoons water

Heap apples into crust shell. Blend granulated sugar, cinnamon and orange juice and pour over apples. Cover with top crust, sealing the edges. Bake in 425° oven for 15 minutes; then lower heat to 325° until apples are tender. When pie is cool, brush mixture of confectioners' sugar and water on top.

GRAHAM CRACKER CRUST

2 cups graham crackers, crushed   ½ cup butter, melted

Combine. Pack into pie pan to form crust. Set in refrigerator to chill. Put frozen mixture in crust and cover with sliced sweetened peaches or strawberries.

HOMEMADE PASTRY MIX

7 cups sifted enriched flour   1¾ cups lard for soft wheat
4 teaspoons salt   flour or 2 cups for hard
                                                    wheat flour

Combine flour and salt. Cut lard into flour mixture with a fork or pastry blender until crumbs are about the size of small peas. Store Homemade Pastry Mix in covered container in refrigerator until ready to use. This mixture will keep at least a month in refrigerator. Yield: 8 single pie crusts.

LEMON CHEESE PIE

1 cup sugar   Salt
¼ cup flour   Juice of 1 lemon
1 cup boiling water   Rind of 1 lemon, grated
2 egg yolks, beaten   2 egg whites
½ cup natural American cheese,   ¼ cup sugar
   grated

Mix sugar and flour together. Add to boiling water, stirring vigorously. Cook until thick. Add egg yolks, cook 2 minutes. Remove from fire. Add cheese, stir until melted. Add salt, lemon juice and rind. Pour into cheese pastry shell. Cover with meringue made by beating egg whites until stiff and adding sugar. Bake in a moderate oven (350° F.) 9 or 10 minutes, or until brown. 9-inch pie.

VENETIAN BEACH LIME PIE

Cool, Green, Hot Weather Dessert

1 baked pie shell—9 inch	3 egg yolks (use whites for
1½ cups sugar	meringue)
6 tablespoons cornstarch	3 tablespoons butter
1½ cups boiling water	¼ cup lime juice
	1 tablespoon lime (grated)

Mix sugar and cornstarch together in top of double boiler. Add boiling water gradually and cook over low heat until mixture thickens and boils. Place over boiling water and cook covered for 10 minutes longer. Pour a little of it over 3 slightly beaten egg yolks. Beat. Add to the mixture in double boiler. Cook and stir the custard for five minutes over boiling water. Remove from heat. Blend in lime juice, rind and butter. Cool custard. Pour in a cold pie shell. Beat egg whites until stiff but not dry; gradually add 6 tablespoons sugar. Beat until stiff and glossy, spread over lime mixture, making sure to spread to edge to anchor meringue. Bake in slow oven (325° F.) for 20 to 25 minutes or until meringue is delicately browned.

(From Venetian Beach Hotel, Venice, Florida)

NESSELRODE PIE

1 tablespoon plain gelatin	¼ each, rum and cherries
2 cups light cream	soaked in rum (optional)
¼ cup sugar plus 6 tablespoons	2 teaspoons lemon juice
4 eggs, separated	1 9-inch pie shell, baked
½ teaspoon salt	Bitter chocolate

Soak gelatin in ¼ cup cold water 5 minutes. Scald cream in double boiler, add ¼ cup sugar and egg yolks, slightly beaten. Cook until somewhat thickened. Remove from fire. Add gelatin and salt and chill until slightly thickened. Beat egg whites stiff, add 6 tablespoons of sugar, and fold into chilled custard. Add rum and lemon juice, and cherries. Pour into pie shell, chill until set. Shave 1 or 2 squares bitter chocolate over the top.

NEW ORLEANS ICE CREAM PIE

1 cup light brown sugar, firmly
    packed
2 tablespoons water
2 tablespoons butter

1 cup pecan halves
⅛ teaspoon cream of tartar
1 quart very firm vanilla ice
    cream
Butterscotch sauce, optional

First make your praline base. Combine brown sugar, water, butter, pecans, and cream of tartar in a saucepan. Heat slowly, stirring until sugar dissolves and mixture boils. Boil, stirring constantly, until mixture reaches 248 degrees, firm ball stage. Remove from heat and pour into waxed paper lined 9-inch pie pan. Cool. When firm, remove waxed paper from candy crust and return praline to pie pan. Pack the ice cream firmly into pan and serve, or wrap and store in freezer for future use. Cut into wedges to serve. Yield: 8 to 10 servings.

NUT CRUST FOR PIES

To any pastry recipe add ½ cup finely chopped pecans, or chopped lightly toasted blanched almonds for each 1 pound of flour in pastry recipe. Add to pastry mix before adding water. Mix in water, roll and bake as usual.

ORANGE PUMPKIN PIE

1 teaspoon ginger
1 teaspoon cinnamon
¼ cup boiling water
⅞ cup brown sugar
½ teaspoon salt

2 eggs
1¼ cups pumpkin
1 cup evaporated milk
    (scalded)
3 tablespoons orange juice

Make a smooth paste of the spices and water. Add with the sugar, salt, and beaten eggs to the pumpkin. Stir to blend thoroughly, then add hot milk. Add orange juice and pour immediately into an unbaked pie shell. Bake in a hot oven (425° F.) 15 minutes, then reduce to a slow oven (300° F.) and bake until filling is just set. 9-inch pie.

ORANGE VELVET CREAM PIE

1 envelope unflavored gelatin
1¼ cups orange juice
⅔ cup sugar
1 tablespoon flour
¼ teaspoon salt

1 tablespoon grated orange
  rind
2 tablespoons lime juice
1 cup heavy cream, whipped or
  ⅔ cup thoroughly chilled
  evaporated milk, whipped
1 9-inch baked pie shell

Soften gelatin in ¾ cup cold orange juice in saucepan. Blend sugar, flour, and salt; add to softened gelatin; mix thoroughly. Place over medium heat; stil constantly until gelatin is dissolved and mixture is thickened. Remove from heat; add orange rind and remaining ½ cup orange juice and lime juice. Chill until mixture is slightly thicker than the consistency of unbeaten egg whites. Fold into whipped cream or whipped evaporated milk. Turn into pastry shell and chill until firm. Yield: 1 9-inch pie.

PARADISE PIE

1 10-inch baked pie shell
2 cups milk
2 tablespoons flour
1 tablespoon cornstarch
⅓ cup sugar

⅛ teaspoon salt
2 egg yolks, slightly beaten
1 teaspoon vanilla
2 tablespoons butter
2 ripe bananas
1 package fruit flavored gelatin

Scald milk. Combine flour, cornstarch, sugar and salt in saucepan. Add small amount of scalded milk, mixing to a smooth paste. Gradually add remaining milk and cook, stirring constantly, until thickened, about 3 minutes. Stir a small amount of hot mixture into egg yolks, gradually add remaining hot mixture. Return filling to saucepan and continue cooking for 3 minutes. Remove from heat, add vanilla and butter. Cool and pour into baked pie shell.

Dissolve gelatin as directed on package. Chill until partially set. Peel and slice bananas and arrange over pie filling. Pour gelatin over bananas. Place in refrigerator and chill until firm.

Note: For a 9-inch pie use only 1 cup of gelatin.

PARTY PARFAIT PIE

1½ cups flour	1 package lemon flavored
¼ cup sugar	gelatin
1 teaspoon cinnamon	1½ cups boiling water
½ teaspoon salt	1 pint ice cream, vanilla
½ cup shortening	2 cups canned applesauce
¼ cup cold water, about	½ teaspoon grated lemon rind
	Blanched almonds

Use pastry mix or make your own as follows: Sift together flour, sugar, cinnamon and salt. Cut in shortening with two knives or pastry blender. Sprinkle cold water over mixture, tossing lightly with fork until dough is moist enough to hold together. Form into ball. Roll out in floured board. Fit into 9″ pie plate; make fluted edge. Prick bottom and sides of pastry with tines of fork. Bake in hot oven, 425° F., 15 minutes, or until brown.

Filling: Add gelatin to boiling water; stir until dissolved. Cut vanilla ice cream into fourths; add to hot gelatin mixture, stirring until ice cream has melted. Add all but ½ cup applesauce; mix well. Put filling in refrigerator until slightly set. Stir; pour into pie shell. Chill until set. To remaining ½ cup applesauce add grated lemon rind. Add few drops yellow coloring. Use as garnish on top of pie with almonds. Yield: 6 servings.

PASTRY FOR SINGLE OR DOUBLE PIE

To make single pie crust, use:

1¼ cups mix for 8-inch; 2 to 4 tablespoons water	1¼ to 1½ cups mix for 9-inch
	1½ to 1¾ cups mix for 10-inch

To make double pie crust, use:

2 to 2½ cups mix for 8-inch;   2¼ to 2½ cups mix for 9-inch
4 to 6 tablespoons water   2½ to 2¾ cups mix for 10-inch

Add water to mix, a small amount at a time, mixing quickly and evenly until dough just holds in a ball. Divide pastry if for double pie crust. Roll to about ⅛-inch thickness and line pie pan, allowing ½-inch crust to extend over edge.

For a double crust pie, roll other half of pastry, making several gashes to allow for escape of steam. Place over filling and cut ½-inch smaller than lower crust. Fold lower crust over top crust. Crimp edges. Bake according to pie recipe.

For baked pie shell, crimp edge of pastry. Prick pastry with a fork before baking. Bake in hot oven (450° F.) 8 to 10 minutes.

PEACH FLUFF FILLING

2 tablespoons sugar
3 tablespoons flour
¼ teaspoon salt
⅔ cup peach juice
16 diced marshmallows (¼ lb.)
1 egg
1 tablespoon gelatin

¼ cup cold water
1½ cups canned, sliced cling
   peaches
1 tablespoon lemon juice
1 teaspoon grated lemon rind
½ cup heavy cream

Combine sugar, flour, salt and juice in double boiler and heat over hot water. Add marshmallows; cook until thick (about 15 minutes.). Stir in beaten egg and cook 2-3 minutes. Add gelatin dissolved in water. Cool slightly, pour over drained peaches. Add lemon juice and rind. Whip cream; fold into cooked mixture. Fill pie shell. Chill. Top with peaches and extra whipped cream.

PHILADELPHIA DATE PIE

1 cup chopped dates
½ cup water
2 teaspoons grated orange rind
1 8-oz. Philadelphia Brand
   Cream Cheese

½ cup sugar
¼ teaspoon salt
2 eggs
½ cup milk
½ teaspoon vanilla
1 9-inch unbaked pastry shell

Cook the dates, water, and orange rind in a small saucepan two or three minutes, until thick. Cool.

Place the cream cheese in a bowl and cream it until soft and smooth. Slowly blend the sugar and salt into it. Add the eggs, one at a time, and mix well after each egg is added. Blend in the milk and vanilla. Fold in the date mixture and pour into the pastry shell. Bake in a hot oven, 400° F., for 10 minutes, then in a slow oven, 325°, for 30 minutes.

PINEAPPLE CHIFFON PIE IN PINEAPPLE COCONUT SHELL

1 envelope unflavored gelatin	4 tablespoons lemon juice
¾ cup sugar, divided	½ cup heavy cream, whipped
⅛ teaspoon salt	1 9-inch baked pineapple pie
4 eggs, separated	shell
1¼ cups pineapple juice	Strawberries

Mix together gelatin, ¼ cup of the sugar and salt in top of double boiler. Beat together egg yolks and pineapple juice; add to gelatin mixture. Place over boiling water and cook, stirring constantly, until mixture thickens slightly and gelatin dissolves, about 5 to 7 minutes. Remove from heat; add lemon juice. Chill until mixture mounds slightly when dropped from a spoon. Beat egg whites until stiff, but not dry. Gradually add remaining ½ cup sugar and beat until very stiff. Fold in gelatin mixture; fold in whipped cream. Turn into baked pineapple pastry shell. Chill in refrigerator until firm. To serve, garnish pie with additional whipped cream and garnish with sliced strawberries.

PINEAPPLE COCONUT PIE SHELL

½ cup less 1 tablespoon	1 teaspoon milk
homogenized shortening	1¼ cups sifted all-purpose flour
3 tablespoons canned	½ teaspoon salt
pineapple juice, heated	4 tablespoons chopped coconut

Put shortening in mixing bowl. Add *heated* pineapple juice and milk and whip with fork until all liquid is absorbed and a thick, smooth mixture is formed. Sift flour and salt onto shortening whip and stir into a dough. Pick up and work until smooth; shape into a flat round. Roll between 2 12-inch squares of waxed paper into a circle ⅛-inch thick. Peel off top paper, sprinkle 2 tablespoons chopped coconut over pastry, leaving a 1-inch border plain. Re-cover with paper and roll coconut into dough. Turn pastry over and repeat, rolling in remaining 2 tablespoons coconut. Peel off top paper; place pastry in 9-inch pie pan, pastry next to pan. Remove paper, fit pastry into pan, trim ½-inch beyond pan, turn back even with pan, flute rim. Prick shell all over with fork. Bake in a very hot oven (450° F.) 12-15 minutes.

PINEAPPLE PIE DELUXE

⅓ cup sugar
1 tablespoon cornstarch
1 cup crushed pineapple (not drained)
1 8-oz. pkg. Philadelphia Brand Cream Cheese

½ cup sugar
½ teaspoon salt
2 eggs
½ cup milk
½ teaspoon vanilla
1 9-inch unbaked pastry shell
¼ cup chopped pecans.

Blend the ⅓ cup of sugar with the cornstarch and add the pineapple. Cook, stirring constantly, until the mixture is thick and clear. Cool.

Place the cream cheese in a bowl and cream it until soft and smooth. Slowly blend the ½ cup sugar and salt into it. Add the eggs, one at a time, stirring well after each egg is added. Blend in the milk and vanilla.

Spread the cooled pineapple mixture over the bottom of the unbaked pastry shell. Pour in the cream cheese mixture and sprinkle with the chopped pecans. Bake in a hot oven, 400° F., for 10 minutes, then reduce the heat to a slow oven, 325°, and bake for an additional 50 minutes. Cool before serving.

PLUM PIE, COUNTRY STYLE

Wash and pit 2½ pounds well-ripened plums. If the plums are large, quarter them; if they are small, halve them. Place pieces in a saucepan with ⅔ cup cold water, 1½ cups granulated sugar and 1 teaspoon salt. Bring to boil, and cook slowly for 3 to 4 minutes. Then add 2 tablespoons plus 1 teaspoon cornstarch dissolved in 3 tablespoons cold water, and cook slowly, stirring constantly from the bottom of the pan, until the mixture is thick and clear. Remove it from the fire, stir in a generous ⅓ cup peeled, coarsely chopped walnuts, and allow the mixture to cool naturally. Line a nine-inch pie plate with the bottom crust, paint the crust with lightly beaten egg white, and chill thoroughly. After chilling, spread the bottom crust with 4 tablespoons orange marmalade, fill it with the cold plum filling, and adjust the top crust in the usual manner. Brush the top crust with beaten egg yolk diluted with equal parts cold milk, and bake the pie in a very hot oven (450-475° F.) for 25 to 30 minutes. Serve warm or cold and, if possible, with a pitcher of fresh cream.

PUMPKIN PECAN PIE

1 can (16 ounces) pumpkin
¾ cup brown sugar
¾ teaspoon salt
¾ teaspoon nutmeg
¾ teaspoon ground ginger
¼ teaspoon ground cloves

1¼ teaspoons ground cinnamon
4 teaspoons molasses
4 eggs
1½ cups milk
½ cup chopped pecans
1 unbaked 10-inch pie crust

Combine pumpkin, brown sugar, salt, nutmeg, ginger, cloves, cinnamon and molasses. Beat eggs and add milk. Add to pumpkin mixture and mix thoroughly.

Sprinkle ¼ cup chopped pecans over bottom of pie crust and press into pastry. Pour pumpkin mixture into unbaked pie crust and sprinkle top with remaining ¼ cup pecans. Bake in a hot oven (400° F.) for 50 minutes or until knife comes clean when inserted.

RAISIN CRUMB PIE

¾ cup water
2 cups seedless raisins
½ cup sugar
1 cup flour
1 teaspoon baking powder

¾ cup sugar
¼ cup butter
1 egg
½ cup milk
9-inch pastry crust

Add water to raisins and sugar, boil 5 minutes. Sift dry ingredients together, mix in butter. Beat egg, add milk and half the flour mixture.

Blend thoroughly, add raisin mixture. Pour raisin mixture into crust. Sprinkle top with remaining flour mixture. Bake in a hot oven (450° F.) 10 minutes, then in a moderate oven (350° F.) 30 minutes. May be served warm or cold. 9-inch pie.

RHUBARB CREAM PIE

2 or 3 cups rhubarb
   Unbaked pie shell
1 cup sweet cream
1 cup sugar

⅓ cup flour
2 egg yolks
Pinch of salt
Egg white for meringue

Put rhubarb in unbaked shell. Mix cream, sugar, flour and salt into beaten egg yolks. Pour over rhubarb.

Bake at 350° about 1 hour, until custard sets.

Make meringue. Top. Brown.

RHUBARB STRAWBERRY PIE

Mix together one cup of sugar and one-fourth cup quick-cooking tapioca. Add two cups rhubarb cut in one-half inch lengths, and two cups crushed strawberries. Put into a pie tin which has been lined with pastry and rubbed with one-half teaspoon flour. Strips of pastry are put across the top of the filling diagonally, making diamond-shaped holes with the pastry latticed. Each strip is fastened to the edge of the lower crust, by moistening with cold water and pressing firmly. When finished, a long strip is placed around the edge of the pie, on top of the other strips, holding them firmly in place and making a higher rim to the pie. While the filling may bubble up, it will not run over the edge. This is a very practical way to make a juicy pie, and attractive.

Bake at 450° F. for forty-five minutes.

SOUR CREAM APPLE PIE

2 tablespoons flour
⅛ teaspoon salt
¾ cup sugar

1 egg
1 cup sour cream
½ teaspoon vanilla
2 cups apples, finely chopped

Sift dry ingredients together. Add egg, cream, and vanilla, beat until smooth. Add apples, mix well. Pour into pastry lined pie tin. Bake in a hot oven (400° to 425° F.) 15 minutes, then in a moderate oven (350° F.) 30 minutes. 9-inch pie.

TOPPING

⅓ cup sugar   1 teaspoon cinnamon
⅓ cup flour   ¼ cup butter

Combine all ingredients, mix thoroughly. Sprinkle over pie. Return to oven and bake in a hot oven (400° to 425° F.) 10 minutes.

IDA'S SOUR CREAM PIE

(Raisins, spice and sour cream—results? Wonderful!)

1 unbaked pie shell—9 inch   1 cup raisins
1 cup brown sugar   1 cup sour cream
¾ teaspoon cinnamon   2 egg yolks, slightly beaten
¼ teaspoon nutmeg   1 tablespoon melted butter
¼ teaspoon allspice   1 teaspoon vanilla

Mix dry ingredients and raisins together. Add eggs, butter and flavoring to sour cream. Combine ingredients, mixing easily. Pour into the unbaked pie shell. Bake for 10 minutes in hot oven (400° F.) then reduce heat to 350° F. and bake for 30 to 35 minutes. Top with meringue made of the 2 egg whites plus 4 tablespoons sugar. Bake meringue in slow oven (325° F.) for 25 to 35 minutes or until delicately browned.

STRAWBERRY DELIGHT PIE

1 8-oz. pkg. Philadelphia Brand   ¾ cup sugar
   Cream Cheese   2 tablespoons cornstarch
2 tablespoons milk   ⅓ cup water
1 baked 9-inch pastry shell   Few drops of red food
1 quart fresh strawberries,   coloring
   washed and stemmed

Place the cream cheese in a bowl and cream it until soft and smooth. Gradually blend the milk into it. Spread half of this mixture on the bottom of the pastry shell. Cover with half of the strawberries. Cut the remaining berries in half.

Combine the sugar and cornstarch. Add the water, stirring until well blended. Add the remaining strawberries and cook until thickened, stirring constantly. Add red food coloring; mix well. Pour immediately over the strawberries in the pastry shell. Chill. Decorate with the remaining cream cheese mixture.

STRAWBERRY SPONGE PIE

Cake and Pie—All in One

1 box strawberries	¼ cup hot water
1 unbaked pie shell—9 inch	½ cup sifted enriched flour
½ cup sugar	1 teaspoon baking powder
2 egg yolks and 1 egg white	⅛ teaspoon salt
	¼ teaspoon vanilla

Wash strawberries and dry thoroughly; mix with sugar. Spread on bottom of pie shell. Beat eggs until light and lemon colored. Add sugar, dissolve in hot water, to eggs, beating constantly. Fold in dry ingredients which have been sifted together; add vanilla. Spread mixture over strawberries.

Bake in hot oven, 400° F., for 10 minutes, then reduce heat to 350° and bake 30 minutes longer.

Remove from oven and spread with meringue made with other egg white plus 2 tablespoons sugar. Return to oven and bake (325° F.) until delicately browned, (about 12 minutes).

SUNGLOW APPLE PIE

6 large apples, sliced	2 tablespoons flour
¼ cup red cinnamon candies	⅛ teaspoon salt
1 teaspoon grated lemon rind	Pastry for 2-crust 9-inch pie
½ cup sugar	2 tablespoons butter

Combine apples, candies, lemon rind, sugar, flour and salt. Divide pastry dough. Roll half of dough to about ⅛ inch thickness and line a 9-inch pie pan allowing ½ inch crust to extend over the edge. Brush 1 tablespoon butter, melted, over the bottom and sides of crust. Fill unbaked pie crust with apple mixture. Dot remaining tablespoon butter on top of filling. Roll out remaining pastry, making several openings to allow for escape of steam. Place pastry over filling. Fold lower crust over top crust. Crimp edges. Bake in hot oven (400° F.) for 40 to 50 minutes.

TAPIOCA LEMON PIE

½ cup quick-cooking tapioca
⅔ cup sugar
½ teaspoon salt
3 cups milk
3 egg yolks, slightly beaten

2 tablespoons butter
⅓ cup lemon juice
1 teaspoon grated lemon rind
1 baked 9-inch pie shell
3 egg whites
6 tablespoons sugar

Combine the tapioca, sugar, salt and milk in a saucepan and mix well. Bring the mixture quickly to a full boil over direct heat, stirring constantly. Remove from fire and pour slowly over the egg yolks, stirring vigorously. Add the butter, lemon juice and rind. Turn into a pie shell. Beat the egg whites until foamy throughout; add the sugar, two tablespoons at a time, beating after each addition until the sugar is blended. Then continue beating until the mixture will stand in peaks. Pile lightly on the pie and bake in a moderate oven until delicately browned. Temperature: 350° F. Time: 15 minutes.

VIRGINIA SWEET POTATO PIE

¼ cup butter
Salt
¾ cup sugar
3 egg yolks
Juice of 1 lemon
¼ teaspoon cinnamon

Nutmeg
Allspice
2 cups sweet potatoes, mashed
1 cup rich milk, scalded
3 egg whites
9-inch pie shell

Blend butter, salt, and sugar, add egg yolks, lemon juice, spices, potato pulp, and hot milk. Fold in stiffly beaten egg whites. Place in pie shell. Bake in a hot oven (425° F.) 10 minutes, then in a moderate oven (350° F.) 30 to 40 minutes, until pie is firm in center. 9-inch pie.

WASHINGTON CREAM PIE

¾ cup cake flour

½ teaspoon cream of tartar

Salt

4 egg yolks

1 cup sugar

½ teaspoon vanilla

4 egg whites

1 cup apricots, sieved

1 cup cream, whipped

Sift dry ingredients together three times. Beat egg yolks, adding ½ cup sugar gradually. Add vanilla. Beat egg whites until foamy, adding ¼ cup sugar gradually until thick and smooth. Fold yolk mixture into whites; fold in flour mixture. Bake in a spring form pan (9-inch) in a moderate oven (350° F.) 45 minutes. Cool. Remove from pan, cut in two crosswise. Combine apricot puree and remaining sugar, fold in cream. Put between two layers. Sprinkle top with confectioners' sugar. Serve with whipped cream.

Serves 6 to 8.

"C LAZY U" DUDE RANCH CHERRY PIE

PASTRY

½ cup butter

½ teaspoon salt

½ cup brown sugar

1 cup flour

Mix all ingredients into thick paste, pat into bottom of greased pie tin, and bake 15 minutes at 325° F.

FILLING

1 cup sugar

4 tablespoons flour

2 teaspoons cornstarch

1½ cups cherry juice (not fruit)

Mix well and cook in double boiler until thick—5 or 6 minutes—stirring constantly to eliminate lumps. Then fold in 2 cups of cherries, pour mixture over pastry in pie tin, and you're ready for

TOPPING

1½ cups dry oatmeal	4 tablespoons flour
½ cup brown sugar	5 tablespoons butter

Mix well, spread over top of the pie, and bake 20 minutes at 325°.

(From "C Lazy U" Dude Ranch, Granby, Colorado)

PRESERVES

Every spring Grandpa used to say "What in the world shall we do with all the pie plant?"

And every spring Grandma would answer patiently that there were a million things to do with the pie plant and, of course, she'd preserve what wasn't going to be used!

Grandma Anderson thought that you could preserve anything and everything! Her rhubarb and orange conserve was a thing of beauty, her end-of-the-garden pickles were a rhapsody of color and arrangement; her cinnamon apple jelly was an accomplished fact long before a commercial distributor dared to put it out under his label! Her pickled peaches were marvelous and her brandied peaches a must for every occasion of great event! She had a way with cherry and rum jam, with preserved figs, with stuffed oranges and with a million and one other vegetables, fruit and sometimes even meat.

Once again we were caught on the horns of a dilemma. What to include; what to leave out? And once again we attempted to bring you the things we were sure you wouldn't find in any other cook book.

If you have the time, the patience, the love it takes to do an immense amount of canning and preserving, then you will bless your activities once winter comes! It's simple, really, and the first requirement is a BIG garden with all manner of things that can be canned, preserved or jellied.

We belong to the school that firmly believes you can preserve or can anything. So here are our recipes with our blessing and we hope for your good luck.

BLACKBERRY JAM

3 pounds blackberries   2¼ pounds sugar

Carefully wash and pick over the berries, discarding any imperfect fruit. In a large preserving kettle put a layer of fruit, then a layer of sugar and continue until the ingredients are used. Should you not have a large enough kettle to hold all, cook small portions at a time, using ¾ pound sugar to each pound of fruit. Let berries and sugar stand at least one hour before cooking. This draws the juice from the berries. Cook until thick. Pour into sterilized glasses and seal.

SPICED BLACKBERRIES

4 cups brown sugar   2 sticks cinnamon
2 cups vinegar   1 tablespoon whole cloves
5 pounds blackberries   ½ tablespoon allspice berries

Make a syrup of the sugar and vinegar, add the blackberries that have been picked over and washed. Tie the spices in a square of cheesecloth and add. Simmer until the mixture is thick, remove the spice bag and pour the berries into clean, sterile jars. Seal with wax.

UNCOOKED CHERRY PRESERVE

Remove the stones from as many cherries as you wish to put up, place in an earthen bowl or other container, and pour over enough white vinegar to cover. Let stand twenty-four hours, then drain off the vinegar (which may be used again for any purpose), weigh the fruit, add a pound of sugar for each pound of cherries, let stand in a cool place and stir thoroughly once every day for ten days. Store in sterile, air-tight jars. These cherries make a delicious preserve, they may be used to flavor tapioca and other puddings or ice creams, or as a garnish for many forms of sweet course. The syrup from them, mixed with a sparkling water, makes a delightful beverage.

CELERY RELISH

1½ cups chopped green pepper
(2 medium)
1½ cups chopped sweet red
pepper (2 medium)
3 cups chopped onions
(5 medium)
2 quarts sliced celery
(4 medium bunches)

2 cups white vinegar
½ cup water
2½ tablespoons salt
1¼ cups sugar
2½ tablespoons whole mustard
seed
¼ teaspoon turmeric

Prepare vegetables. Combine vinegar and water with remaining ingredients; heat to boiling. Add vegetables. Simmer, uncovered, 3 minutes. Quickly pack one hot sterilized jar at a time. Fill to ⅛-inch from top. Be sure vinegar solution covers the vegetables. Seal each jar at once. Makes 5 pints.

GROUND CHERRY CONSERVE

1 quart ground cherries
1 orange

1 lemon
Their weight in sugar

Proceed as for peach and tomato conserve.

CORN RELISH

18 cups fresh corn
4 cups chopped, peeled onions
2 cups chopped, seeded green
peppers
1 cup chopped, seeded red
peppers

1 cup brown sugar, firmly
packed
1 cup corn syrup
¼ cup salt
3 tablespoons celery seed
3 tablespoons mustard
1½ quarts cider vinegar

Cut the corn from the ears (do not scrape). Combine corn, onions and peppers. Then add remaining ingredients. Bring to a boil, cover and simmer 15 minutes, stirring occasionally to prevent scorching. Pour into hot sterilized jars and seal.

Yield: about 8 pints.

CRANBERRY JELLY

4 cups cranberries   1½ cups water
                                2 cups sugar

Wash and pick over cranberries. Cook cranberries with ¾ cup of water until very soft. Press through a sieve. Combine the sugar and remaining ¾ cup of water and cook for 10 minutes. Add the strained cranberries and cook 10 minutes longer. Strain again and pour into a moistened mold. Chill. When firm, unmold and serve.

GOOSEBERRY CONSERVE

5 pounds green gooseberries   1½ pounds seeded raisins
4 pounds sugar   (chopped)
                                4 large oranges

This makes 15 glasses.

SWEET PICKLED CONCORD GRAPES

Crush four pounds of ripe Concord grapes in a preserving kettle and cook over gentle heat until the seeds separate. Sift through a colander, rubbing the skins through, but removing the seeds. Return the grape pulp to the kettle with two pounds of sugar and one heaping teaspoonful of mixed spices, tied in a cheesecloth and crushed with a wooden mallet. Let come to a boil, add one and one-fourth cup cider vinegar, and cook the whole for half an hour, stirring now and then keeping kettle uncovered. The mixture should be thick when poured into the glasses, and should jell when cold. This is particularly good with roast meat. It is good also with chilled, sliced roast veal.

GRAPE CONSERVE

3 pints Concord grapes pulped   2 oranges
1 cup pecan nuts   1 package raisins
    8 cups sugar

First boil pulp to remove seeds. Add skins, also sugar and raisins, cook 5 or 10 minutes, add orange juice and grated rind, cook a few minutes more, add nut meats last. Excellent. This recipe makes about 2 quarts.

SPICED GRAPES

5 pounds ripe Concord grapes   1 teaspoon cinnamon
3 pounds white sugar   1 teaspoon allspice
¼ cup cider vinegar   ½ teaspoon cloves

Separate grape skins and pulp. Cook pulp until seeds separate. Remove seeds. Cook skins slightly, then add pulp, sugar, spices and vinegar. Cook until skins are tender and mixture begins to jell when cold. Seal in glasses.

SPICED SECKEL PEARS

2 pounds Seckel pears   3 cups brown sugar
1 cup water   1 dozen cloves
1 cup vinegar   1 dozen allspice berries
    1 stick cinnamon

Wash the Seckel pears, remove the blossom end and pare, leaving the stems intact. Make a syrup from the water, vinegar and brown sugar, in which is placed a cheesecloth spice bag containing the cloves, allspice and cinnamon. Simmer for five minutes, then add the pears, and cook until clear and tender. Pack in hot, sterile jars, fill to overflowing with the remaining syrup, and seal.

Remove the seeds from ten large, sweet red peppers. Wash and chop. Sprinkle with one and one-half teaspoon salt and allow to stand overnight. In the morning drain and put into a kettle with one pint of cider vinegar and three cups of granulated sugar. Place the kettle over

RED PEPPER JAM

heat. Stir until the sugar is well dissolved. Bring to the boiling point and allow to cook gently until the mixture is thick, of the consistency of jam. Pour into hot jelly glasses and seal.

NEW ENGLAND RED PEPPER RELISH

12 red bell peppers
6 green bell peppers
3 large onions
6 peeled tomatoes

1 lemon, sliced
1 quart cider vinegar
2 cups sugar
1½ tablespoons salt

Chop up the gaily-colored peppers (seeding them first of course), cover with boiling water, let stand 10 minutes, drain and cover with more water, let stand 5 minutes, drain again. Add the onion chopped fine and the chopped tomatoes, and the lemon, very thinly sliced and cut into pieces.

Heat the vinegar, sugar and salt and boil 5 minutes before adding to it the chopped pepper-onion-tomato mix. Boil all together for 10 minutes. Let it cool and stand a few hours to amalgamate the flavors, and again boil 10 minutes before putting into glass jars. Delicious with any meat or fish.

AUNT MAHALA'S MUSTARD PICKLE

2 quarts small cucumbers
2 quarts button onions
1 large cauliflower

4 red peppers (for color)
2 cups small whole carrots
2 cups salt
2 quarts water

Cut up vegetables and cover with brine of salt and water. Let stand overnight. In the morning, heat to the boiling point (don't boil) and drain. Pour dressing over vegetables and bring to the boiling point. Just simmer until vegetables are tender. Pack in hot, sterile jars.

DRESSING

1 cup flour
6 tablespoons dry mustard
1½ cups sugar

1 tablespoon turmeric
2 quarts vinegar
1 teaspoon whole peppercorns

Mix the dry ingredients together. Add a little vinegar to make a smooth paste; then stir into the remaining vinegar and cook until smooth and creamy.

SWEET PICKLED PLUMS

2 pounds plums
1 cup water
1 cup vinegar

3 cups brown sugar
1 dozen cloves
1 dozen allspice berries
1 stick cinnamon

Wash the plums. Make a syrup from the water, vinegar and brown sugar, in which is placed a cheesecloth spice bag containing the cloves, allspice and cinnamon. Simmer for five minutes, then add the plums, and cook until clear and tender. Pack in hot, sterile jars, fill to overflowing with the remaining syrup, and seal.

RHUBARB MARMALADE

4 pounds rhubarb
5 pounds sugar
1 pound seeded raisins

1 lemon, rind only
2 oranges, juice only
½ teaspoon cloves
1 teaspoon cinnamon

Wash and scrape rhubarb and cut into 1-inch pieces. Cover with sugar and let stand overnight. Add remaining ingredients. Place on stove and bring to the boiling point. Reduce heat and simmer about 40 minutes or until mixture becomes thick. Stir frequently to prevent mixture from burning. Pour into sterilized glasses, cool and seal.

GREEN TOMATO CONSERVE

4 cups green tomatoes, chopped   4 cups sugar
     and drained   1 lemon, chopped fine
                               ½ cup nut meats

Boil until thick and put in glasses. Do not put in nuts until done.

PARADISE JELLY

4 quarts of red apples or   12 quinces
     crab apples   2 quarts cranberries
                          Granulated sugar

Wash the apples and quinces and remove the stems and blossom ends. Cut in quarters, cover with cold water and cook until tender. Wash the cranberries and cook in 1 quart of water until tender. Pour the apples, quinces and cranberries into a jelly bag and let drain overnight. To every two cups of juice, add 1 pound of granulated sugar and boil for about 10 minutes. Remove the scum which forms while boiling. Pour into sterilized jelly glasses and seal.

THREE-FRUIT CONSERVE

6 cups granulated sugar   4 cups sliced fresh pears
4 cups sliced fresh peaches   1 cup seedless raisins

Mix sugar with peaches and pears, and allow to stand 1 to 2 hours, until juice forms. Rinse and drain raisins and add to fruit mixture. Boil slowly 1½ to 2 hours, until fruit is clear and syrup thick. Seal in sterilized jars. Makes about 4 pints.

WINE JELLY

2 tablespoons granulated gelatin   1 cup sugar
½ cup cold water   2 cups boiling water
1 cup sherry wine   ¼ cup lemon juice
                           ¼ cup orange juice

Soak the gelatin in the cold water for 5 minutes. Add the wine and sugar to the boiling water and boil for 1 minute. Dissolve the gelatin in the boiling liquid and then add the orange and lemon juices; strain and pour into one large mold or individual molds which have been rinsed in cold water. Chill. Serve with whipped cream.

HOW TO COOK WITH WINE

Like magic, wine brings out the natural goodness of food, creating many rich, new flavors.

If cooking with wine is a new experience for you, the chart below will be a handy guide to the amount and kind to use in various dishes. Post it in your kitchen, and see how it helps you make simple everyday dishes taste even better.

The amounts given are minimum, so taste as you go, and continue to add wine until it tastes just right. (The alcohol in wine passes off in cooking just as it does from vanilla.)

A Word About Marinating

To give added flavor and texture to the less expensive cuts of meat (pot roasts, stews, etc.), before cooking, marinate them overnight in California table wine to cover. Turn meat occasionally. Seasonings (including salt, whole peppercorns or ground peppers, onion and garlic, bay leaves and other herbs, cloves and other spices) may be added as desired. When you're ready to cook the meat, strain this marinade, if necessary, and use some of it as all or part of the liquid in cooking the meat. You'll be well rewarded with extra flavor and a new tenderness in the finished dish.

Chicken that is to be broiled or barbecued is especially good if marinated in white table wine for several hours before cooking.

SOUPS: *Amount*   *Wines*
Cream Soups   1 tsp. per serving   Sauterne** or Sherry
Meat and Vegetable Soups   1 tsp. per serving   Burgundy* or Sherry

SAUCES:
Cream Sauce and Variations   1 tbsp. per cup   Sherry or Sauterne**
Brown Sauce and Variations   1 tbsp. per cup   Sherry or Burgundy*
Tomato Sauce   1 tbsp. per cut   Sherry or Burgundy*
Cheese Sauce   1 tbsp. per cup   Sherry or Sauterne**
Dessert Sauces   1 tbsp. per cut   Port or Muscatel

MEATS:
Pot Roast—Beef   ¼ cup per lb.   Burgundy*
Pot Roast—Lamb and Veal   ¼ cup per lb.   Sauterne**
Gravy for Roasts   2 tbsps. per cut   Burgundy*, Sauterne**
                                                              or Sherry
Stew—Beef   ¼ cup per lb.   Burgundy*
Stew—Lamb and Veal   ¼ cup per lb.   Sauterne**
Ham, Baked—Whole   2 cups (for basting)   Port or Muscatel
Liver, Braised   ¼ cup per lb.   Burgundy* or Sauterne**
Kidneys, Braised   ¼ cup per lb.   Sherry or Burgundy*
Tongue, Boiled   ½ cup per lb.   Burgundy*

FISH:
Broiled, Baked or Poached   ½ cup per lb.   Sauterne**

POULTRY & GAME:
Chicken, Broiled or Sautéed   ¼ cup per lb.   Sauterne** or Burgundy*
Gravy for Roast or Fried
  Chicken and Turkey   2 tbsps. per cut   Sauterne**, Burgundy*
                                                              or Sherry
Chicken, Fricasse   ¼ cup per lb.   Sauterne**
Duck, Roast—Wild or Tame   ¼ cup per lb.   Burgundy*

Venison, Roast, Pot Roast
  or Stew   ¼ cup per lb.   Burgundy*
Pheasant, Roast or Sautéed   ¼ cup per lb.   Sauterne**, Burgundy*
                                                              or Sherry
FRUIT:
Cups and Compotes   1 tbsp. per serving   Port, Muscatel, Sherry,
                                                              Rose Sauterne** or
                                                              Burgundy*

* Or California Claret, Zinfaudel or other red table wine.
** Or California Rhine Wine, Chablis or other white table wine.

EPILOGUE

The book is done, the recipes compiled, the chapter headings written and little essays on Grandma Anderson ready for the printer.

And I am off to South America by way of Puerto Rico to study the food customs of Twelfth Night or Three Kings Day which is part of their Double Christmas. Accompanied, of course, by Belle Anderson Ebner and my mother Verna Anderson MaCaffrey.

We are the eatingest tourists in the country! This time we are taking the long way home, coming back into the country by way of our beloved New Orleans, spending a gourmet holiday here before going on up to Cherry Grove Plantation at Natchez, Mississippi, for more authentic Southern Plantation Food and taking a long road home via some of the South's finest eating places.

It's all an attempt to learn the new, the different, to capitalize on the old and revered and to bring from far away places something of their charm to our own little Hotel.

Will we ever learn all there is to learn about food? Never ever for food customs and habits change, there is always some new discovery, some new ways of service, and there are always eager students such as we are.

It all makes for a new book to follow this one. I can see Belle Ebner and Ann starting new recipe collections now—Again we thank God for the Mayo Clinic at Rochester practically at our door steps; from here comes our greatest rush of customers and from all corners of the earth. And from them come some of our choicest recipes.

We hope you have liked our book and the one before this. We are irrepressible writers, for more will follow. If there are questions we have all the time in the world to answer. Life in Wabasha moves at a slow pace!

JEANNE HALL SENDERHAUF

295

INDEX

297